IMAGES
of America

RESERVE

On the Cover: Charles "Brother" Alltmont, right, managed Alltmont Store until it closed in November 1973. The store, located on West Seventh Street, was referred to as the "company store" and supplied groceries, food, shirts, pants, underwear, socks, suits, shoes, washing machines, radios, televisions, comic books, magazines, and hardware. Standing next to Charles Alltmont are Dasise Labat, center, and Leo Lasseigne. (Courtesy of Norine Alltmont.)

IMAGES
of America

RESERVE

Gerald J. Keller, PhD, and
E. Darroch Watson

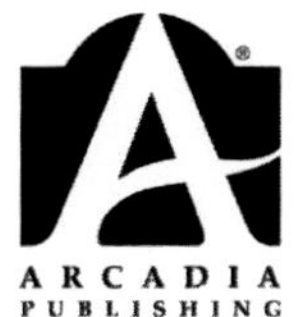

ISBN 978-0-7385-8774-5

Published by Arcadia Publishing
Charleston, South Carolina

Printed in the United States of America

Library of Congress Control Number: 2011922215

For all general information, please contact Arcadia Publishing:
Telephone 843-853-2070
Fax 843-853-0044
E-mail sales@arcadiapublishing.com
For customer service and orders:
Toll-Free 1-888-313-2665

Visit us on the Internet at www.arcadiapublishing.com

CONTENTS

Acknowledgments

Many individuals and organizations helped make this book possible. The authors thank Joy Donaldson McGraw, Shirley Casseigne Terrio, Gerard Montz, Wayne Boudreaux, the Carl L. Levet family, and Dr. Douglas Starr, all for sharing their personal collections. Willie Robert, Lucian Cambre, Keith Perilloux, J.L. and Peggy Robichaux, Sylvia Taylor Dunn, Mary Dorothy Mitchell, and Albertha Henderson are but a few names of folks who shared photographs and personal stories. We thank Mary Dorothy Mitchell, Judge Sylvia Taylor Steib-Dunn, and Albertha Henderson for their unselfish dedication in the development of this book. This book also could not have been completed without the help of Claude Levet.

The Reserve150 Sesquicentennial Committee members and organizations deserve special recognitions: Judge Sterling Snowdy, chair; Randy Desoto and Jamey Boudreaux, lecture series; Darroch Watson, Education Committee; Rita Perrilloux, time capsule; Charles Daigle, logo; Calvin Rousse, bookkeeper; Debbie Craighead, media; Dawn and Suzette Remondet, Fun Day and sesquicentennial souvenirs; Jamey Boudreaux, Jane Montz DeRoche, and Gail Boudreaux Castay, cemetery walk; Jeff Duhe, Reserve DVD production; Lennen Madere, video and archival project; Ronnie Keller Michel, *Reserve Commemorative Book*; Ingram Barge Company, doubloons; St. John Theatre, meeting area; Pete McGraw and the LaPlace Boy Scouts, Troop 406, Christmas bonfire; and to the many community sponsors that supported the Reserve150 celebration.

Amy Perryman, of Arcadia Publishing, guided the authors though the development of this book, and we would like to thank her for her support, advice, and patience. Proceeds of this book will go to Reserve150, thus allowing historic preservation of the town of Reserve to continue. We especially thank the many Reserve residents who made this area a great place to live.

INTRODUCTION

Reserve, Louisiana, is a town rich in history—a town in the Mississippi River region of southeast Louisiana that figured prominently in the growth and development of Louisiana. Part of the Louisiana German Coast settlement in the 1700s, Reserve is embedded with German, French, and African American families who have been in the area for nearly 300 years. The first German settlers came in 1718 and were promised the "Garden of Eden." Instead, they found a land rich in mosquitoes, swamp, and hardship. They survived, and other German immigrants followed in 1759. The area soon became the food basket for New Orleans as settlers paddled their pirogues down the river to market. The Acadians from Nova Scotia came in the late 1760s and brought with them customs that are still found today.

The village of Reserve is part of St. John the Baptist Parish and was originally called Bonnet Carré. The name Bonnet Carré originated from a right-angle turn in the levee from Reserve to the lower end of LaPlace, Louisiana, giving the levee the shape of a square bonnet—hence Bonnet Carré. The first post office for the East Bank of the parish received its mail from the St. John the Baptist train station in Edgard, Louisiana, and the area was called Bonnet Carré to conform to the name first given to the village. In 1864, the first church of St. Peter was built, and the village assumed the name St. Peter; however, the post office retained the Bonnet Carré name. In 1883, the railroad constructed a train station behind St. Peter Catholic Church cemetery, and mail was received at that station. The name of the village was changed to St. Peter to conform to the name of the religious parish. In the late 1800s, the Yazoo & Mississippi Valley railroad station was moved to the Reserve Plantation, where a railroad maintenance office is now situated. The name of the village was changed to Reserve because it was customary to give all railroad stations on plantations the same name as the plantation. Naming the station Reserve caused the people to file a petition with the US government to change the village name to Reserve. The petition was approved, and the name of the post office was officially changed to Reserve. The town of Reserve would eventually extend from the upper boundary of the Belle Pointe Plantation to the lower boundary of the Reserve Plantation and would later extend to include Dutch Bayou, Star Plantation, and Lions.

The name Reserve has conflicting origins, but its development can be traced to the sugar industry that prospered before and after the Civil War. Leon Godchaux, an illiterate immigrant from France, had much to do with the development of Reserve. He founded a sugar industry that became one of the largest sugar providers in the South. He centralized his sugar mills, installed a narrow-gauge railroad system that brought his sugar cane to the mill at a faster rate, used the latest technology, and purchased state-of-the-art equipment to increase both production and efficiency.

The 100th anniversary of Reserve in 1960 gave claim to Leon Godchaux for naming his plantation Reserve, but documents support that the Reserve Plantation existed prior to 1850. Sugar records indicate that Antoine Boudousquie applied the name Reserve to his plantation before Leon Godchaux officially purchased it in 1869. An 1850–1851 sugar report noted sugar production at the Reserve Plantation, and an 1850 Mississippi River Plantation map listed a "Mrs. A. Boudousquie, Reserve Plantation." Whatever its true origin, the people, events, triumphs, and heartbreaks of the area have helped to make Reserve what it is today.

Looking back over the past 150 years, Reserve has seen monumental change. The area shifted from an agrarian to an industrial society as the petrochemical industry now supplies the community with employment. A rebirth in recent years includes a veterans hospital, airport, National Guard armory, and small commercial strip malls. In the collection of photographs presented, the authors hope to give just a glimpse of the diversity of Reserve and its history. The photographs have been divided into chapters focusing on people, community, commerce, and celebrities that came from the community.

One

The Beginning

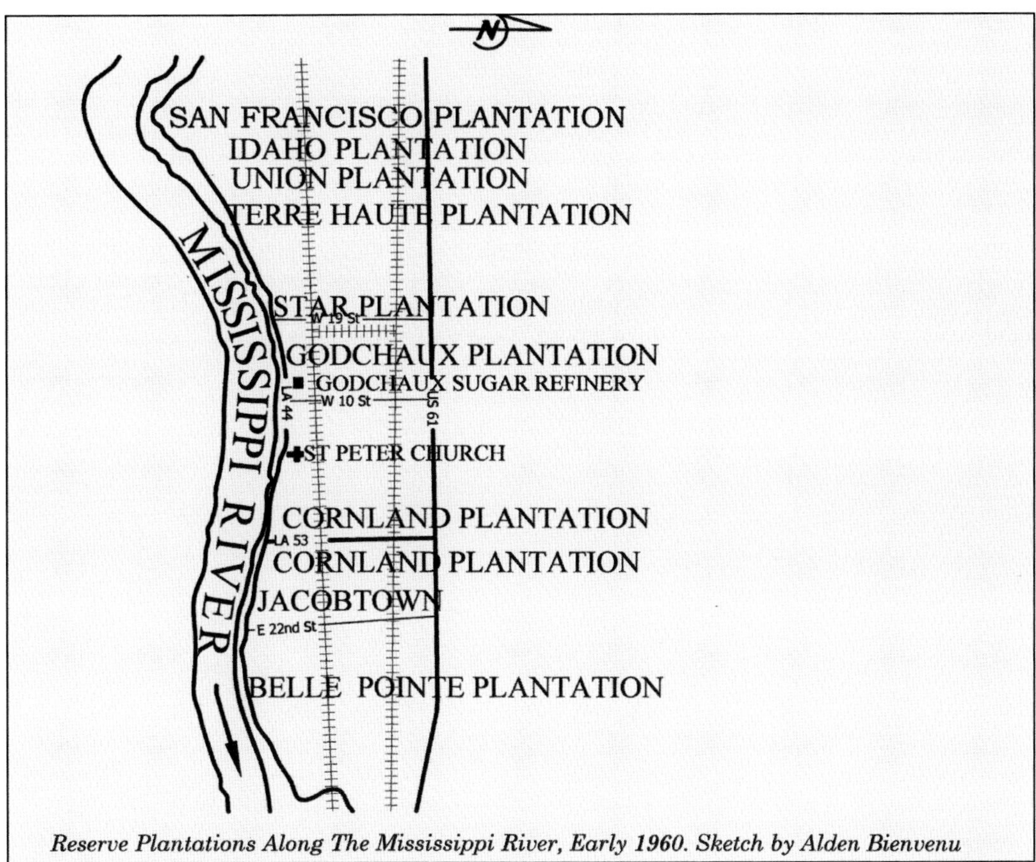

Reserve Plantations Along The Mississippi River, Early 1960. Sketch by Alden Bienvenu

The effects of milling centralization cut swiftly into sugar production. In 1880, Louisiana had 1,114 large plantation mills. By 1889, there were 746 plantation and central mills. In 1900, there were 300 sugar mills in Louisiana, and by 1910, that number dropped to 214. The 1900 Reserve plantation map, sketched by Alden Bienvenu, indicates that only five large sugar plantations existed in Reserve during that period. The Godchaux family farmed the Star, Godchaux, and Belle Point Plantations, and a narrow-gauge railroad system brought sugar cane to the mill during the grinding season. Leon Graugnard and his successors, the Guidry family, harvested sugarcane from the Terre Haute Plantation site. The Levet-Ory family grew sugarcane and had a sugar mill that harvested sugarcane from the Union, Idaho, and San Francisco Plantations. Maurice Edrington, and later C.I. James, grew sugarcane on the Cornland Plantation. The Edrington family also had a railroad system that brought sugarcane to their mill in Reserve. (Sketch by Alden Bienvenu.)

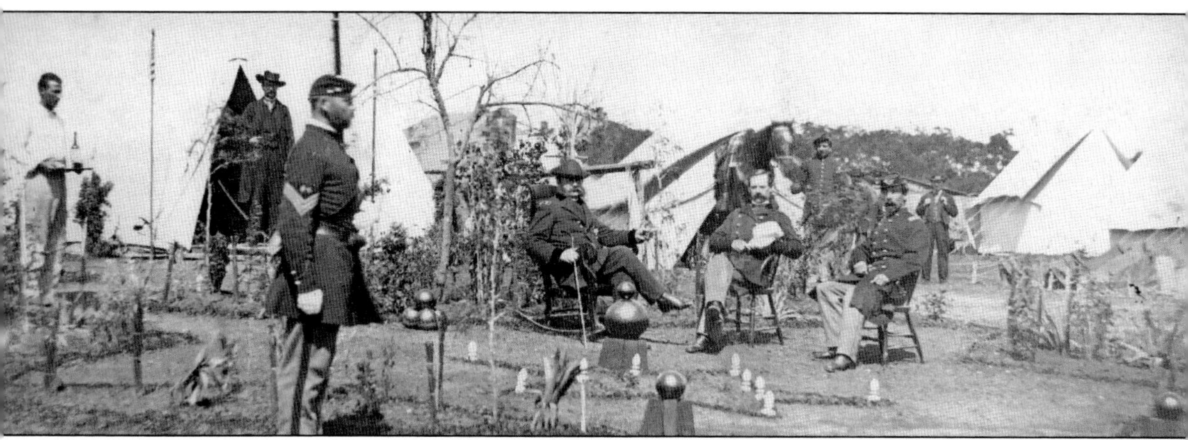

With the onset of the Civil War, Reserve was called Bonnet Carré until 1864. Pictured are unidentified Union soldiers during the occupation period. At the fall of New Orleans, Bonnet Carré was placed under military rule, and the provost marshal set up headquarters at the Belle Pointe Plantation. This was not a coincidence, as Belle Pointe plantation owner Andréa Deslonde's two daughters married leading Confederates John Slidell and Maj. Gen. Pierre Toutant Gustave Beauregard. Federal troops from the 24th Maine Volunteers Infantry, the 177th New York Regiment, the 28th Iowa Infantry, and the 38th Iowa Infantry served in the Bonnet Carré area until Union occupation ended in 1868. The Confederate army did make life difficult. From Thibodaux, Louisiana, Capt. Felix Pierre Poche led a raiding party on March 23, 1865, from Lake Maurepas through Boudousquie and Marmillion Canals, to capture provost marshal Captain Darling. When Poche found out the provost was in New Orleans, he waited at Belle Pointe. As he heard the steamboat signal that the provost's party had returned and was stopping to let Captain Darling disembark, Darling was arrested by the Confederates. (Photograph by Andrew D. Lytle; courtesy of Louisiana State University Special Collections Library.)

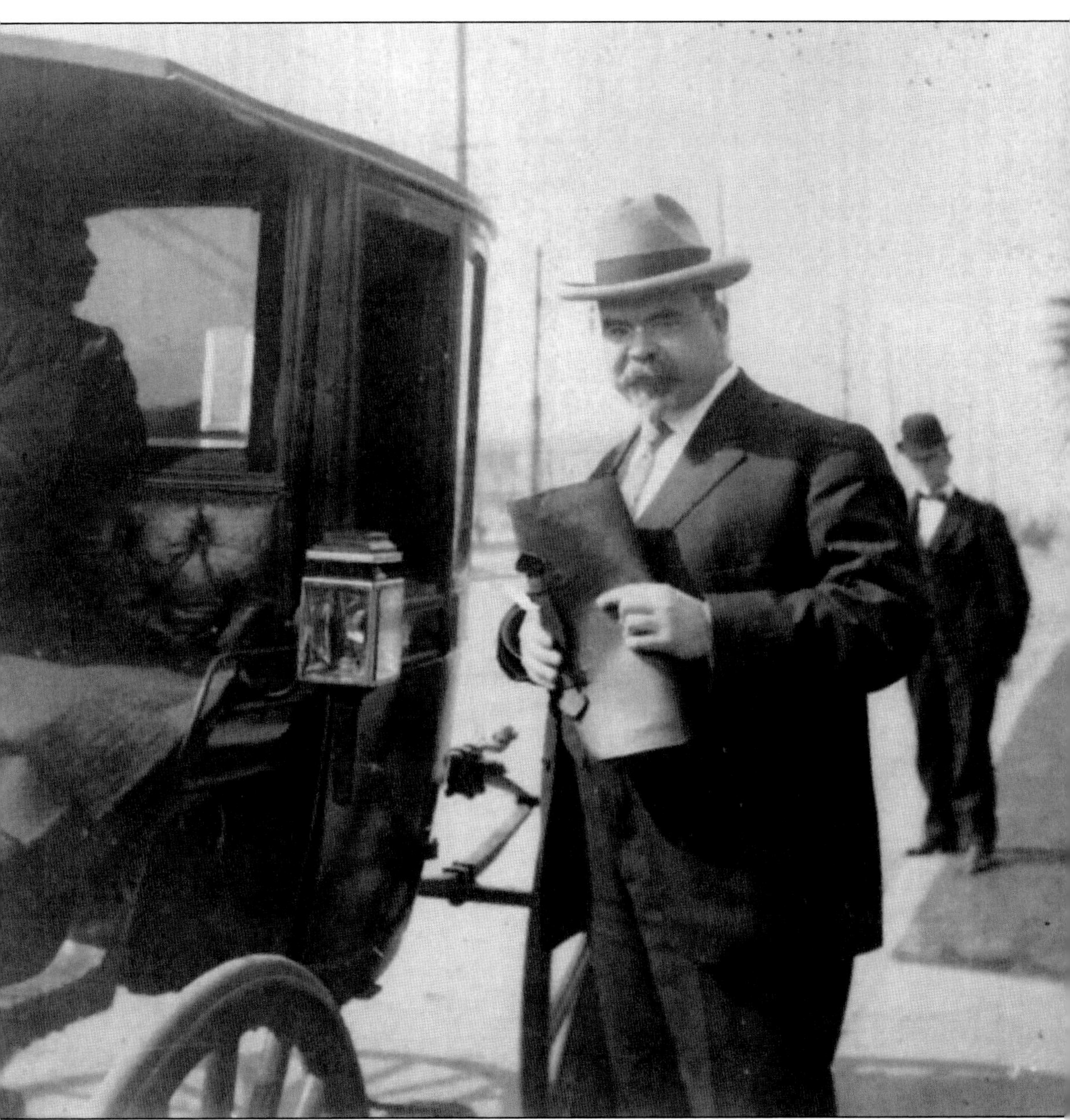

Dr. Rudolph Matas was born in Bonnet Carré on September 12, 1860. His parents, natives of Spain, returned to that country while Rudolph was very young. In 1867, the family came back to the United States, where his father, also a physician, found work, necessitating moves from New Orleans to Texas to Mexico, and then back to New Orleans. The young Matas entered, in 1877, the Medical School of the University of Louisiana, now Tulane University, receiving his doctor of medicine degree in 1880, at age 19. Dr. Matas's life remained, at all times, intimately associated with Tulane. He taught in the University Medical School for 42 years. Dr. Matas was a surgical giant and is hailed as the "Father of Vascular Surgery." He died on September 23, 1957, at age 97, a loss to the world of one of its most eminent pioneering thoracic and vascular surgeons. Rudolph Matas Elementary School in Metairie, Louisiana, is named in his honor. (Collection of Tulane University.)

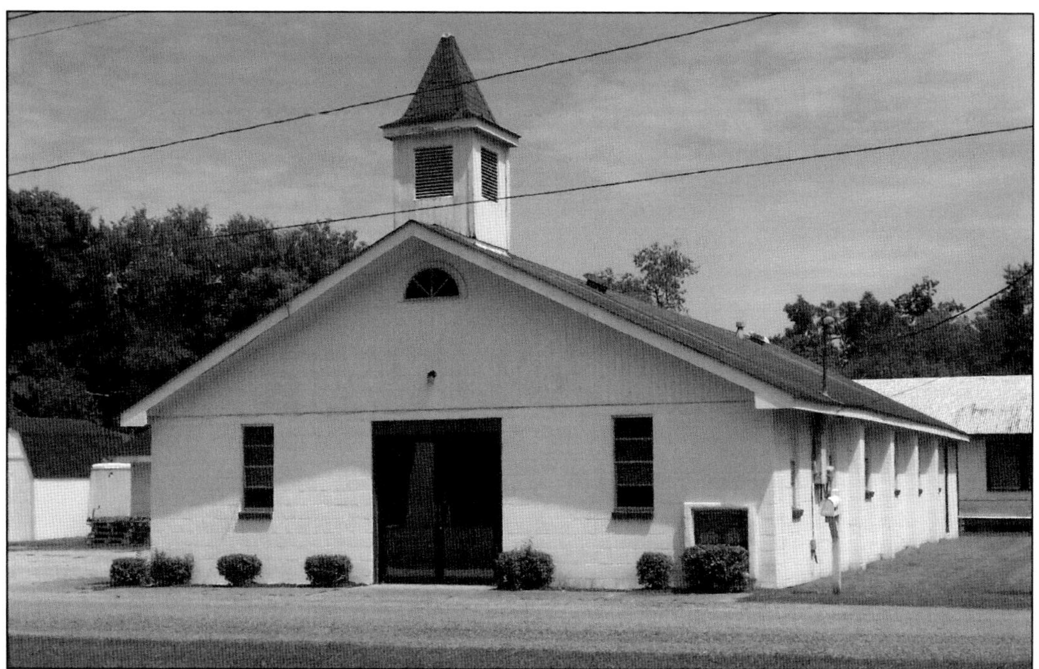

Founded in 1865, the Bethlehem Baptist Church is the oldest African American Baptist congregation in Reserve. In 1901, Rev. John Wallace and his membership rebuilt Bethlehem at its present site on East Twentieth Street, and property was purchased for a church cemetery. In 1965, the church was destroyed by Hurricane Betsy but was later rebuilt (pictured above). Today, Rev. Forrel Bering Sr. is the pastor of Bethlehem Baptist Church. (Courtesy of Judge Sylvia Taylor Steib-Dunn.)

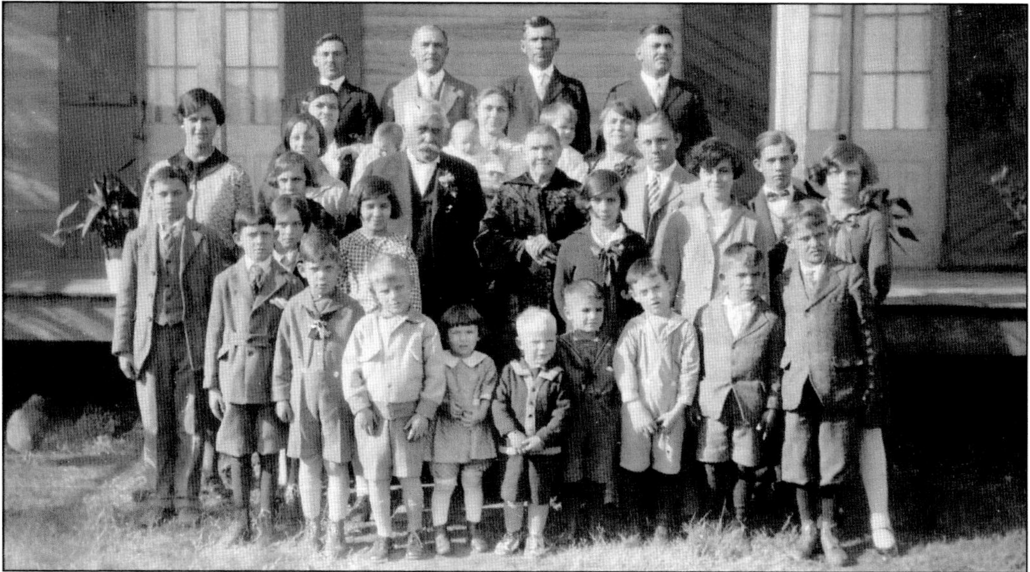

Philemon Guidry and Marie Adele Guidry are surrounded by family members and grandchildren. Edwin Guidry, top right, married Eve, the daughter of Terre Haute Plantation owners Leon and Marie Eve Graugnard. In time, Edwin and his wife assumed full ownership of this plantation and managed the sugarcane operation of the plantation. The management of this plantation was passed on to their children and grandchildren. (Courtesy of Trisha Guidry Aucoin.)

Pictured is Raoul "Happy" Luminais Sr., who grew up in an orphanage in New Orleans and moved to Reserve in the early 1900s. Raoul married Andrea Keller and opened a plumbing business in Reserve. Raoul's sons continued in the plumbing, heating, and air conditioning business. Earl Luminais opened Green Acres in 1949 in Metairie, Louisiana, and Floyd Luminais opened Luminais and Son, on Central Avenue in Reserve, in the 1970s. (Courtesy of Jill Luminais Bordelon.)

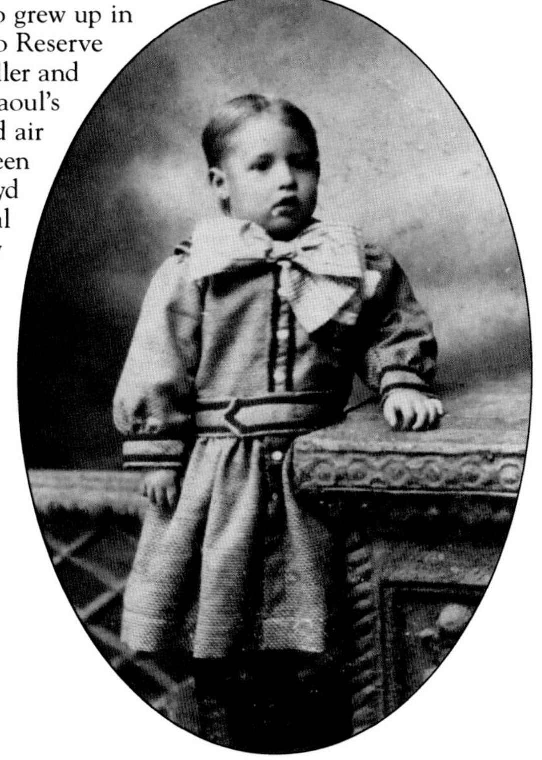

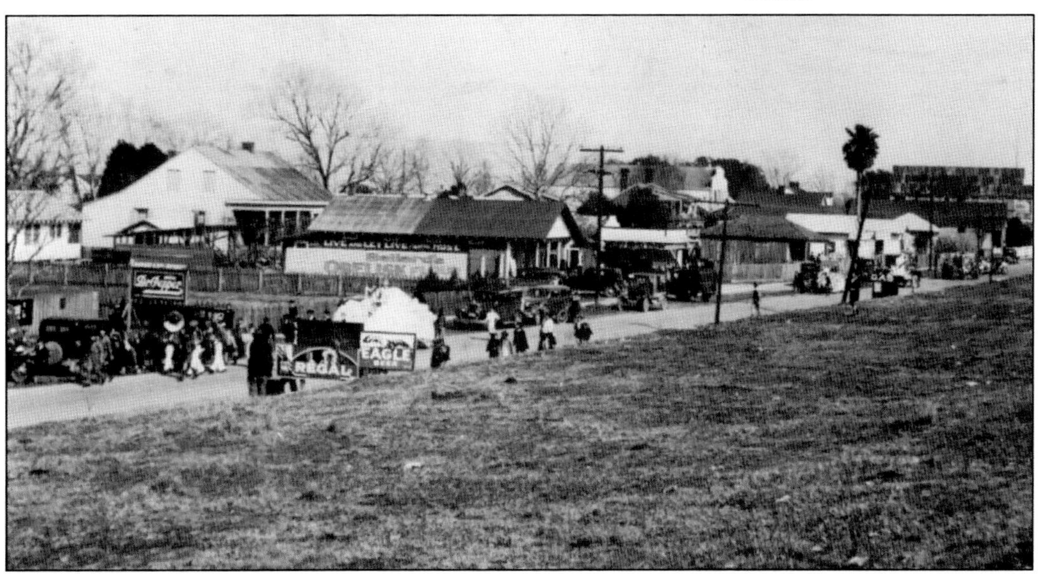

Pictured on May 27, 1938, is the Eucharistic Day procession as part of the observance at St. Peter Catholic Church. Buildings identified include, in the foreground, Lucien Troxler's Live and Let Live Store No. 2 and his Gulf service station, Dr. Oscar J. Ory's dental office, Alonzo J. Boe and Company Economy Meat and Market Store, Alex and Tewfix Haik's Store, and Nash Smith's Social Club. In the background are the Entremont house, the Freddie Fossier house, the Hart house, the LeBrun house, the Maurin Park Dance Pavilion, and Louis J. Maurin's movie theater. (Courtesy of Shirley Casseigne Terrio.)

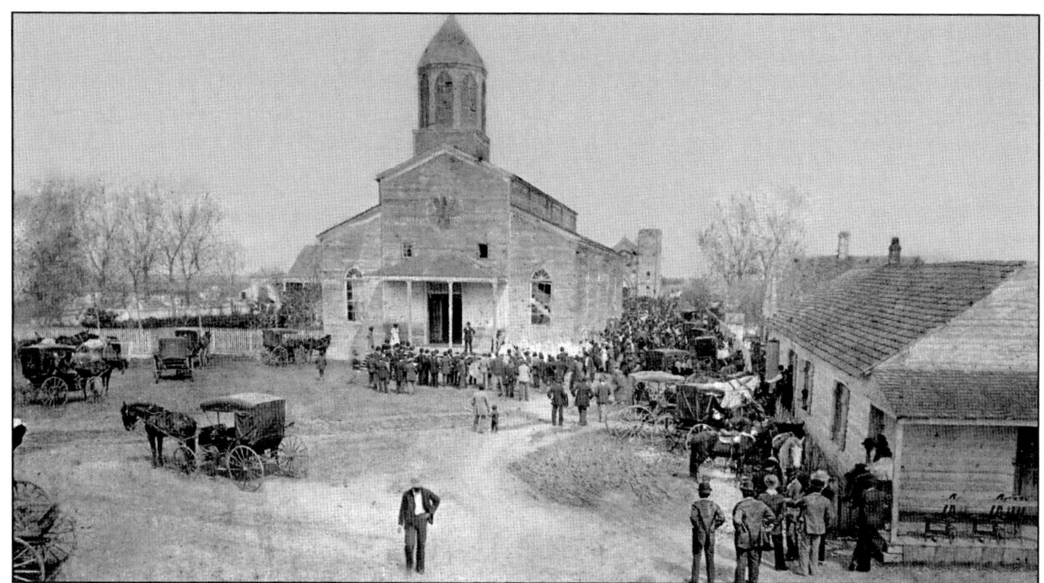

The growth of St. Peter Catholic Church in the late 1890s required a larger building, and in 1894, Fr. Etienne Bodoil and his parishioners began building a new church. Pictured is the 1897 dedication, as parishioners gathered outside and moved to the new St. Peter Catholic Church in the background. The church and altar was built by well-known carpenters John Ernest and Jules Albert Pastureau. (Courtesy of Shirley Casseigne Terrio.)

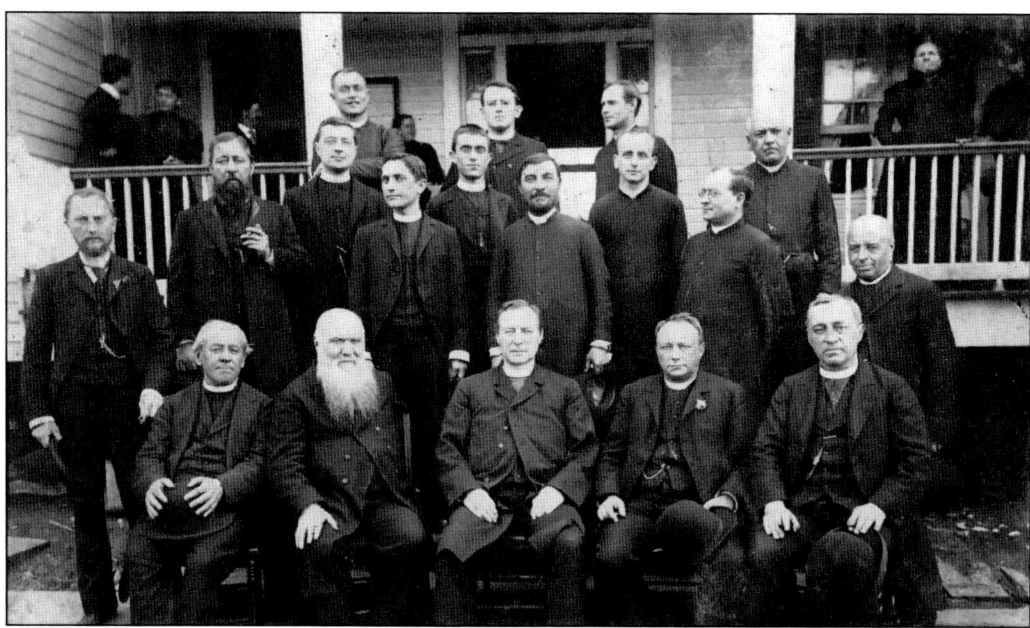

In 1897, although it was not finished, the new St. Peter Catholic Church was dedicated by Fr. Etienne Bodoil (second row, fourth from left) and Archbishop Francis Janssens, of the New Orleans Diocese (third row, center). They are surrounded by dignitaries of the archdiocese and Marists of Jefferson College. The pews, confessional, and other church relics were moved from the old church. (Courtesy of Shirley Casseigne Terrio.)

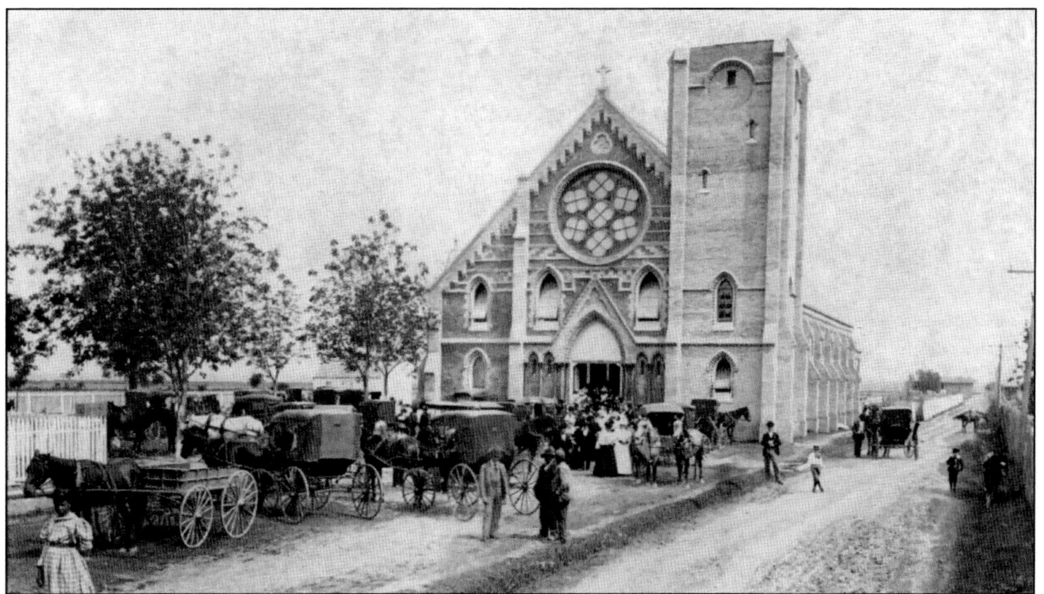

Bride and groom appear outside St. Peter Catholic Church following their wedding in the early 1900s. The couple was taken away in horse and buggy. In the background of this photograph is an oak tree that still stands today. The oak tree was a popular meeting place for many Reserve youths. The Yazoo & Mississippi Valley Railroad Station can be seen in the background behind the church cemetery. (Courtesy of Shirley Casseigne Terrio.)

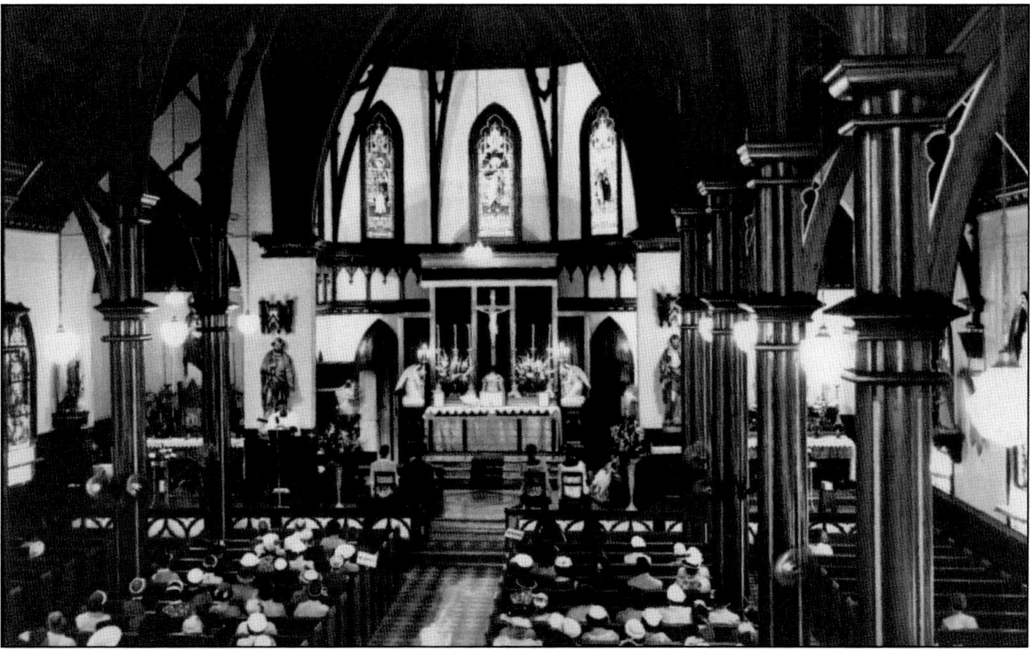

St. Peter Catholic Church was renovated in 1922 with the help and generosity of Edward Godchaux and the Godchaux Sugar Refinery. The church was electrically rewired, and the interior of the church was completely replaced. In 1930, three stained glass windows were installed in the church to honor the contribution of the Edward Godchaux, a Jewish member of the community. The church was completely destroyed in 1965 by Hurricane Betsy. (Courtesy of Shirley Casseigne Terrio.)

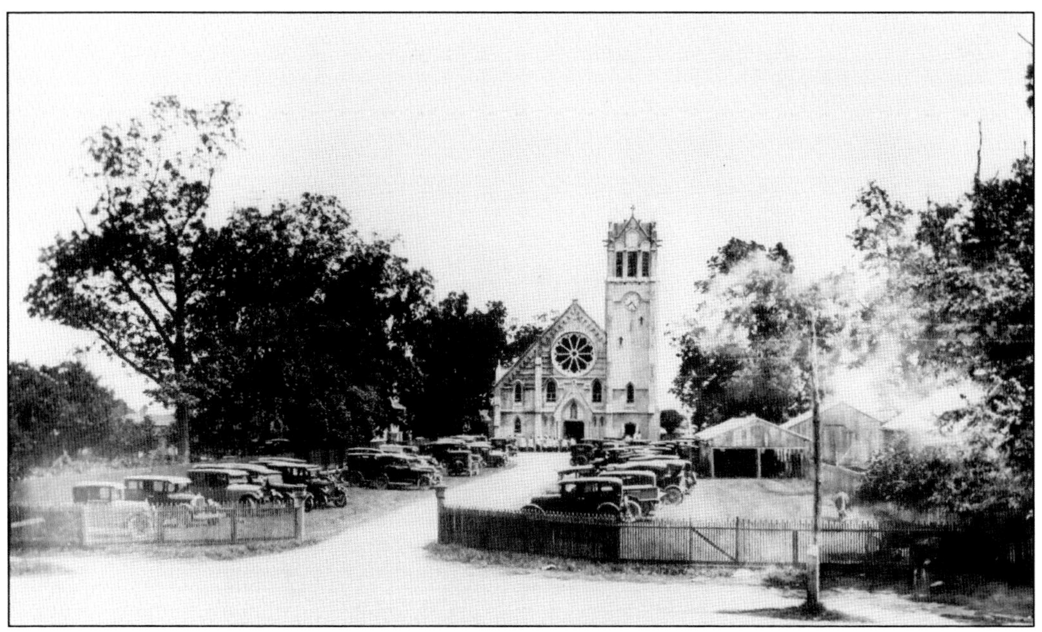

In the late 1920s, priests are entering St. Peter Catholic Church, which now has a steeple and a clock. Ford Model A cars line the parking lot, and to the right of the stables is the Pierre René Montz property. Montz maintained a surrey that rented light carriages with four wheels and two seats to traveling salesmen. The Montz property was eventually purchased by St. Peter Catholic Church. (Courtesy of Shirley Casseigne Terrio.)

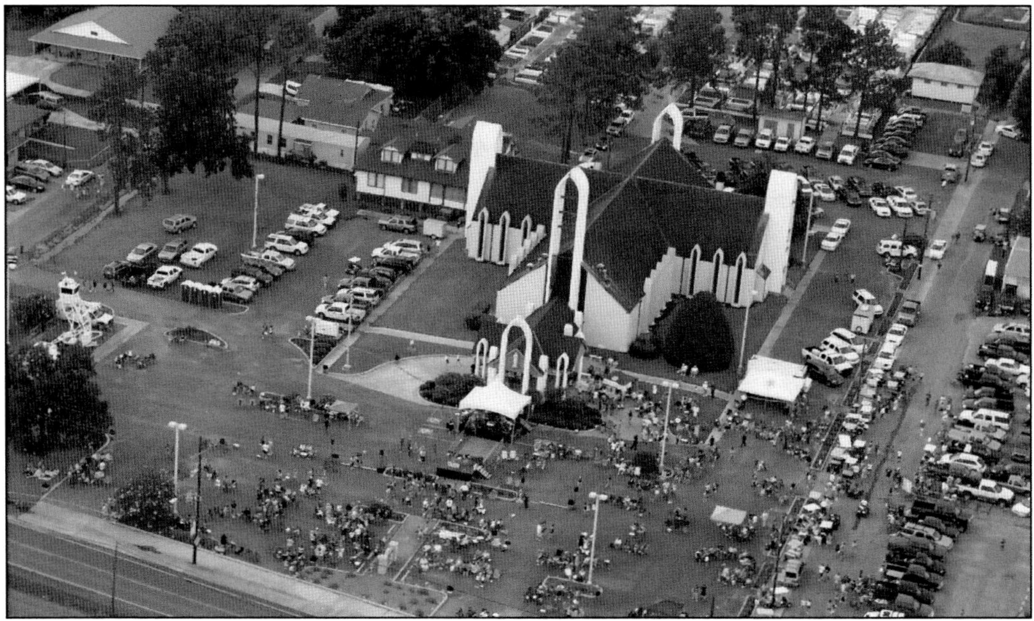

On January 24, 1968, the new St. Peter Catholic Church replaced the 75-year-old building that was destroyed by Hurricane Betsy. Most of the construction funds came from insurance and from an intensified fund drive. The new church was built in the form of a cross, with the altar in the center and a seating capacity of 860, almost double the 440 capacity of the old church. The church was later modified by Fr. Rodney Bourg. (Courtesy of Eugene Beaver Borne.)

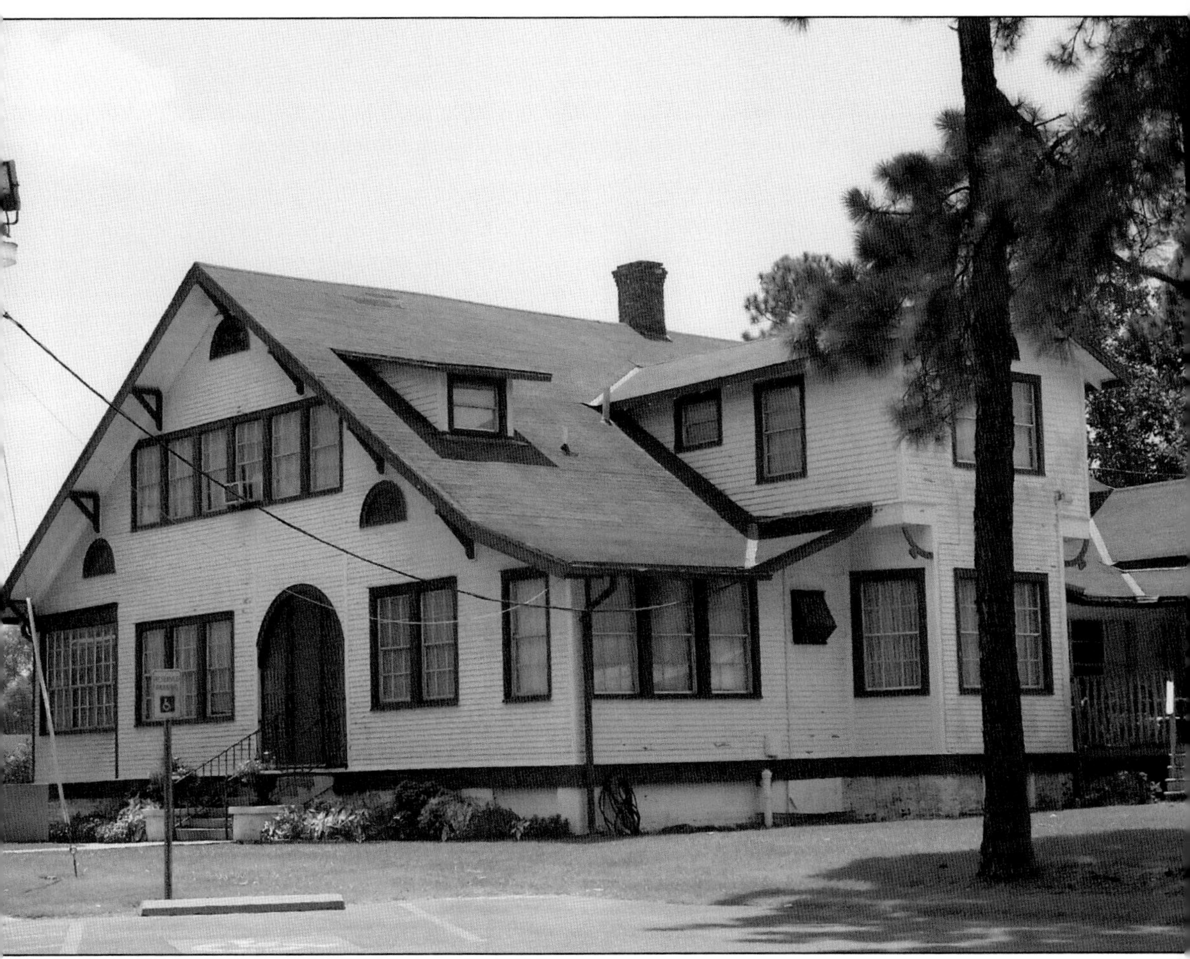

The St. Peter Catholic Church rectory, located near the Mississippi River, was built by Antoine Vicknair around 1850. Insulation in the walls of the house was made of dried mud and Spanish moss, called *bousillage*. In 1864, the home was sold to the St. Peter Catholic Church and moved to its present site by Fr. Pierre Lacour. The parlor was used for mass until a church was built in 1867. (Photograph by Peter Forest.)

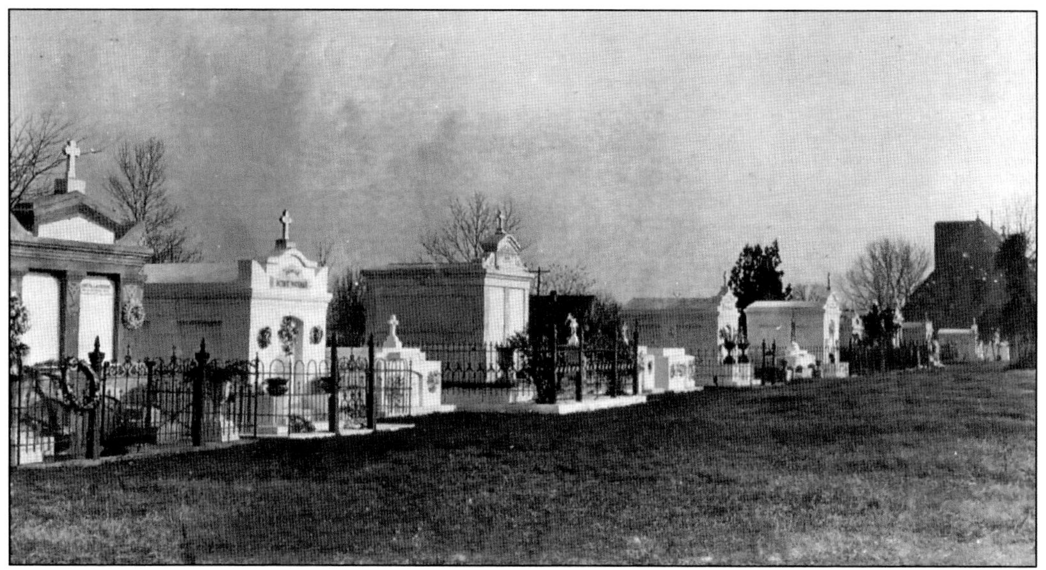

In 1908, the St. Peter Catholic Church cemetery was captured by photographer Guy Donaldson. Located to the rear of St. Peter Catholic Church, the church cemetery opened in 1871. Because of flooding along the Mississippi River, tombs were built above ground. Prior to the opening of the cemetery, church burials were conducted in the St. John the Baptist Church cemetery in Edgard, Louisiana. (Courtesy of Marion Donaldson.)

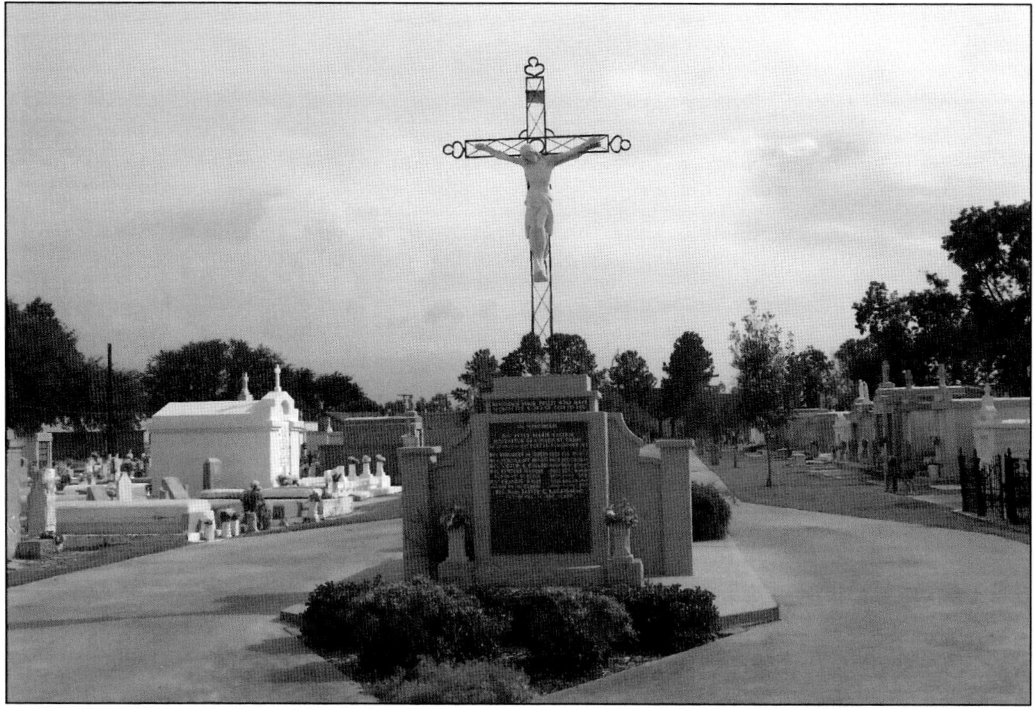

Located in the St. Peter Catholic Church cemetery is a beautiful monument to the former pastors of St. Peter Catholic Church parish. A wrought-iron cross, salvaged from the original wooden church, rests on the tomb of Msgr. Jean Eyraud, pastor of St. Peter for 47 years. Other former pastors buried at the monument are Fr. Pierre Lacour and Fr. Etienne Badoil. (Courtesy of Darroch Watson.)

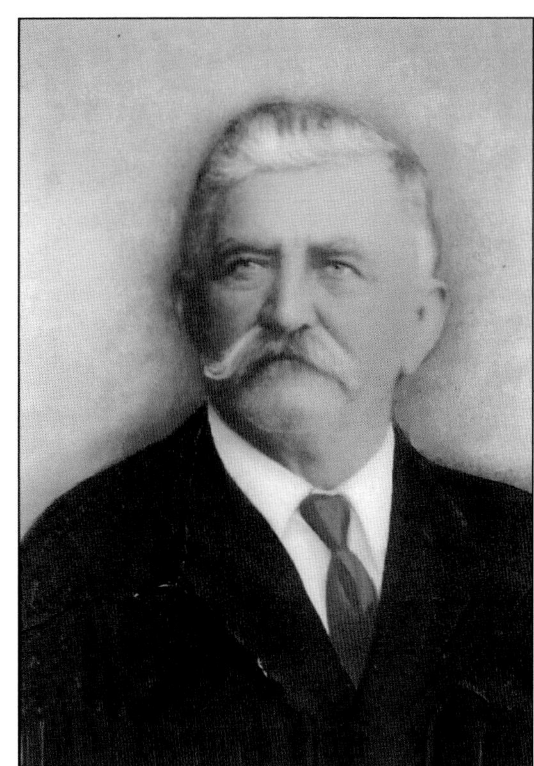

In days long gone, one family's place in village life produced a legacy that has endured. Pictured are Reserve farmer and school board member, Joseph LeBrun, right, and his wife, Marie Monet LeBrun, below. The pair entertained ship passengers from the paddlewheel boats that stopped along the Mississippi River. Their antebellum home was referred to as the "Welcome House." A walkway was built on the levee for passengers. (Courtesy of Gerard Montz.)

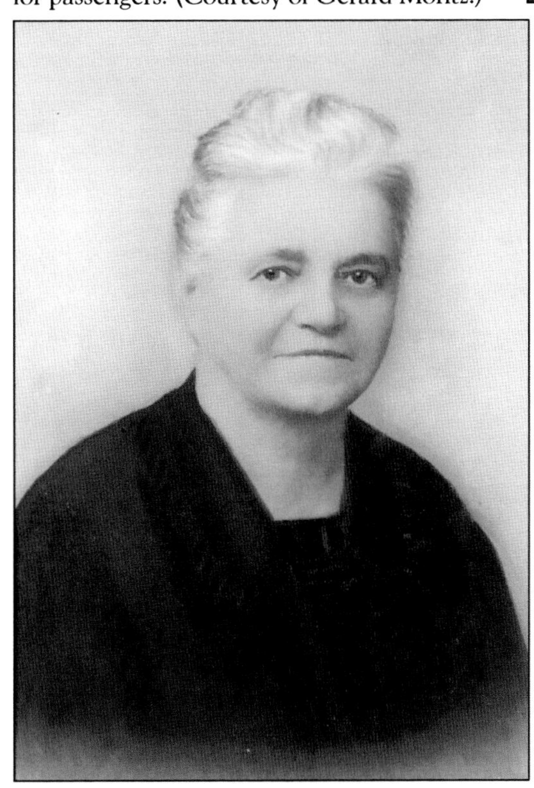

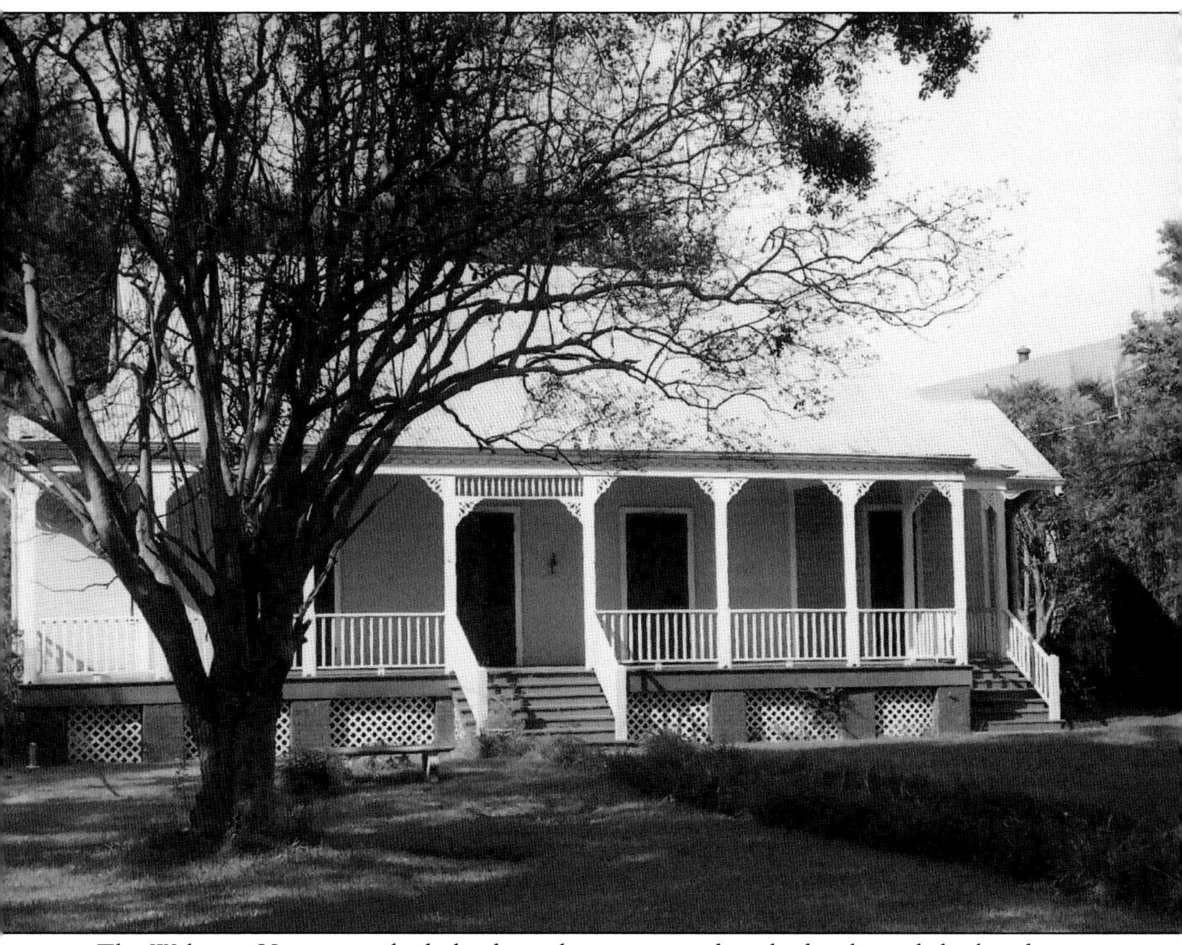

The Welcome House was the hub of social activities as friends, family, and the less fortunate shared the family's bounty. At the LeBrun house, fun was always on the menu as each who visited indeed felt a part of the family. Memories from the LeBrun house, built by John Ernest and Jules Albert Pastureau in the late 1890s, include showboat entertainment on the river, yard games, and parties. (Courtesy of E. Darroch Watson.)

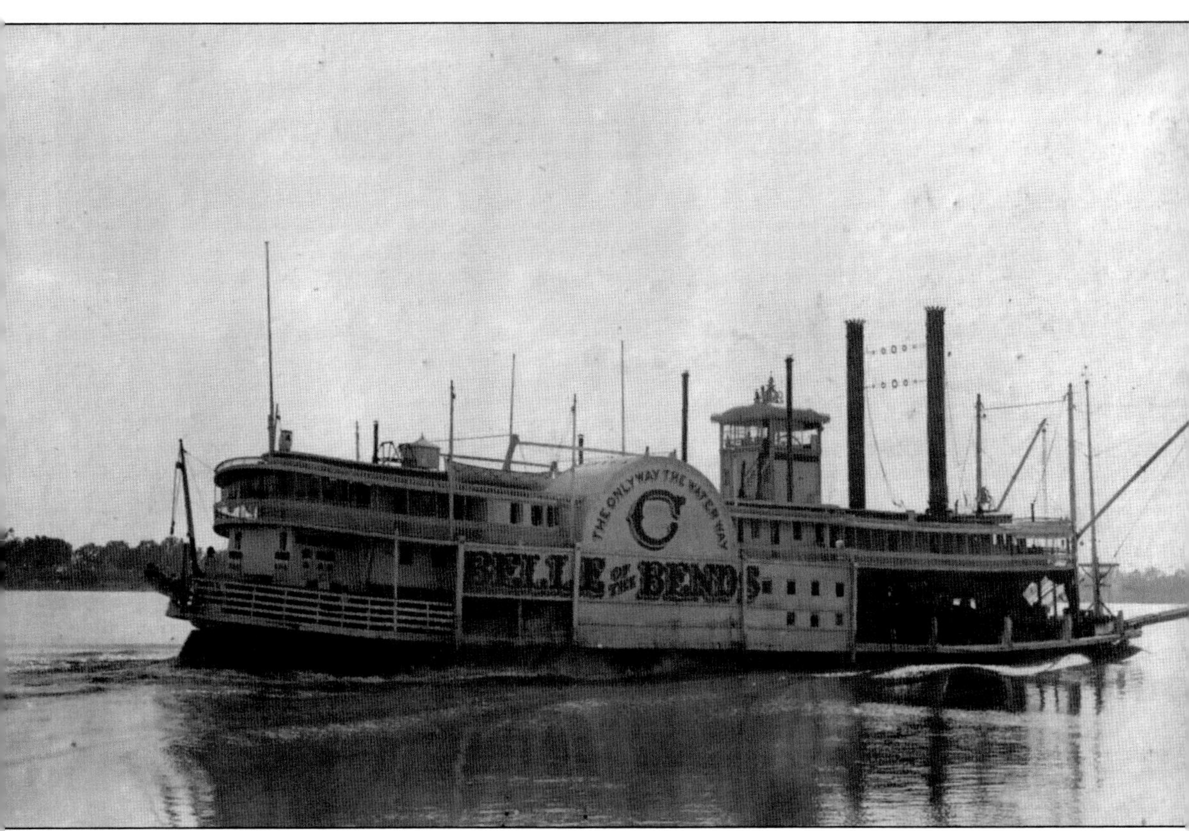

Next to church activities, the most anticipated event was the arrival of the showboat. When the first faint notes of the calliope were heard just around the bend, all hearts beat faster and all heads whirled. Work was abandoned for the day; in the house, the field, and the school, every task was dropped. Everyone raced up the levee to welcome the arrival of the romantic, the glamorous, and the exotic. One watched every exciting and interesting move of the showboat: the landing, the putting down of the gangplank, the formation of the parade, the calliope blaring forth its medley all the while, and then the band, the horses in their gay trappings, and the beautiful ladies—the parade! Showboats declined by the Civil War, but began again in 1878, focusing on melodrama and vaudeville. (Courtesy of Joy Donaldson McGraw.)

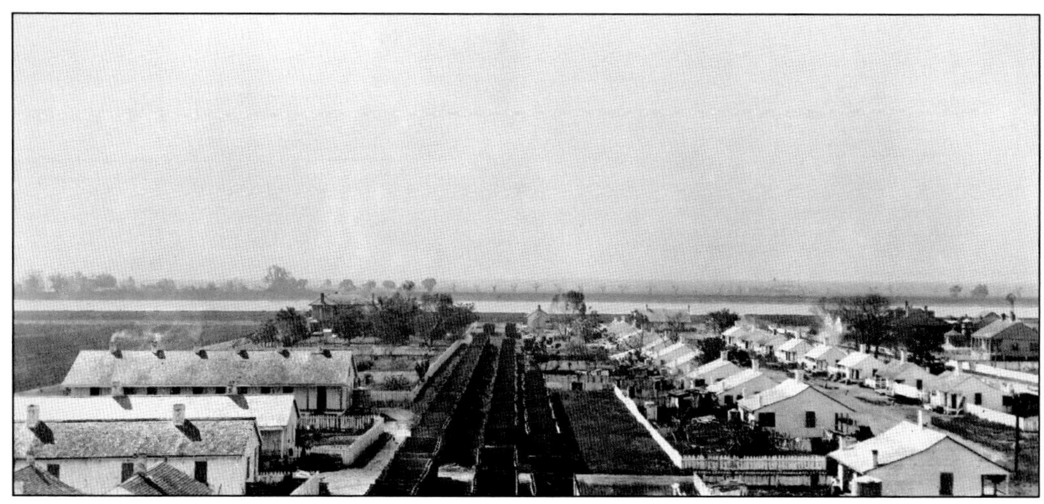

A unique photograph taken from the Godchaux Sugar Refinery, looking toward the Mississippi River, shows the housing pattern near the sugar refinery in the early 1900s. A series of houses was built by the Godchaux family to house employees. Sugarcane carts three rows deep are stored between two rows of houses. Across the Mississippi River is the Columbia Sugar Refinery, operated by Etienne Joseph Caire and Jean-Baptiste Graugnard. (Courtesy of Marion Donaldson.)

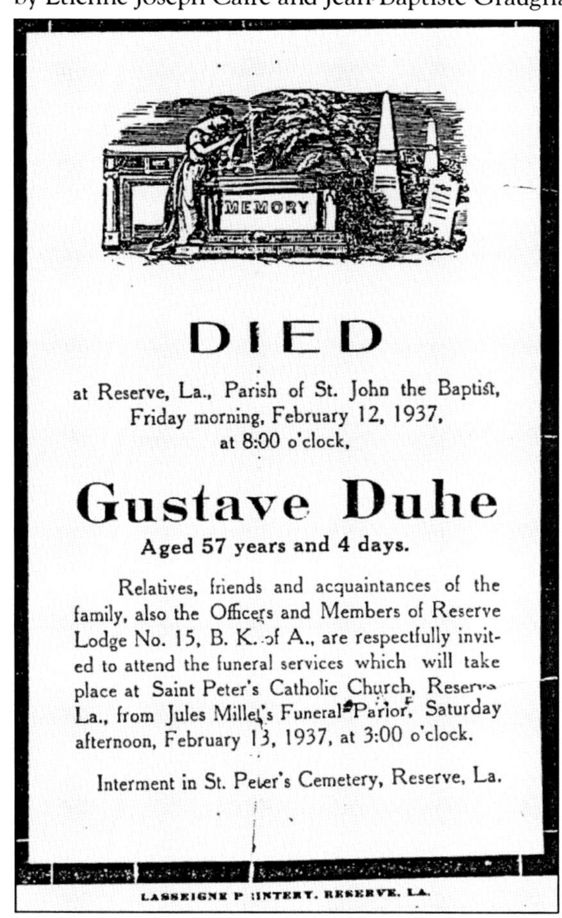

MEMORY

DIED

at Reserve, La., Parish of St. John the Baptist, Friday morning, February 12, 1937, at 8:00 o'clock,

Gustave Duhe

Aged 57 years and 4 days.

Relatives, friends and acquaintances of the family, also the Officers and Members of Reserve Lodge No. 15, B. K. of A., are respectfully invited to attend the funeral services which will take place at Saint Peter's Catholic Church, Reserve La., from Jules Millet's Funeral Parlor, Saturday afternoon, February 13, 1937, at 3:00 o'clock.

Interment in St. Peter's Cemetery, Reserve, La.

LASSEIGNE PRINTERY. RESERVE. LA.

Communication between plantations was quite limited, and messages of deaths were delivered on horseback or posted in a public place for all to see. Generally, a white sheet of paper bordered in black was tacked to the gateposts along the River Road. These notes announced the demise of the individual, listing the time and place of religious services and internment. (Courtesy of Melba Duhe Hymel)

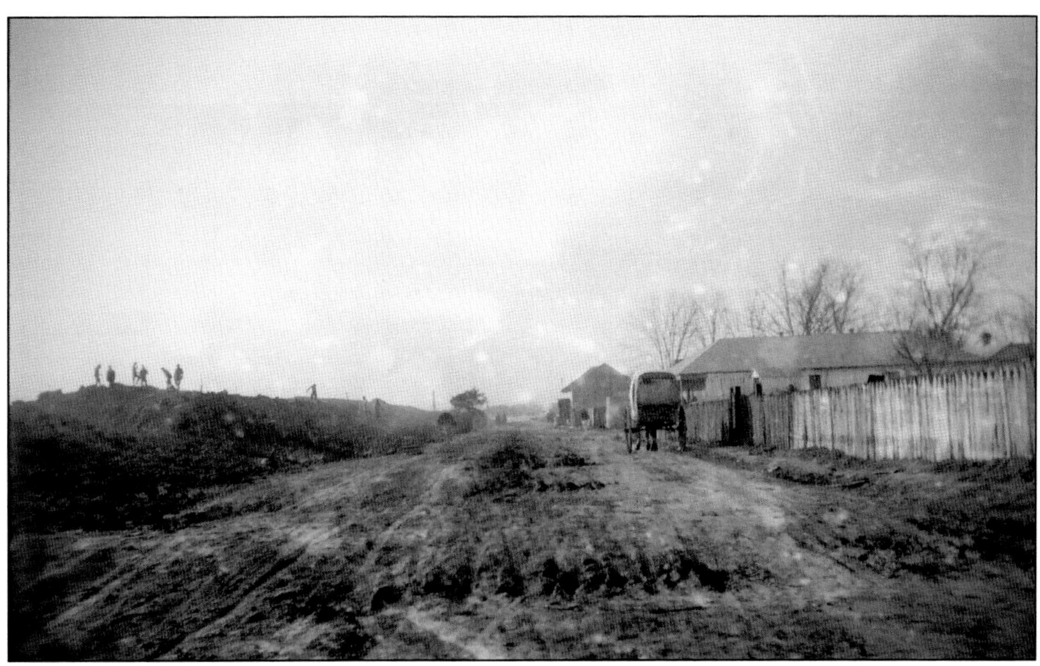

The first Mississippi River levees were built in 1820 and raised in 1885; new levees were built in 1898, 1908, 1916, and 1919. When the levee of 1916 was built, half of the Leon Godchaux High School land was taken, and the people living along the public roads from Cornland Plantation were forced to move back from the levee. Pictured, top, are convicts working on the Mississippi River levee as it moved from Donaldson's Drug Store to Dr. Louis T. Donaldson's home. The bottom photograph shows the dragline operations in front of Dr. L.T. Donaldson's home. Prior to 1916, land in Reserve extended 100 yards into the Mississippi River, and a park with gazebos was built in front of Cornland Plantation. (Courtesy of Marion Donaldson.)

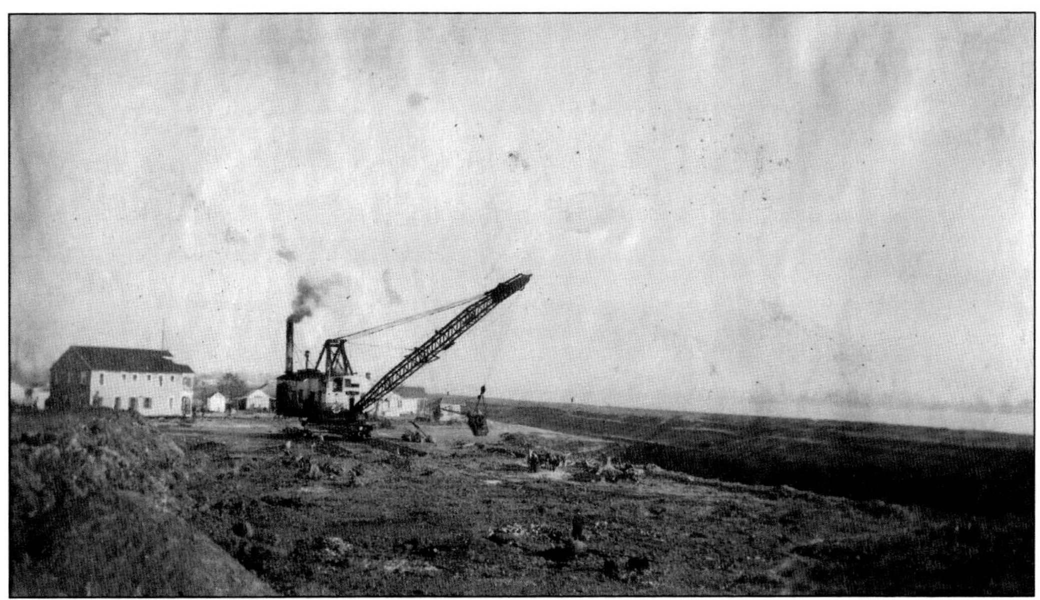

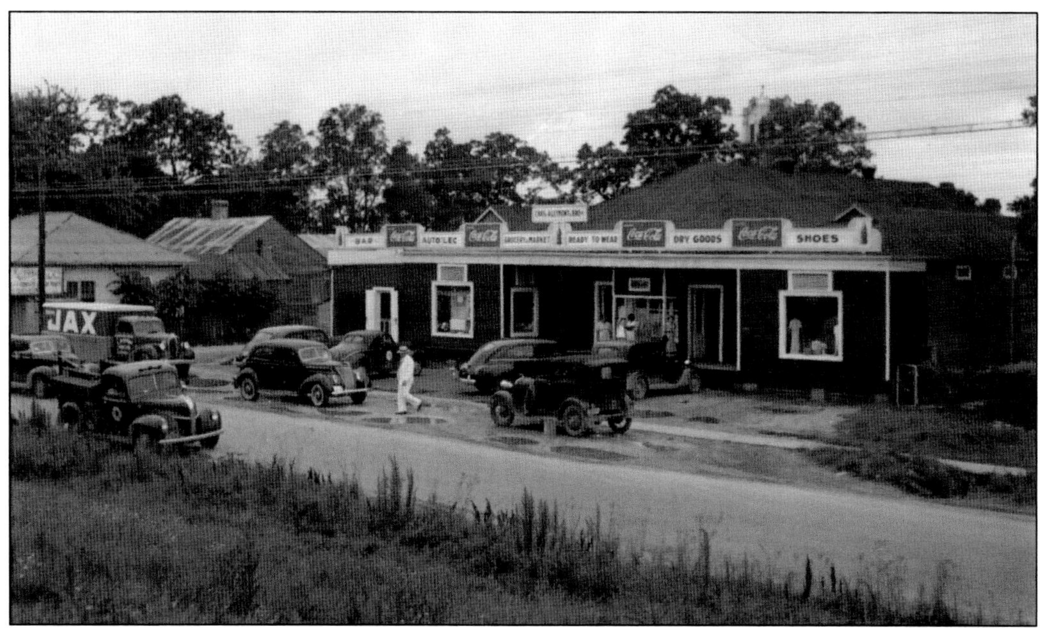

Originally called the Reserve Star Store in the 1880s, the cypress wood store was a commissary for the Reserve Sugar Refinery and referred to as the company store. In 1904, Charles Alltmont leased the property until his death in 1928, and additions were added to the store. In the years that followed, two other generations—Alfred C. and his son Charles Alltmont—managed the store. (Courtesy of Norine Alltmont.)

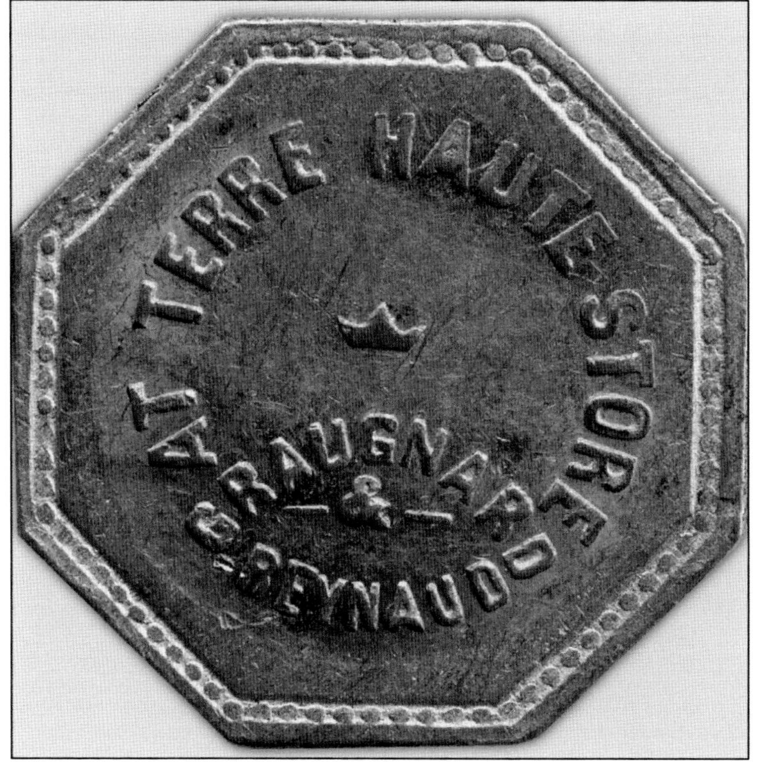

Tokens were predominately used by plantation owners to pay employees. These tokens were good only at the country store and could be redeemed as cash. The coins were of different shapes and sizes to distinguish them from the tokens of other plantations. Tokens were also used in bakeries, restaurants, bars, and pool halls. The practice of using store tokens was discontinued in the 1950s. (Courtesy of Trisha Guidry Aucoin.)

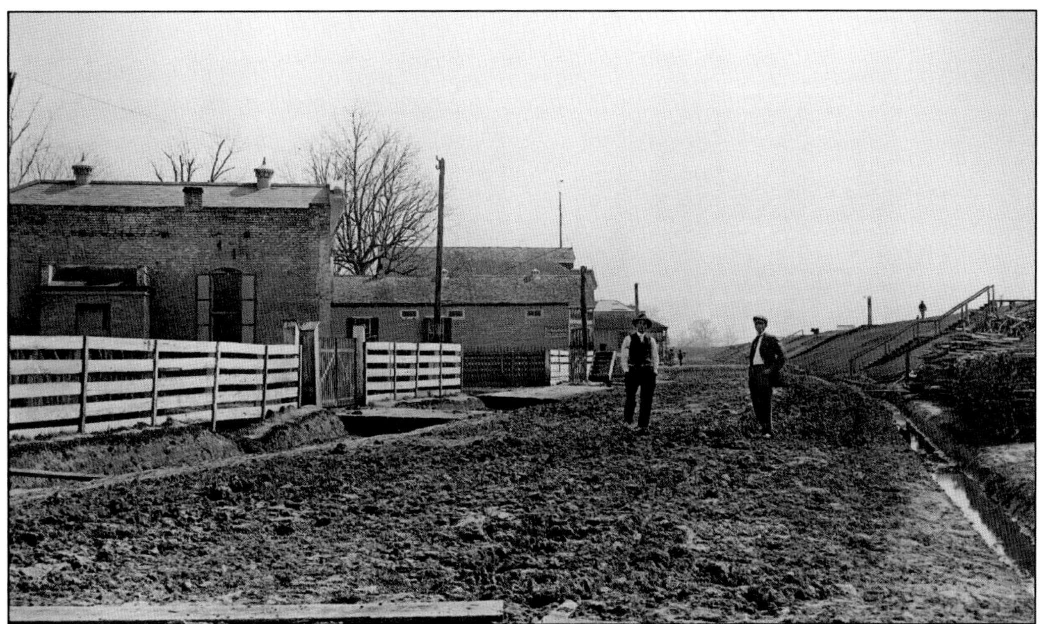

In 1908, the Donaldson brothers, Henry and Guy, are pictured walking down River Road, now US Highway 44. Buildings include the Bank of St. John, Donaldson's Drug Store, and the New Sugar Belt Club. Roads were so poor that travel from Reserve to New Orleans took as many as three to four hours. Motorists stopped frequently to fix flat tires. (Courtesy of Marion Donaldson.)

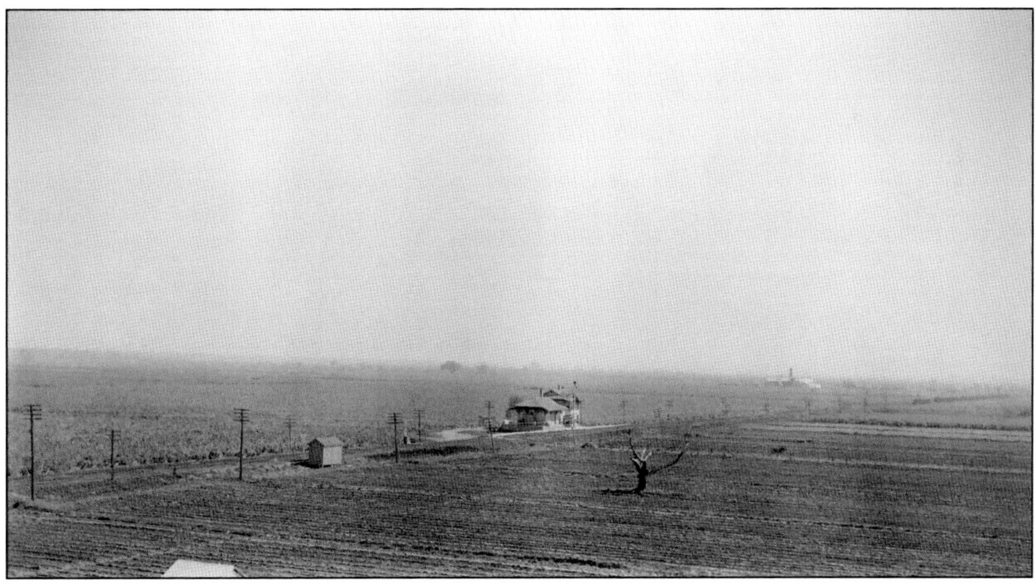

In 1908, the Reserve train station, located on West Tenth Street, is pictured. To the extreme right of the train station is the Maurice Edrington sugar mill. Since Edrington also grew corn, the area was called Cornland. The Edrington Plantation was sold to C.I. James, who subdivided a portion of the property and developed Reserve's first subdivision, West First Street, in the 1920s. (Courtesy of Marion Donaldson.)

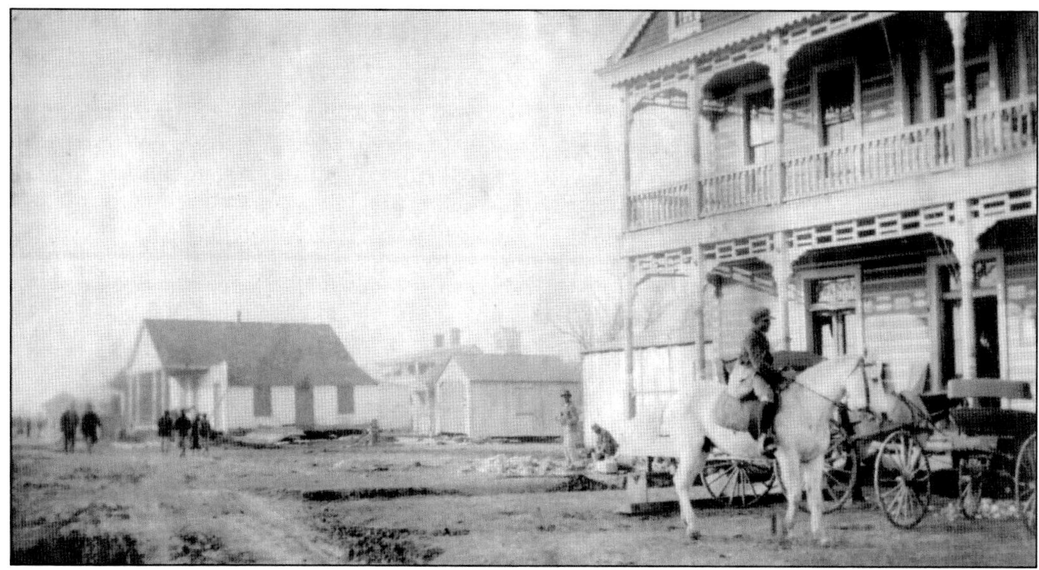

The New Sugar Belt Club was a social club that was built by John Ernest and Jules Albert Pastureau in 1897 on property owned by Joseph LeBrun. Ahead of its time, it had indoor toilet facilities, a central unit of gas lights, and running water from a double deck of cisterns. In 1904, the building was purchased by Pierre René Montz and moved near St. Peter Catholic Church. (Courtesy of Gerard Montz.)

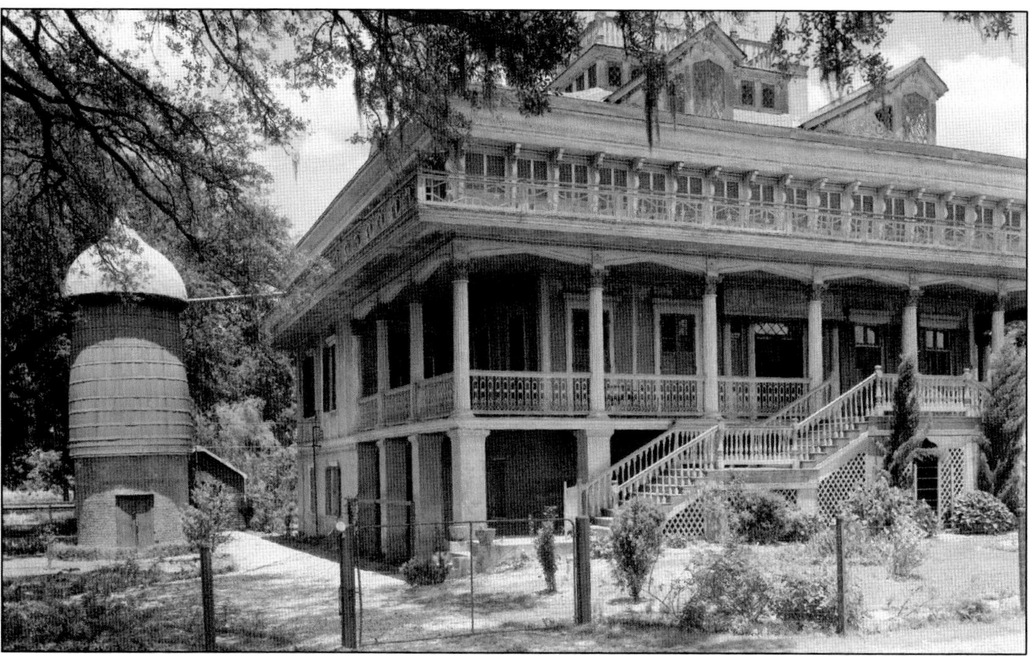

The San Francisco House, located in Lions, was constructed in 1849 by Antoine Valsin Marmillion following the purchase of a sugar mill by his father, Edmond. Antoine Valsin married Louise von Seybold, a Bavarian girl, and they named the plantation San Francisco. An accomplished organist, Louise became a regular at St. John the Baptist Catholic Church in Edgard, Louisiana, and performed in July 1865 for the memorial mass for Caroline Deslonde, the late wife of General Beauregard. (Courtesy of Carl L. Levet and family.)

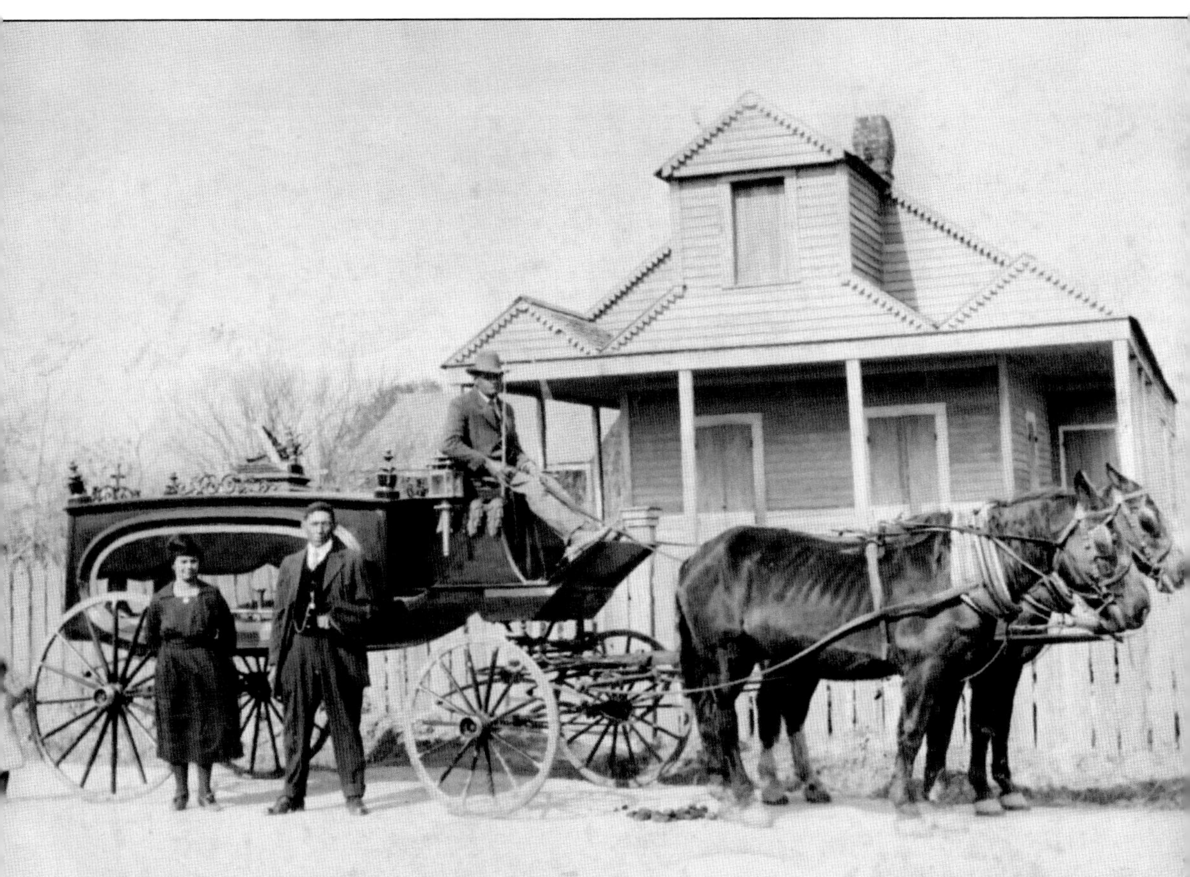

In 1922, this horse-drawn hearse carried the bodies of African Americans for burial. Pictured are, from left to right, two-year-old Ethel Cureau Robottom, mother Leah Perrilloux Cureau, and father Oureelian Cureau. The driver of the hearse is Ethel's uncle Joseph "Pa-Chot" Perrilloux. Ethel married Harry Robottom Sr., founder and owner of Robottom Mortuary, which is currently located on East Twenty-Sixth Street in Reserve. (Courtesy of Dale Thomas.)

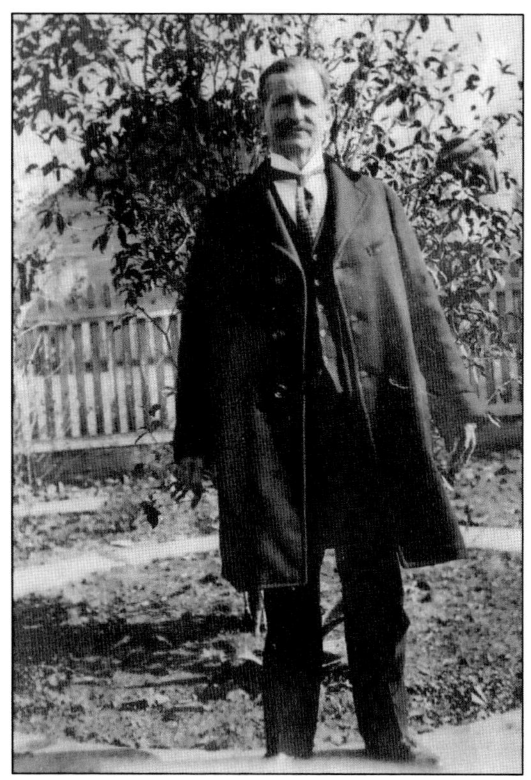

Dr. Louis T. Donaldson, left, and his wife, Antoinette, below, settled in Reserve and raised a family of nine children. Sons Louis and Armand followed in their father's footsteps to become doctors. Henry and Guy served as druggists, and Sidney was a dentist. Daughter Rosa married into the Maurin family, and Antoinette and Claire lived on the homestead. (Courtesy of Joy Donaldson McGraw.)

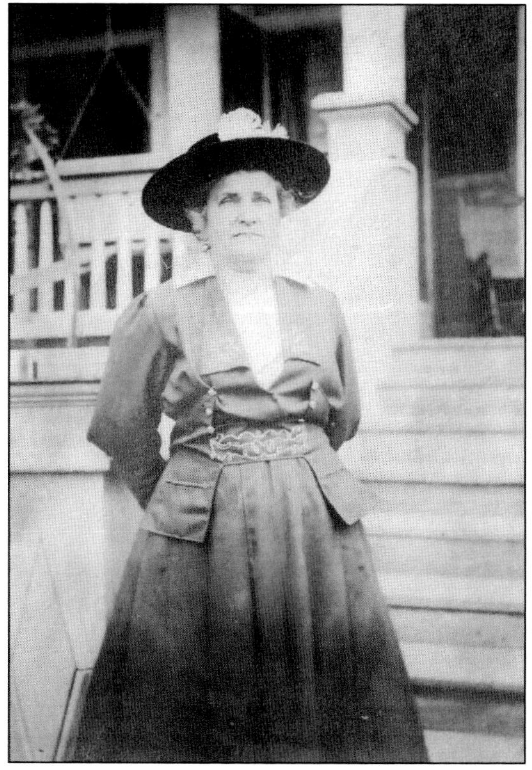

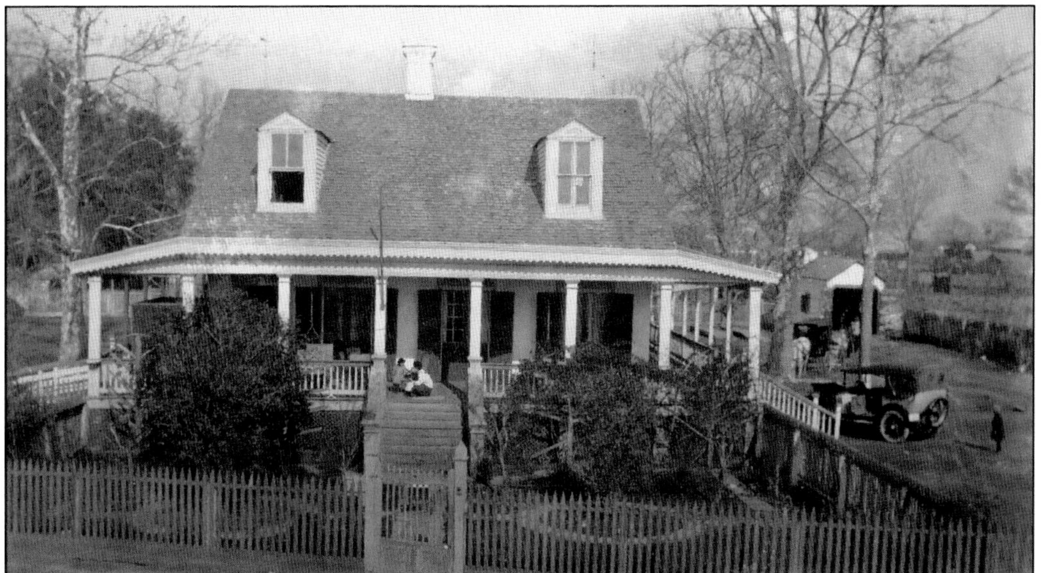

Pictured on January 1, 1918, is a front view of Dr. Louis T. Donaldson's home. Playing on the porch are Rose and Beulah Donaldson. Standing near the 1914 Oakland automobile is Dr. Donaldson's grandson Guy Donaldson Jr. The house is currently owned by Dr. L.T. Donaldson's great-grandson Alfred Walden Donaldson. (Courtesy of Joy Donaldson McGraw.)

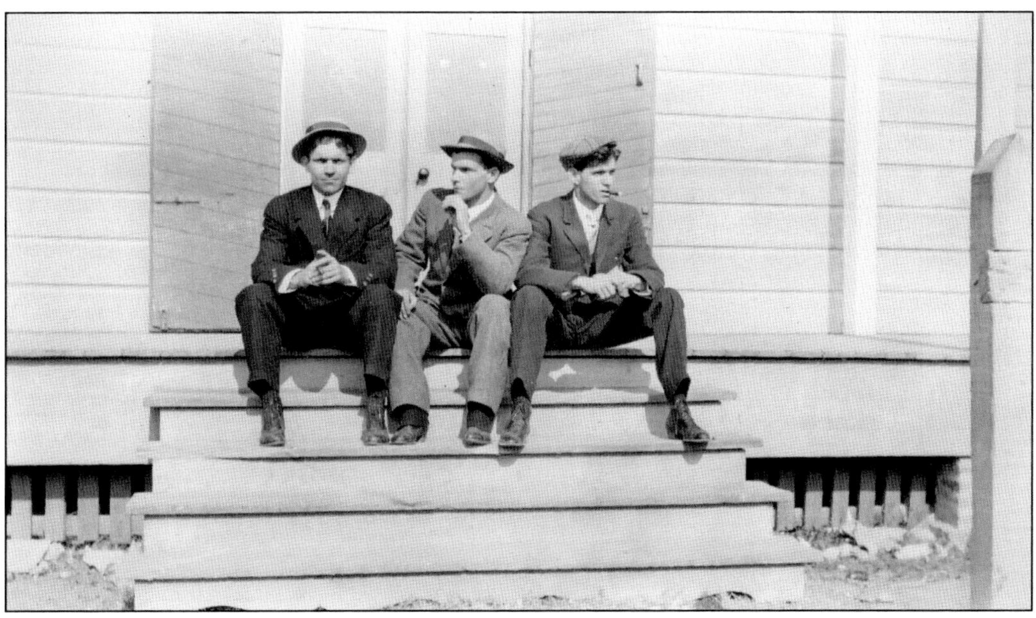

In 1908, three of Dr. Louis T. Donaldson's sons—Sidney (left), Guy (center), and Henry—are pictured sitting on the steps of People's Pharmacy. The pharmacy was located near St. Peter Catholic Church and was purchased by Henry Donaldson and renamed Donaldson's Drug Store. Eventually, the property would be sold to St. Peter Catholic Church and is now part of the church parking lot. (Courtesy of Marion Donaldson.)

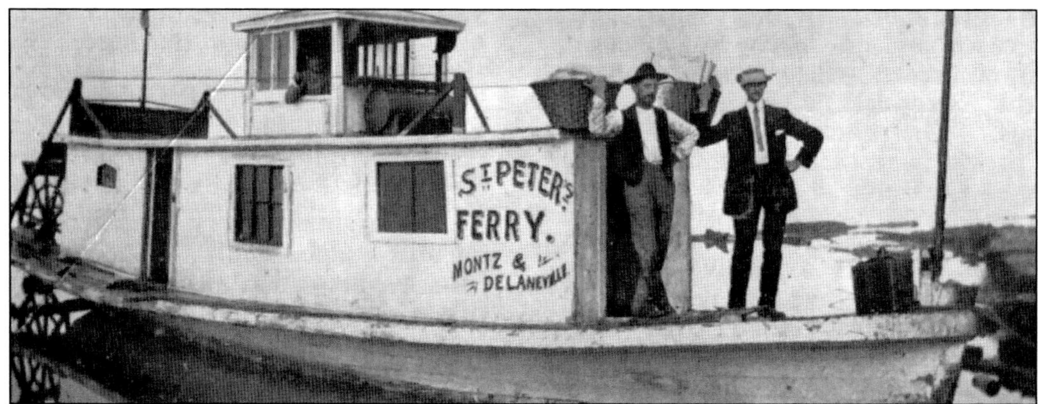

In the early 1900s, the St. Peter's Mississippi River Ferry was operated by Pierre René Montz and Horace Delaneuville. The ferry service took passengers back and forth across the Mississippi River to conduct business at the parish courthouse in Edgard, Louisiana. Montz was very entrepreneurial, as he operated a hotel, silent movie house, stable, and the Reserve Electric Company. (Courtesy of Shirley Casseigne Terrio.)

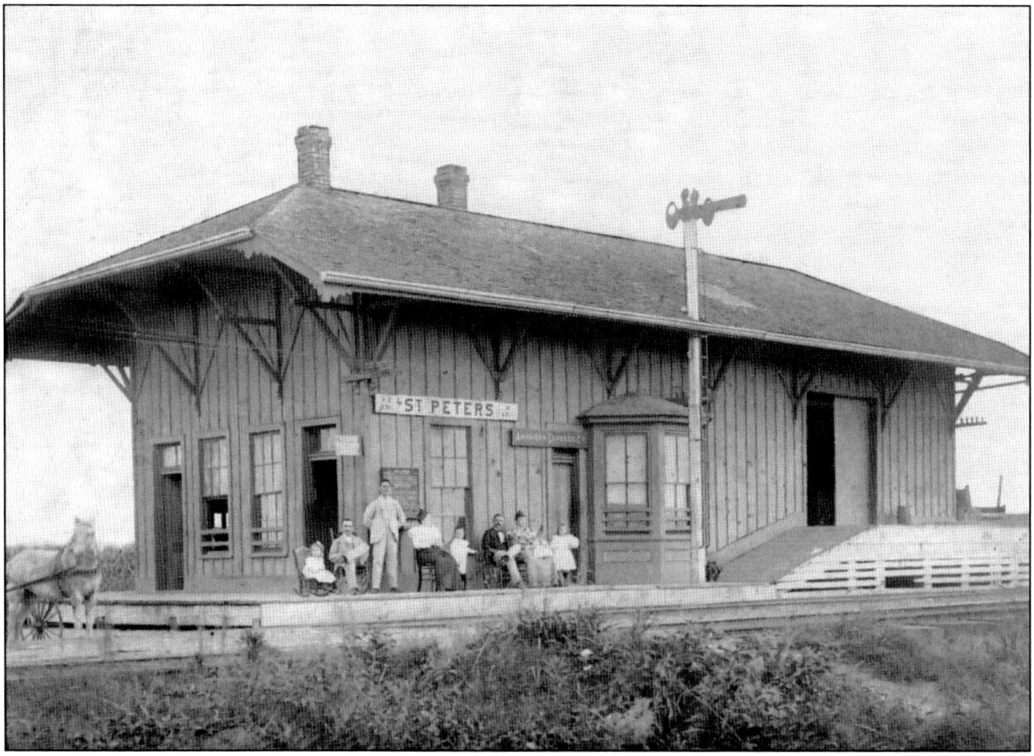

The Yazoo & Mississippi Valley Railroad Company completed their railroad through St. Peters (Reserve) in 1883. Pictured is Andre Perilloux, the first manager of the train station. Located behind St. Peter Catholic Church cemetery, the train station took the name of the town in which it was located, as was customary; thus the train station was named after the town—St. Peters. (Courtesy of Carl L. Levet and family.)

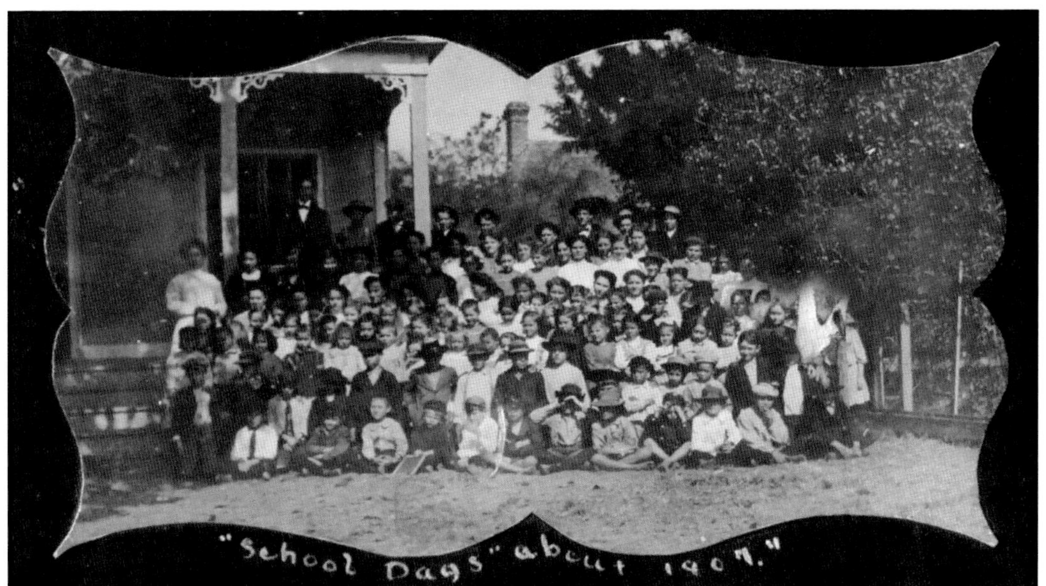

Pictured in 1907 is a private school in Reserve. Private schools in Reserve began in the late 1860s and 1870s. French noblemen opened private schools. One was Furrate du Bois, a pioneer of teaching reading using the phonetic method, and his school was situated on James Humphrey's (Old Cornland) plantation. The other was Amedee Papet, and his school was on Union Plantation in Lions, Louisiana. (Courtesy of Joy Donaldson McGraw.).

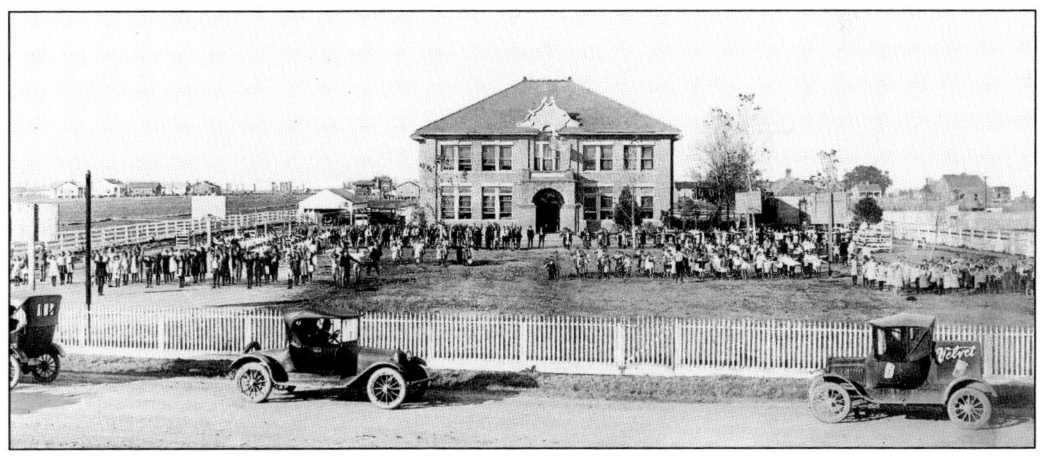

In 1909, a public high school was built in Reserve by the St. John the Baptist Parish School Board to serve East Bank students of the parish. The school was built at a cost of $15,000 on land donated by the Leon Godchaux family. For this donation, the St. John the Baptist Parish School Board named the new school Leon Godchaux High School. (Courtesy of Joy Donaldson McGraw.)

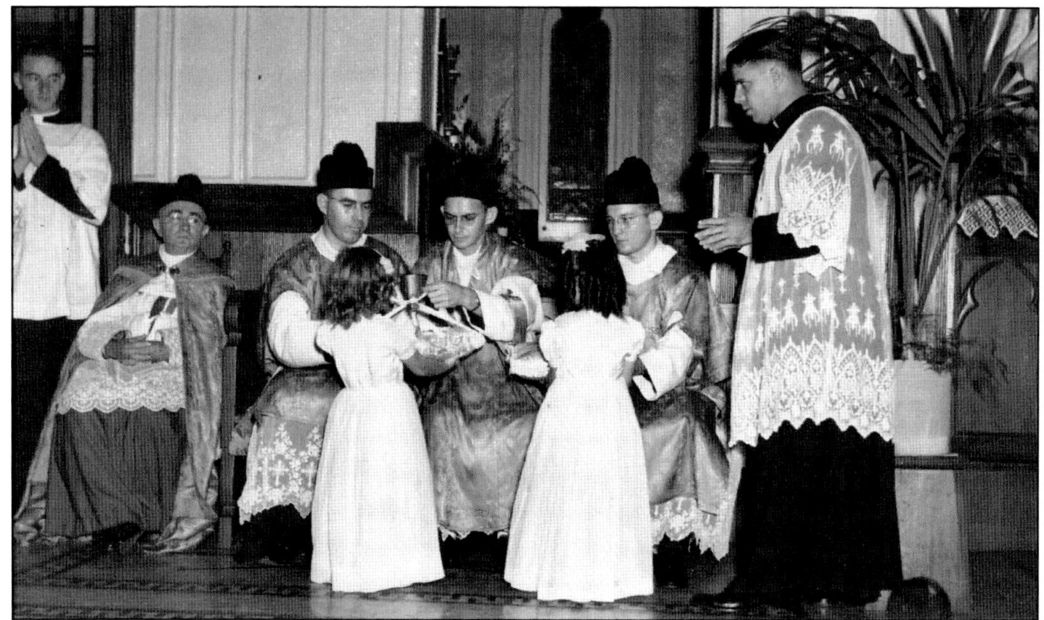

Reserve native and former St. Peter Parochial School and Leon Godchaux High School student John Warren Barrios celebrated his first mass following his ordination at St. Peter Catholic Church on Sunday, September 22, 1946. Pictured in the photograph are, from left to right, Msgr. Jean Eyraud, unidentified, Father Barrios, unidentified, and Fr. George Hebert. Bringing the gifts are chalice bearer Diane Benoit and paten Charlene Thibodaux. (Courtesy of St. Peter Catholic Church.)

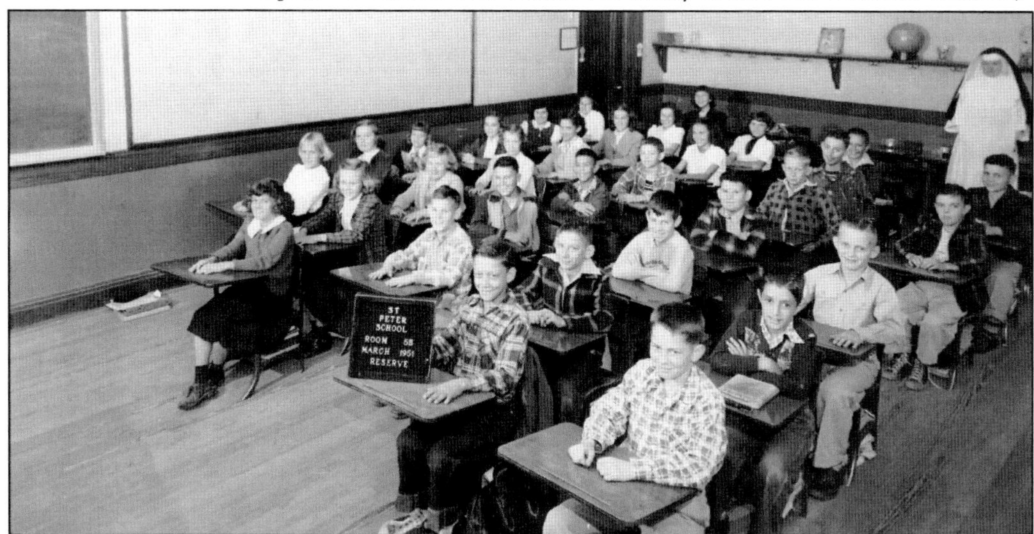

Sr. Mary Robert's St. Peter School fifth-grade class is pictured in 1951. The students include, from front to back, (first row) Lynn Robichaux, John Falgoust, Sheldon Vice, Ronald Stein, and Winton Waguespack; (second row) John Brady, Gerald Keller, Wilton Madere, Blaine Weber, Nolan Landeche, Manton Duhe, and Bryan Torres; (third row) Bertram Madere, Leonard Torres, Remy Hahn, Richard Granier, Mary Ann Torres, and Brenda Audiffred; (fourth row) Lorraine Scioneaux, JoAnn Delhommer, Linda Sue Englade, unidentified, Shirley Tassin, Joan Scioneaux Brady, Julie Hymel Brady, and unidentified; (fifth row) Carol Ory, Katherine Brignac, Marilyn Fabre, Melanie Fulton, Sherry Weber Millet, and Jerrye Brady St. Martin. (Courtesy of Gerald Keller.)

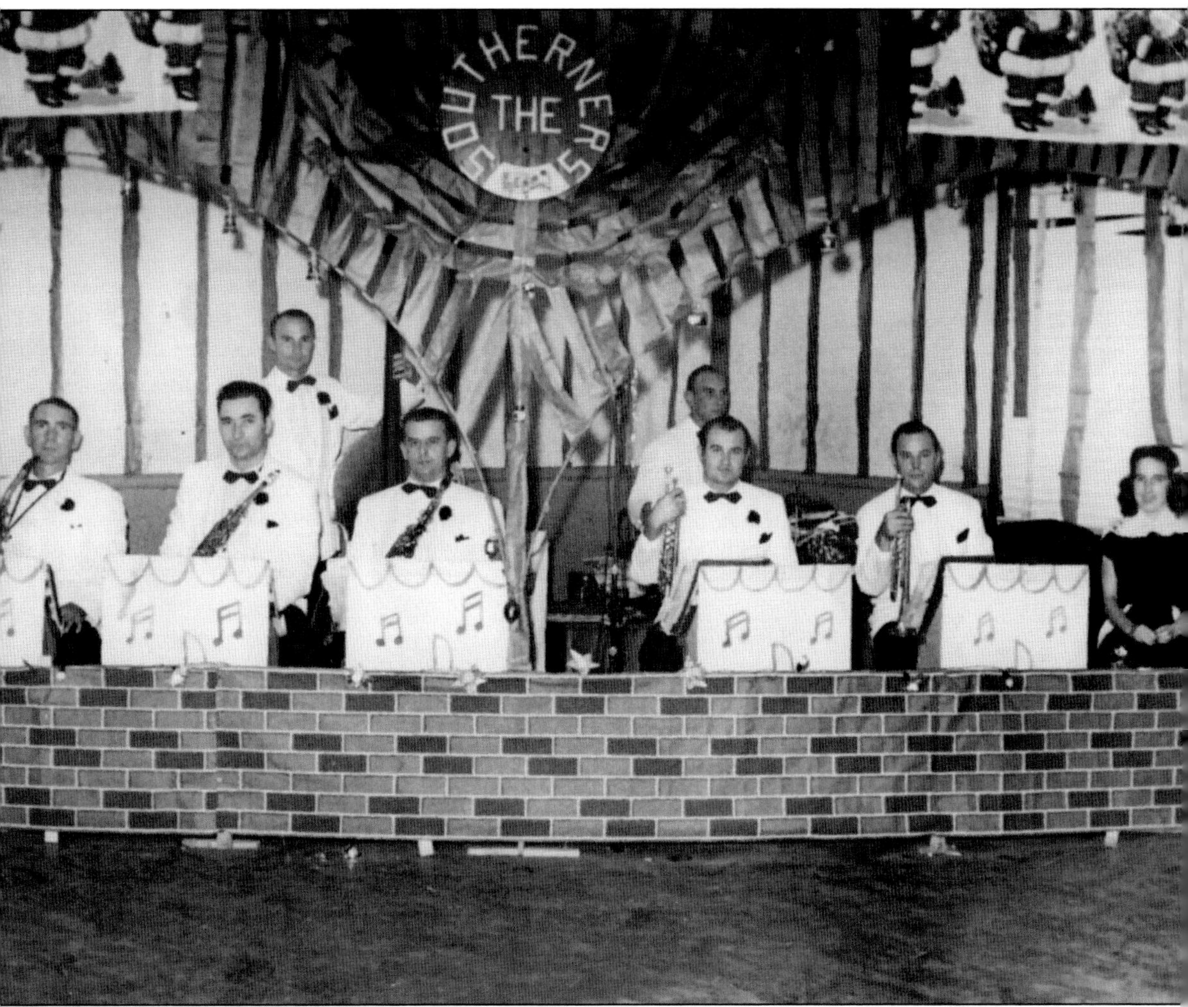

Originally known as Lester Louque and His Orchestra, the Southerners played during the last of the Big Band swing era of the late 1940s and early 1950s. This picture shows the Southerners performing during a Christmas dance at the Godchaux Community Club Pavilion. Members of the band include, from left to right, (first row) James Haydel Jr., two unidentified, Sidney Dufresne, unidentified, and singer Iris Boudreaux Rousse; (second row) Lester Louque Sr. and unidentified. (Courtesy of Fay Louque Reine.)

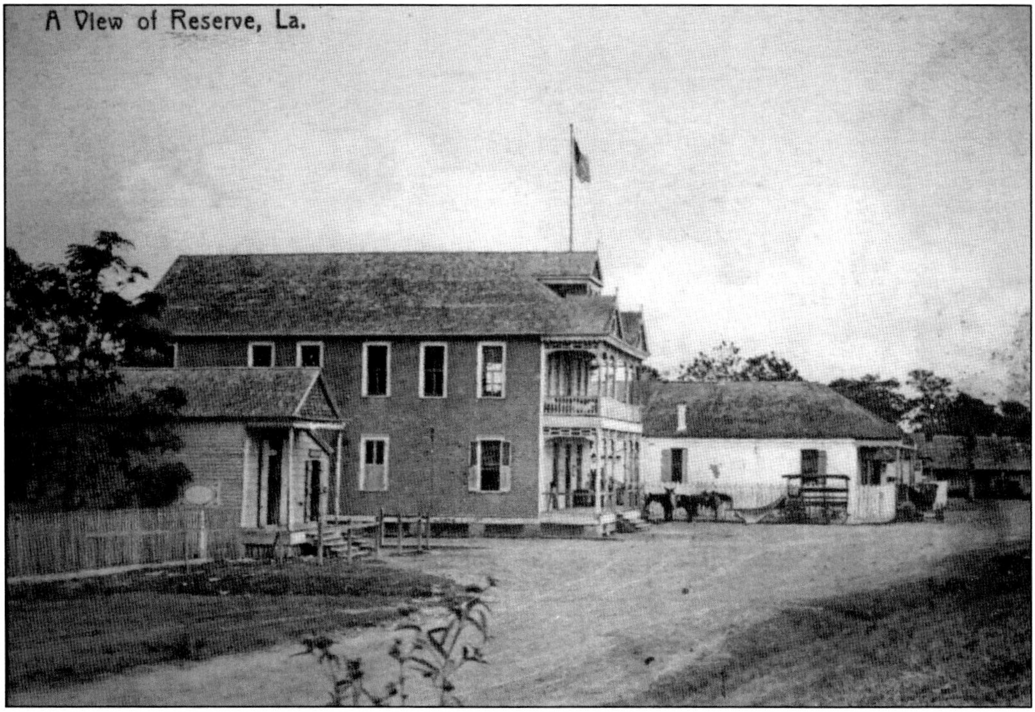

A View of Reserve, La.

Pictured in 1912 is the New Sugar Belt Club and Alltmont's Store. Not in view was the Sugar Belt Hotel, owned by Pierre René Montz. The hotel was a rest stop for salesmen who arrived by paddlewheels and needed an overnight stay or those who were waiting for passage on the Yazoo & Mississippi Valley Railroad. A color postcard was made of this photograph and distributed in 1913. (Courtesy of Gerard Montz.)

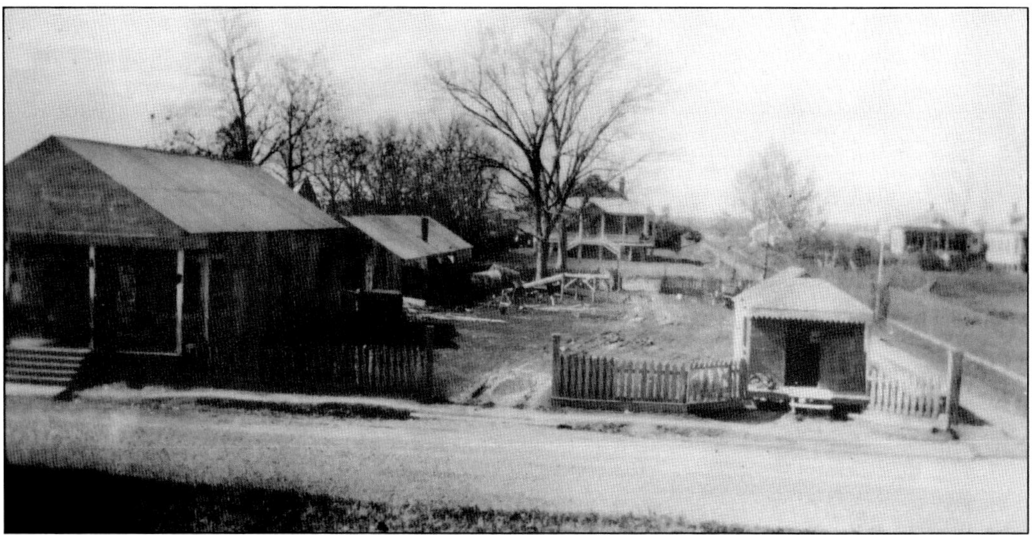

This 1920 photograph shows the home of Albert Millet (background) and the home of Leon Graugnard (right). The buildings on River Road include the Edward Millet Sr. store and the Lions Post Office. Behind Millet's store is a cistern shop owned and operated by Albert Millet. Graugnard was a successful sugarcane farmer on Terre Haute Plantation. (Courtesy of Joseph L. and Peggy Robichaux.)

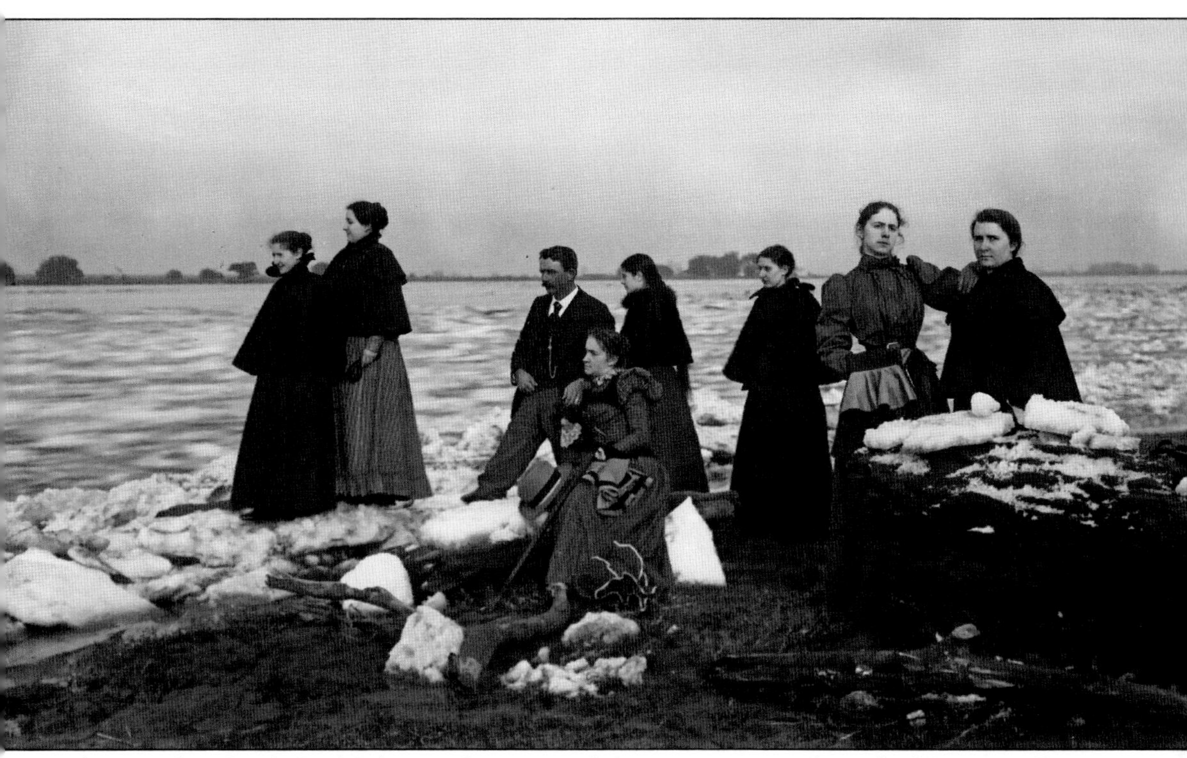

Photographer Ovidé Paul Schexnayder captured this winter scene along the Mississippi River in February 1899. Although it was not as cold as the winter of 1823, the Mississippi River was filled with ice in such quantity and of such huge sizes that all navigation along it was completely stopped for two weeks. The ground remained frozen for eight days, making travel on the roads almost impossible, as the horses could not be used and there were no automobiles. The sugarcane was so hard that the planters did not begin cutting until 10:00 a.m., and the mills had to steam the cane to extract the juice. Most of the cane crop was lost, and the grinding season lasted only two to three weeks. However, the corn crop was prolific, with unusually large ears of excellent quality, as the freezing temperatures had destroyed the insects and weeds. (Courtesy of Louisiana State Museum.)

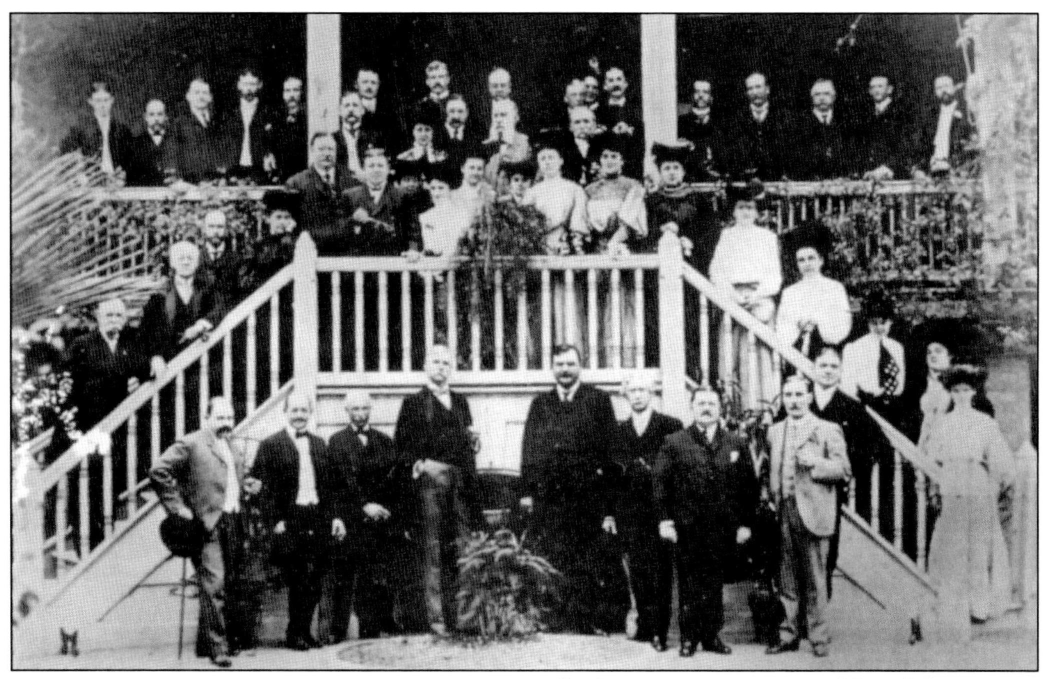

On his convention trip to New Orleans, Pres. William Howard Taft anchored at Reserve in October 1909 with his entourage of 117 senators, 24 governors, and three diplomats. Taft was invited to a luncheon and visited the Godchaux Sugar Refinery. From the left stairwell of the Godchaux House, Taft, left, gave a speech. Standing next to President Taft is plant manager Edward Godchaux, right. (Courtesy of Shirley Casseigne Terrio.)

Follow the CROWD to

RESERVE!

The Amusement Center of St. John Parish

WHERE YOU WILL ENJOY YOUR

HOLIDAY DANCES

SUNDAY, DECEMBER 23rd---AT COMMUNITY CLUB

—MUSIC BY—

Lawrence CLUB PINE Orchestra

MONDAY, DECEMBER 24th---XMAS EVE

AT RESERVE COMMUNITY CLUB

—MUSIC BY—

Claiborne Williams

Tuesday, December 25--Christmas Night

AT MAURIN'S PAVILION

—MUSIC BY—

CELESTIN'S TUXEDO ORCHESTRA

SUNDAY, DECEMBER 30th--At MAURIN'S PAVILION

MUSIC BY

Peerless Revelers

MONDAY, DECEMBER 31st---NEW YEAR'S EVE

AT MAURIN'S PAVILION

This 1934 poster features some of the leading orchestras in the area. Jazz was sweeping the nation, and Papa Celestin's orchestra was one of the leading bands hired for social functions—both African American and white—and was a regular on Bourbon Street in New Orleans. Claiborne Williams's orchestra, from Ascension Parish, and the Peerless Revelers Orchestra, from Independence, Louisiana, were always local favorites. (Courtesy of Gerard Montz.)

Two

Godchaux Sugar Refinery and Industrial Growth

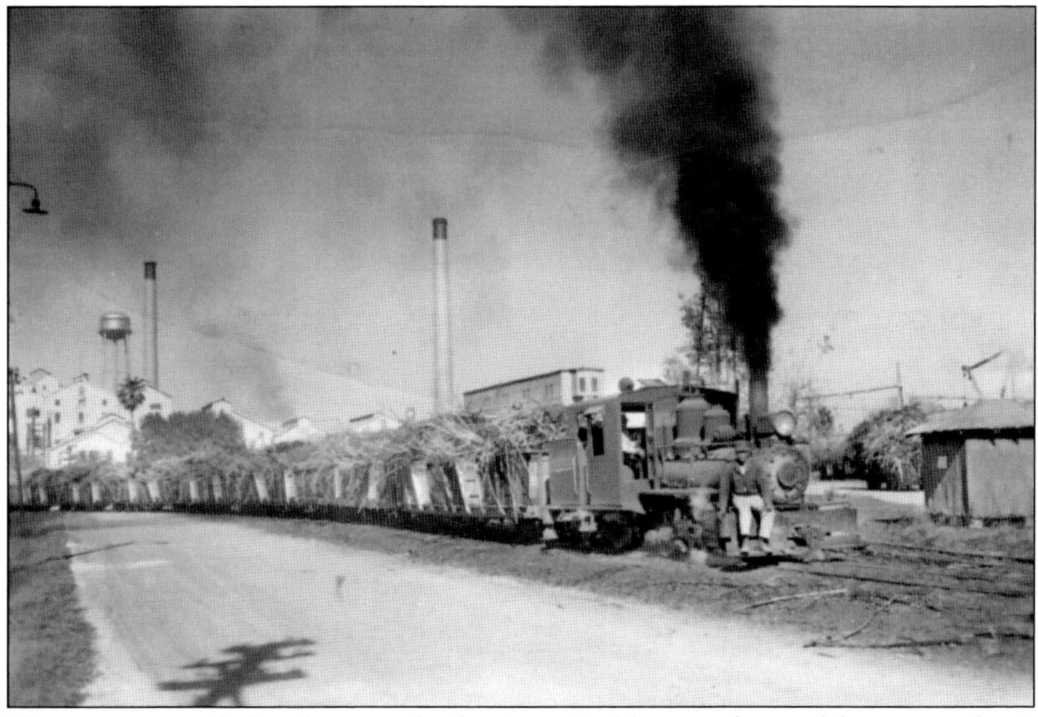

There are no records that show exactly when Leon Godchaux made use of the tramway, but it is believed to be around 1890. The tiny steam locomotives became popular after the advent of the narrow-gauge rails, and Leon Godchaux got on the bandwagon by adding steam engines to this railroad. The small steam trains were called "dummies" by those who ran them. (Courtesy of Joy Donaldson McGraw.)

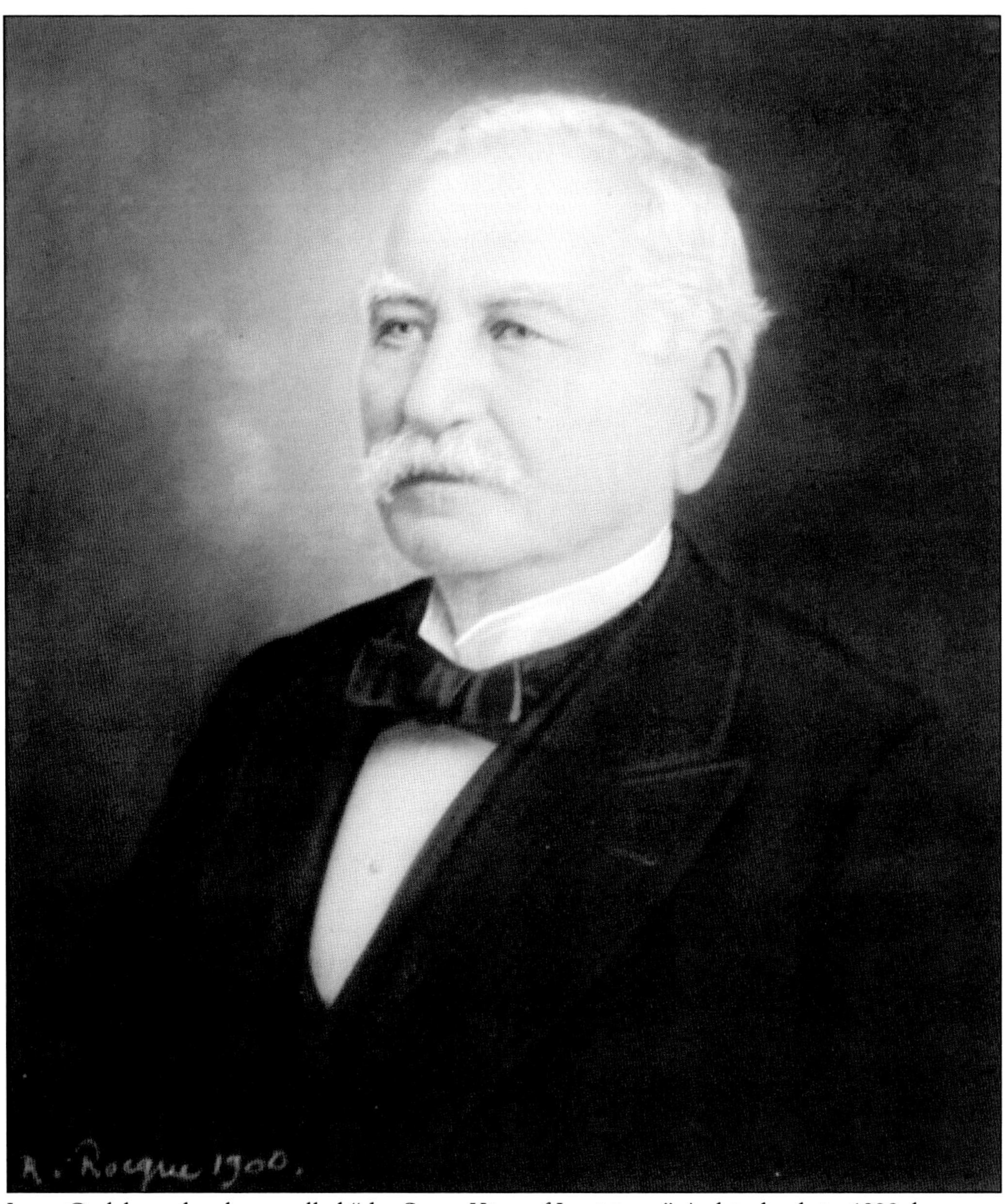

Leon Godchaux has been called "the Sugar King of Louisiana." At his death in 1899, he was a multimillionaire from the profits of the sugar industry, investments, and a clothing store in New Orleans. The rag-to-riches story began in Herbeviller, France, where he was born Lion Godchot, on June 10, 1824. At age 16, he used virtually all his money for passage to New Orleans in 1840. Seeing the vast number of plantations, he reasoned there was a good market for needles, ribbons, lace, and other notions that the plantation ladies had a hard time buying. The business was so good that he opened a New Orleans clothing store near Decatur Street and later moved to Canal Street. Although he was a successful merchant, his prize was the purchase of the Reserve Plantation. Eventually, he owned 14 plantations and promoted the idea of centralizing his sugar manufacturing. The Godchaux Store in New Orleans catered to the middle and upper classes and kept in stock neckties that sold for $1,000–$2,000. (Courtesy of the Leon Godchaux family.)

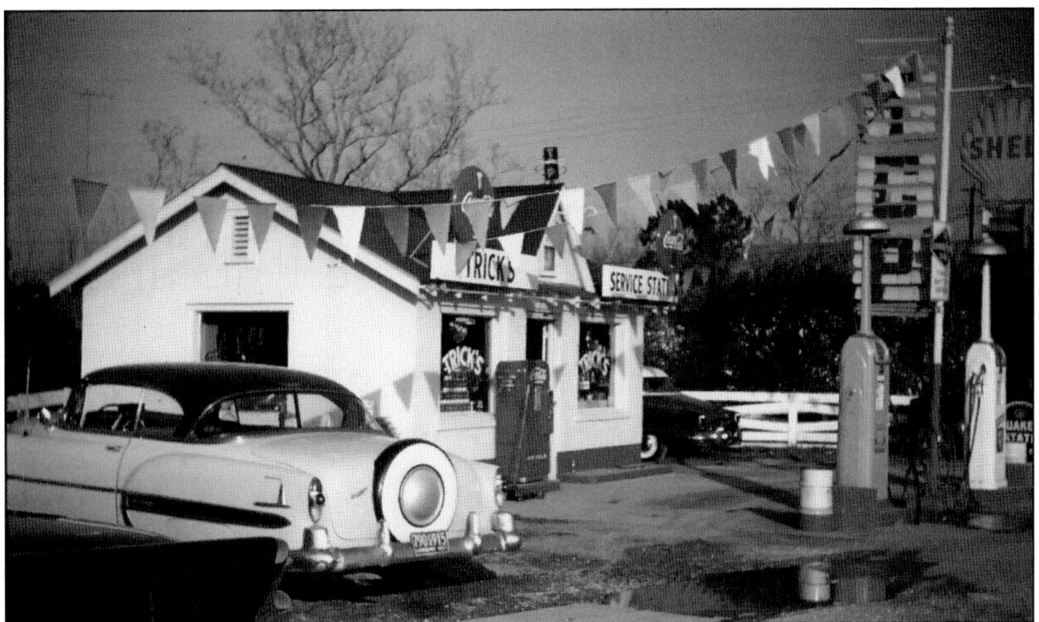

Former Reserve Wildcat star Leon "Treky" Duhe owned and managed an automobile repair shop and fueling station in a section of Reserve called Silvertown. One of 14 children, he was the son of former sheriff Willie J. Duhe and Leonie Millet Duhe. Treky was a bus driver for the St. John the Baptist Parish School Board and moved his repair shop to LaPlace, Louisiana. (Courtesy of the Reserve150 Picture Committee.)

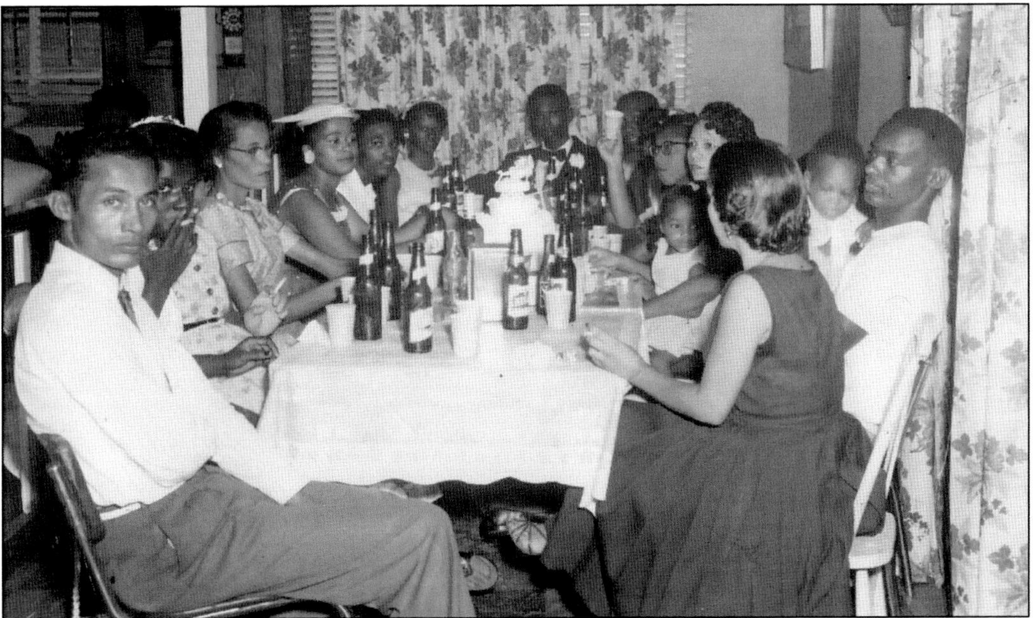

Jo Ann Cook Dunn and Lester Dunn (center) celebrated their wedding reception at the Rhythm Club in Reserve in the mid-1950s. The Rhythm Club was a local nightclub in the African American community, and it rocked each Friday and Saturday night. Rhythm-and-blues and rock-and-roll music were the order of the night as an overflow crowd danced until the early mornings. (Courtesy of Dale Thomas.)

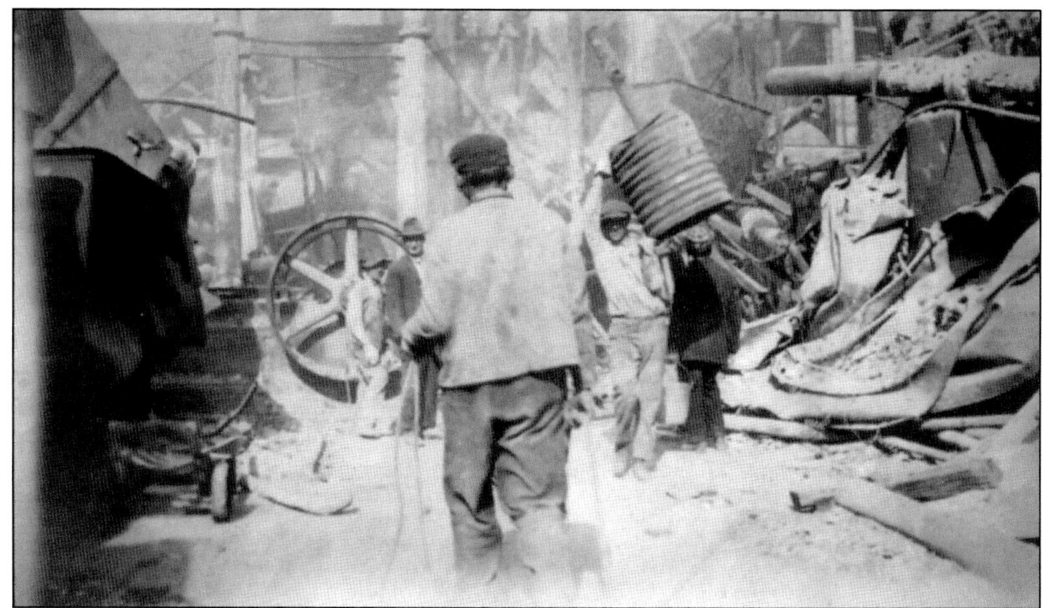

Pictured in 1912 is the Godchaux Sugar Refinery. A fire totally destroyed the sugar refinery in 1917. The Godchaux family took advantage of the adversity by modernizing and rebuilding the sugar refinery in 1918. In 1933, an additional product was added. Sold under the name Servall, this scientifically produced material was used for horticultural humus, poultry litter, animal bedding, and was processed from bagasse, a cane by-product. (Courtesy of Joy Donaldson McGraw.)

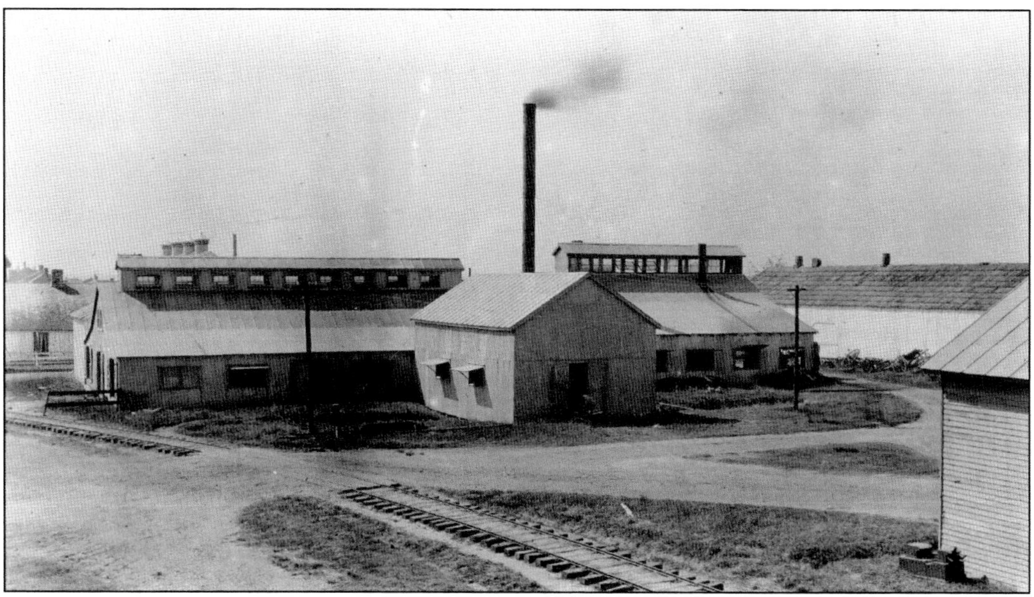

Pictured in 1908 is the Godchaux Refinery mechanic shop. Dantes Keller operated the mechanic shop, and his workers built whatever parts they needed to operate the sugar mill. The mechanic shop was also responsible for a volunteer fire department that utilized a fire alarm system. Long and short blasts from the Godchaux Sugar Refinery whistle indicated each fire location. (Courtesy of Joy Donaldson McGraw.)

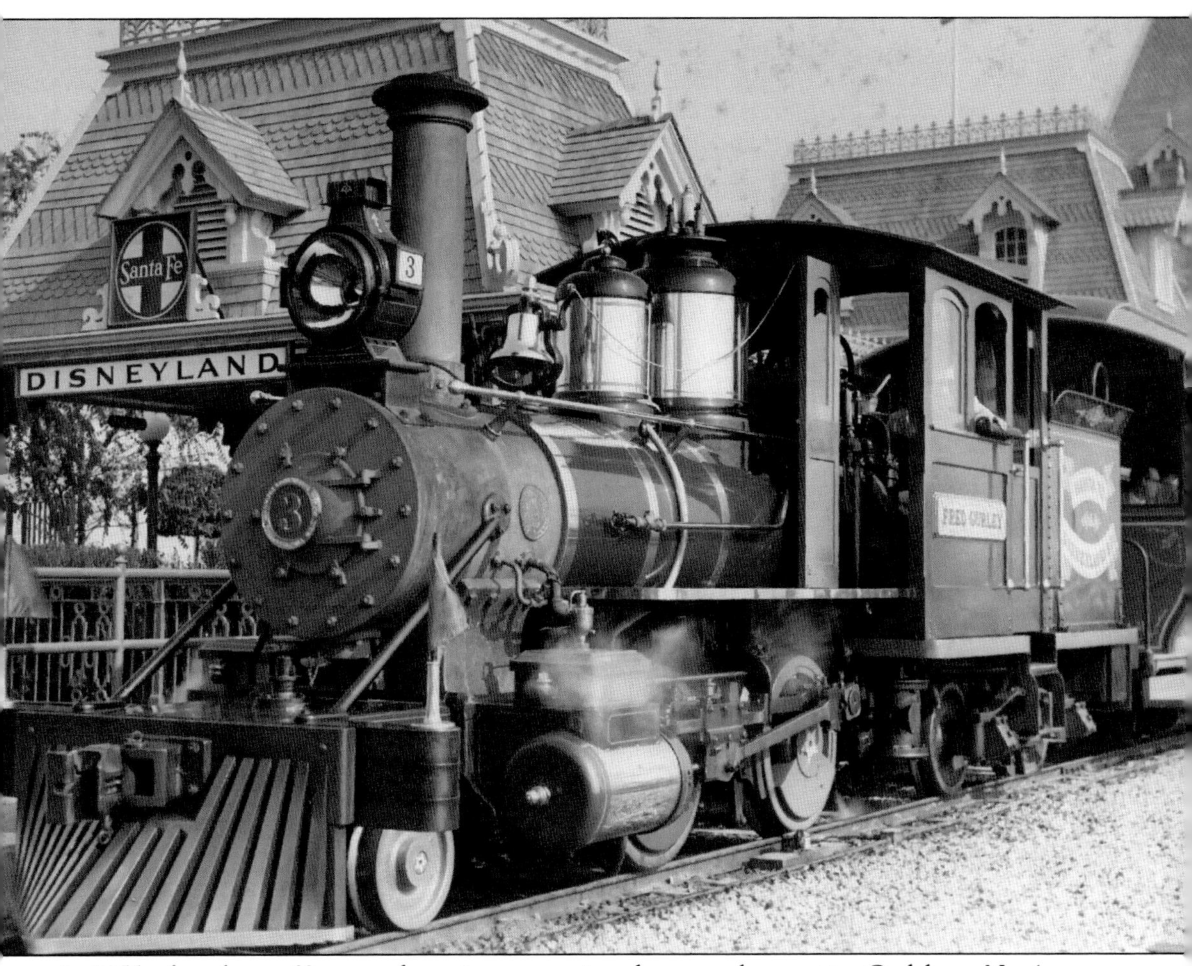

In 1955, after almost 60 years of continuous service, the steam locomotive Godchaux No. 1 was condemned by the insurance company and scheduled for the scrap pile. However, the engine would have a more interesting future: it was sold to Walt Disney and Disneyland. The engine was rebuilt, renumbered, renamed the *Fred Gurley*, and is now part of the Main Street Santa Fe Railroad in Anaheim, California. (Courtesy of Margaret Cambre Cerami.)

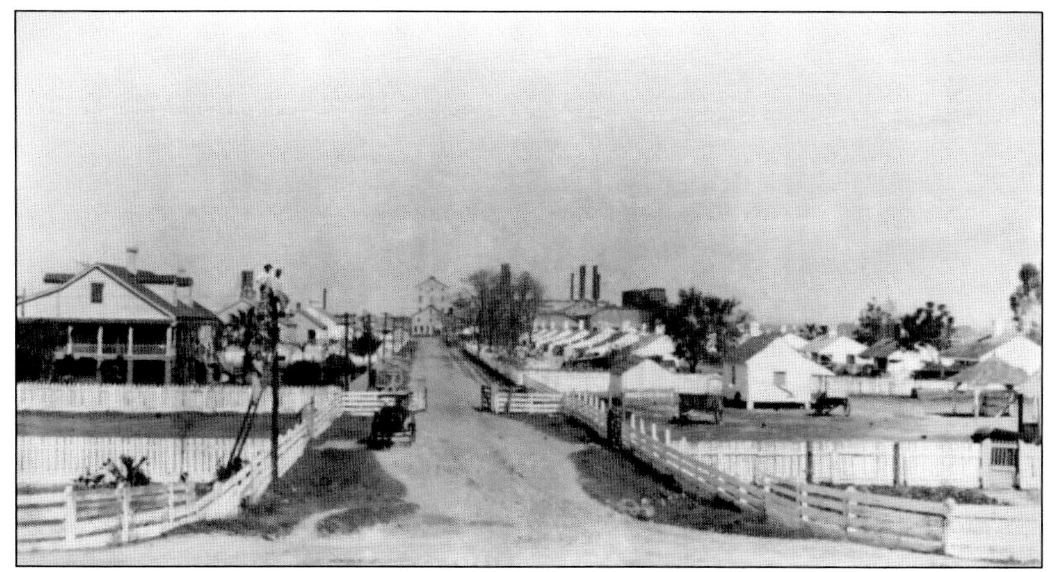

Pictured in 1908 is the entrance to Godchaux Sugar Refinery. The photograph shows the Boudousquie-Godchaux house (left) that was moved to this site around 1900. Originally built by free African Americans and expanded by the Boudousquie family, the home was occupied by the Godchaux family during the initial period of their ownership. Later, it was used by the plant managers that operated the sugar refinery for administrative purposes. (Courtesy of Joy Donaldson McGraw.)

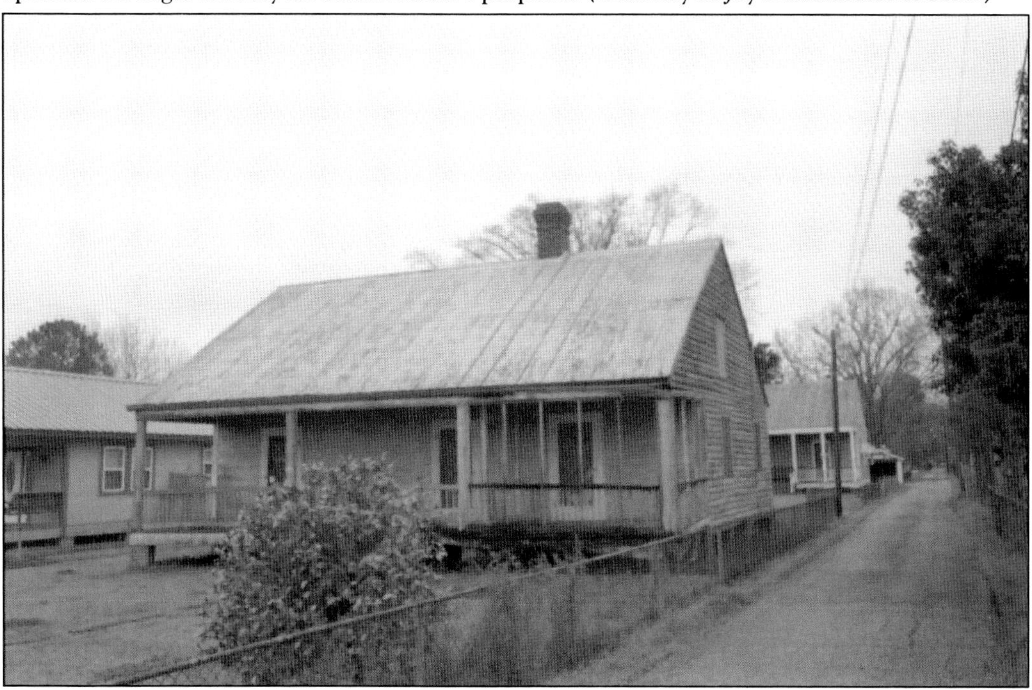

Ernest and Julia Keller Duhe moved into their Creole-style home in 1875. The Creole house was a one-story, timber-frame house, raised above ground level with a wide, hipped roof extending over a porch, or gallery. It had four adjoining rooms, one room in each corner of the house, but no interior hall. Armoires were commonly used to solve storage problems in Creole cottages. (Courtesy of Gerald Keller.)

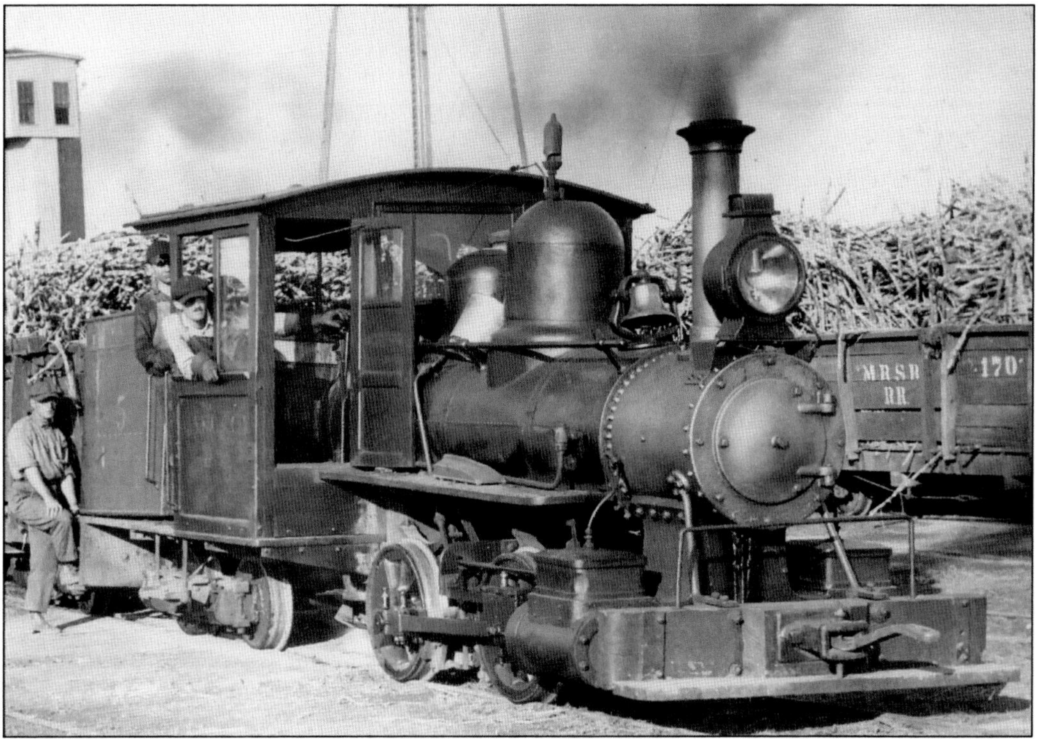

Leon Godchaux, in realizing his dream of the centralization of the grinding and refining of sugar on his many plantations, purchased and relied upon an amazing system of tramways. In a class of its own, Godchaux's narrow-gauge railroad line extended from St. James Parish into the spillway area of St. Charles Parish. The *MRSBRR* lettering on the trains stood for "Mississippi River Sugar Belt Railroad." (Courtesy of Dr. Douglas Starr.)

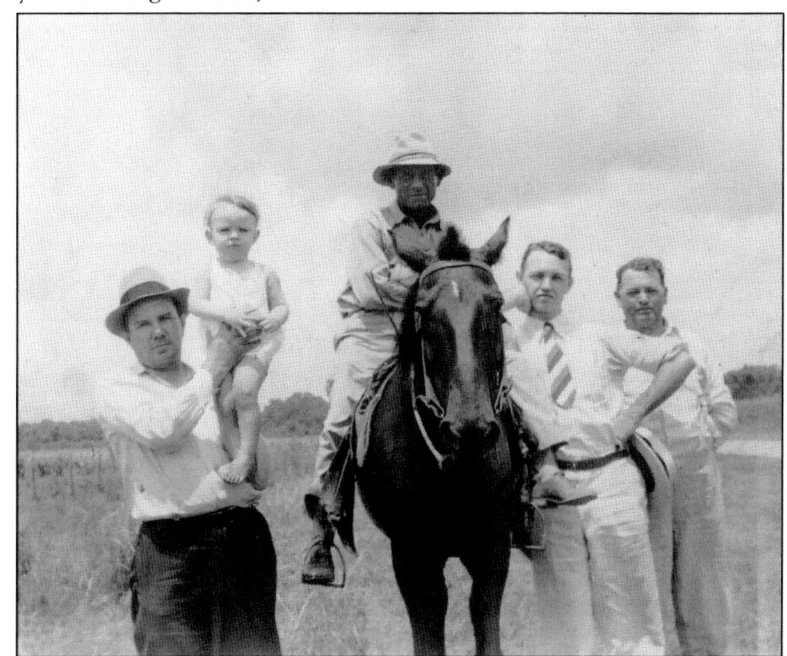

This 1939 photograph, taken at the San Francisco Sugar Mill in Lions shows, from left to right, Lester Millet Sr., two-year-old Sidney Levet III, overseer George Haydel, Sidney Levet Jr., and unidentified. The Millet family (Jean Ovide, Lester Sr., and Lester Jr.) served as St. John the Baptist Parish assessors from 1916 to 1974. (Courtesy of Steven Levet.)

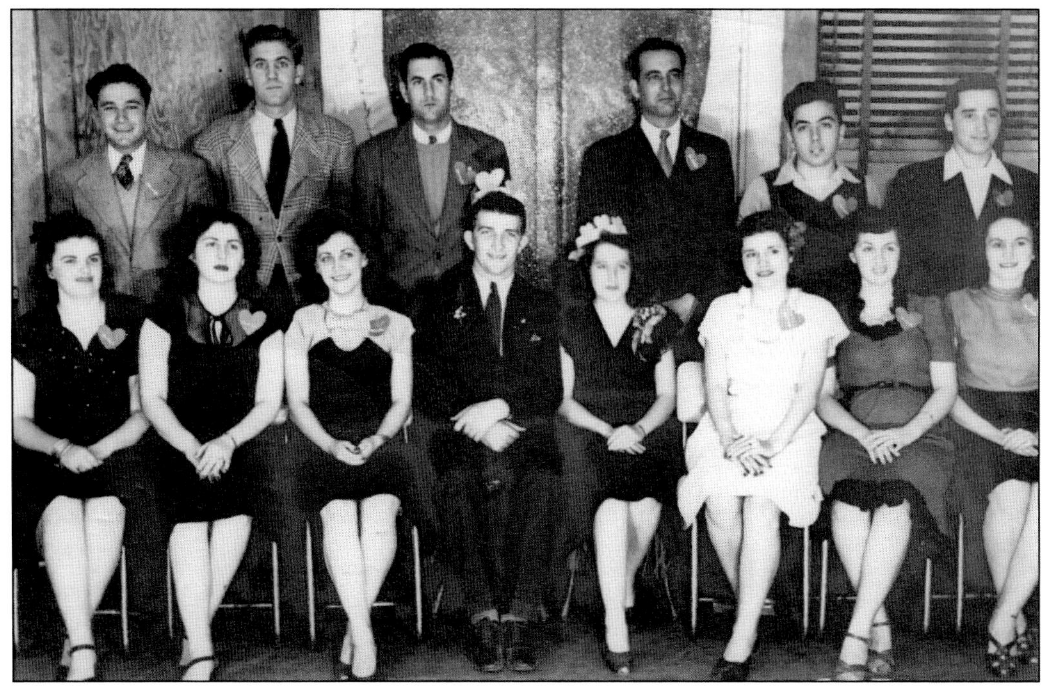

On February 14, 1946, members of the St. Peter Catholic Church Senior Sodality are pictured at a Valentine's party. From left to right are (first row, seated) Marjorie Clement, Elsie Fremin St. Pierre, Inez Madere Millet, Frank Rome (king of hearts), Iris Boudreaux (queen), and Jo-Ann Maurin Montz, Sally Ann Madere, and Marie Therese Maurin Montz; (second row, standing) Prentice Madere, Don Maurin, Milton Bienvenu, Sidney Montegut, Anthony DiCarlo, and Richard Oubre. (Courtesy of Gerard Montz.)

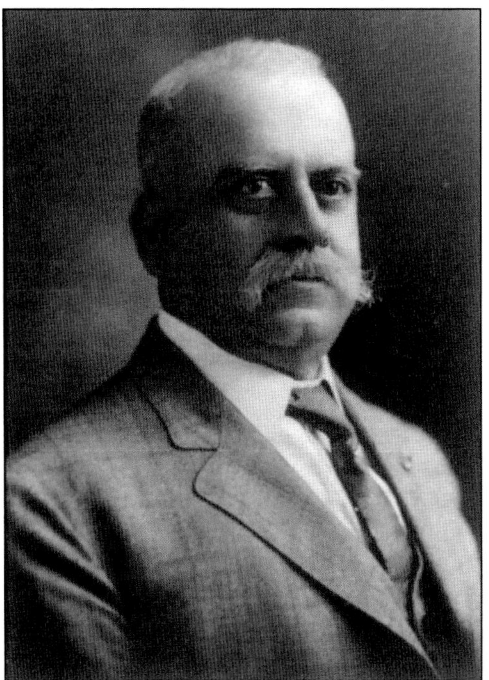

The expansion of the Reserve community includes a village called Lions, which was first known as Terre Haute and received its new name from merchant and postmaster Francois P. Lions, who operated the Willowbridge Store and post office. Perhaps the most recognizable landmark is the San Francisco Plantation. Barrel making, or cooperage, thrived in the Lions area between the 1860s and the early part of the 20th century. (Courtesy of Brent Tregre.)

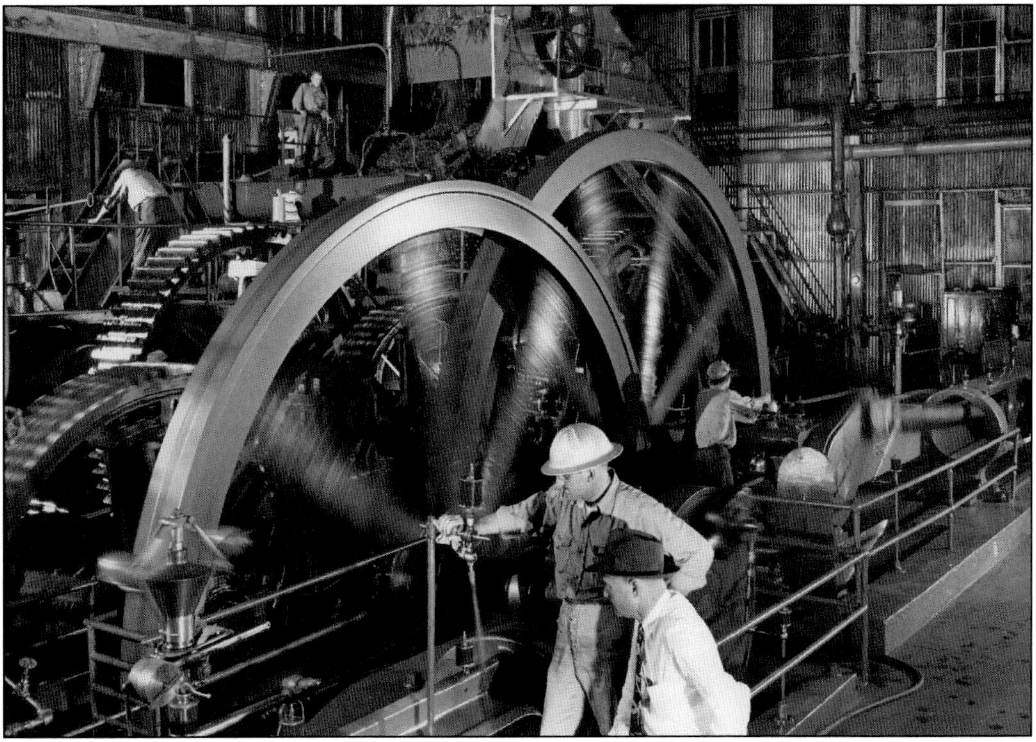

Pictured inspecting equipment are Godchaux Sugar Refinery chief engineer Hamilton J. Boudreaux Jr. and plant superintendent Charles Avrill (wearing hat and tie). The Godchaux Sugar Refinery was the major source of work for many Reservians, and entire families worked at the refinery. Many locals contributed to the development of the sugar refinery, such as George Williamson, who developed the Williamson clarifier. (Courtesy of Hamilton J. Boudreaux, Jr. and family.)

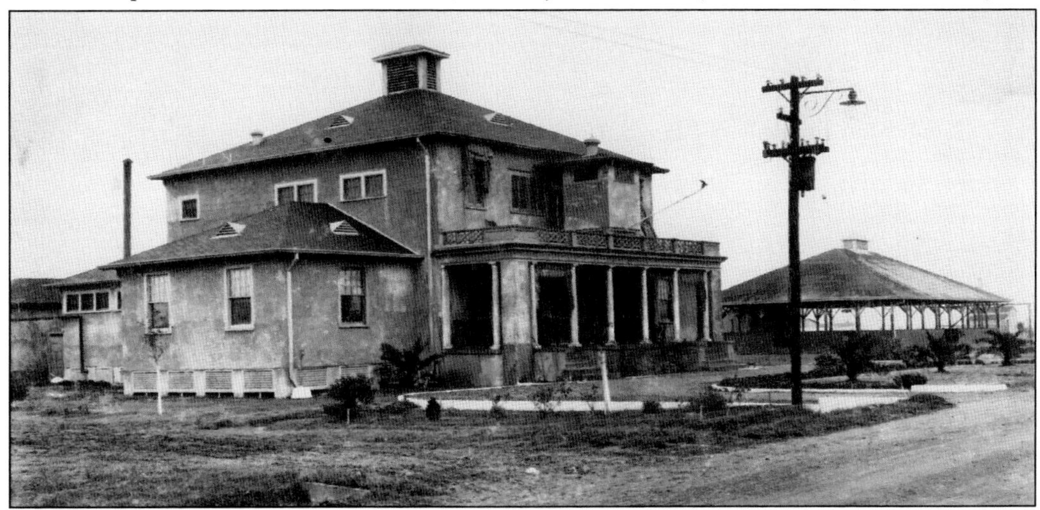

As a dream of Edward Godchaux, the Reserve Community Club was opened in 1922 for its employees. Members enjoyed a library, movie theater, snack area, swimming pool, baseball field, tennis court, and a dance pavilion. The building was the first air-conditioned building between New Orleans and Baton Rouge. Under construction, to the right, is the dance pavilion. (Courtesy of Phil Breaux.)

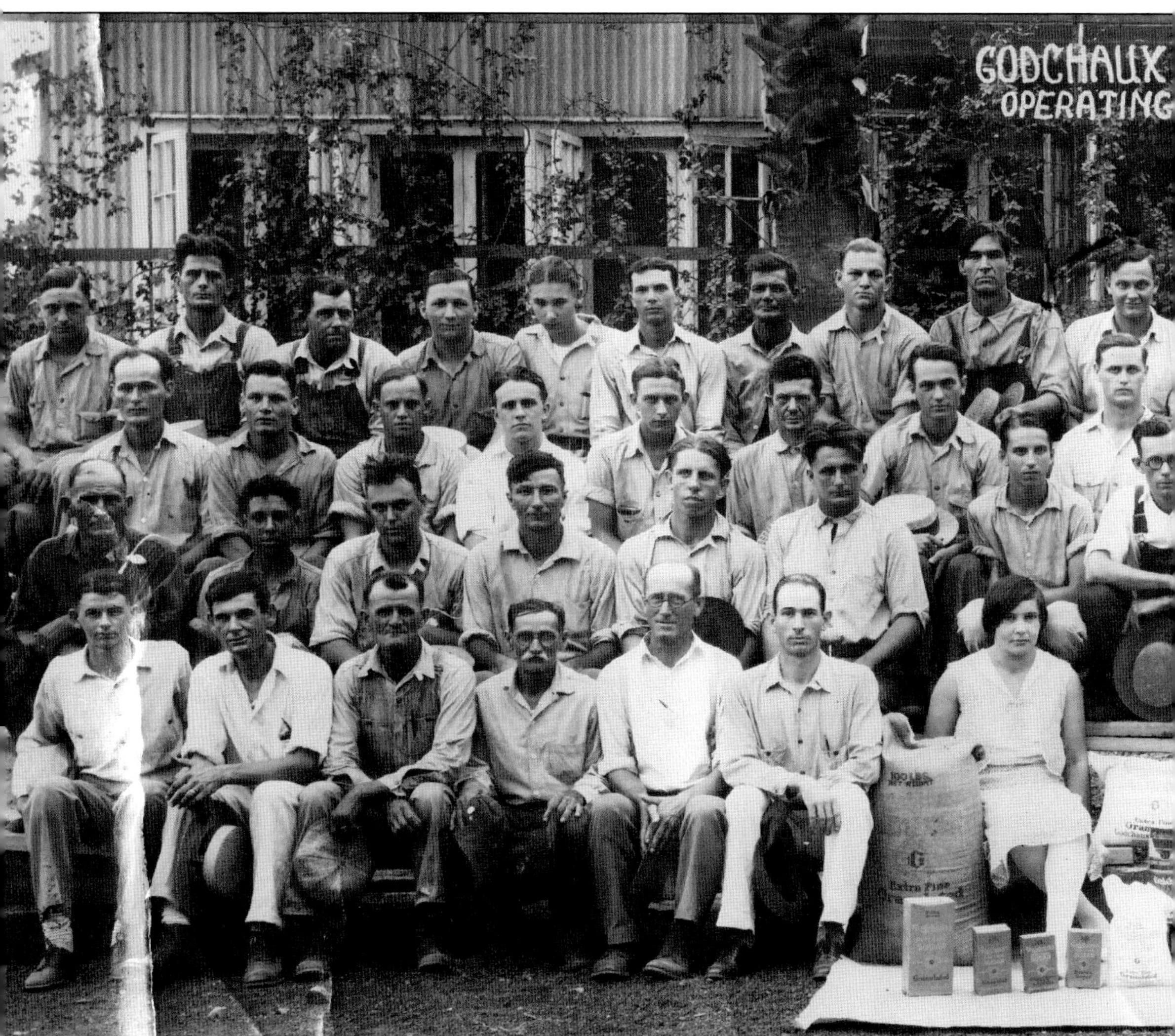

Gathered for a photograph on July 10, 1930, are day shift workers of Godchaux Sugar Refinery. They include, from left to right, (first row) Irving Millet, Dewey Weber, two unidentified, Etienne Klibert, unidentified, Bridget Williams Duhe, Cecile Triche Vice, Louis Hotfelter, Edwin Lumar, Thomas Reine, Elphege Aucoin Sr., unidentified, Arthur Borne, and Oliver Oubre; (second row) two unidentified, Leonard Daigle, Medric Vicknair, Rene Miller, Arthur Hymel, Francois Cambre, Theophile "Spec" Jacob, Ben Elfer, Sidney "Kaiser" Audiffred, Clay Delaneuville, Henry Klibert, ? Madere, two unidentified, and Stan or Guy Catoire; (third row) J.D. Vicknair

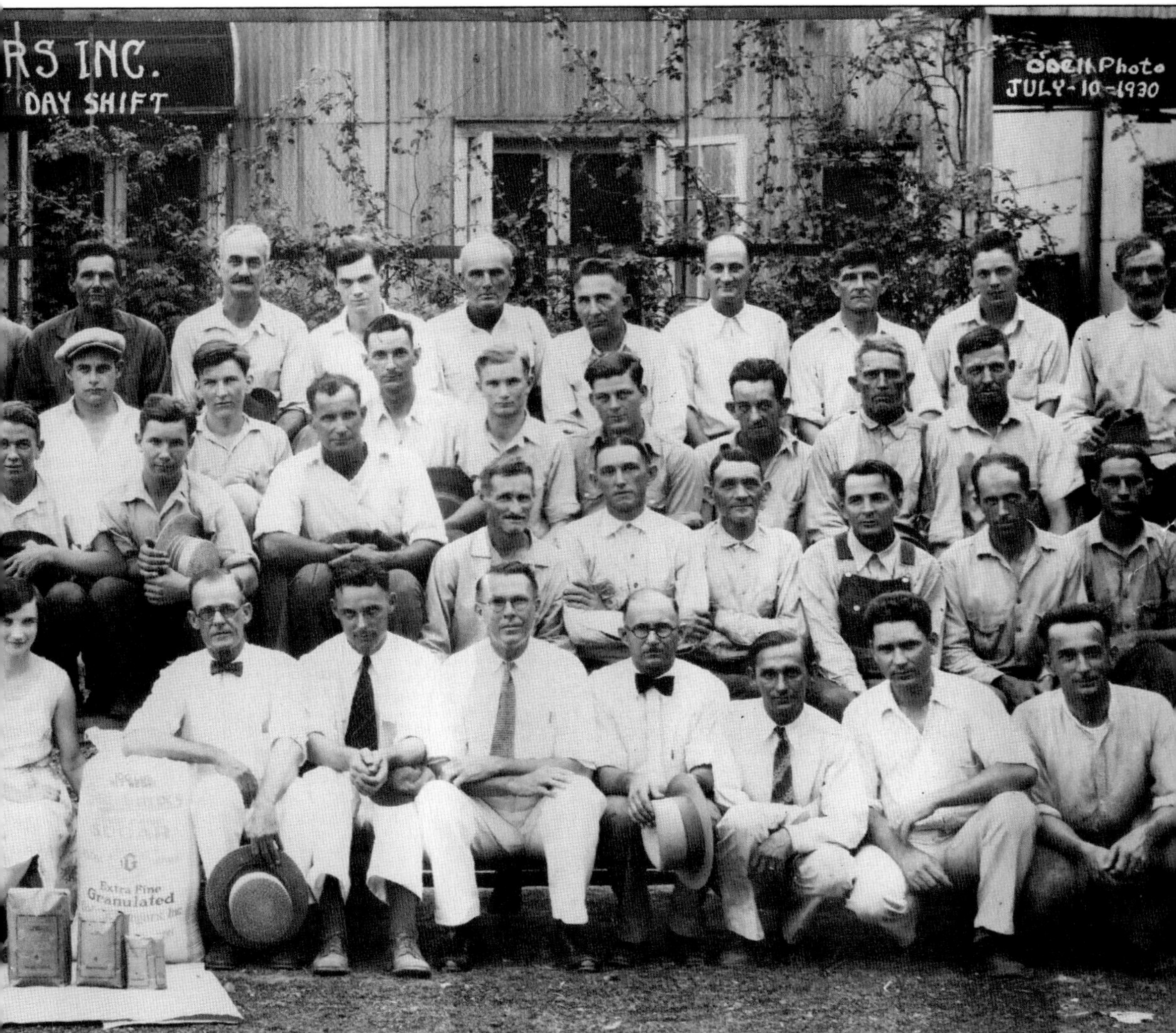

Sr., unidentified, Joseph Haydel, two unidentified, Leon Waguespack, Telsema "Noon" Vicknair, Felix Jacob, Robert LeBlanc, Alexander Brady, unidentified, ? Levet, "Red" Roussel, McAllen Brignac, State Hidalgo, Clifton Vicknair, and unidentified; (fourth row) two unidentified, Sidney Dupre Sr., three unidentified, William Bercegay, Paul Clement, Frank Vicknair, Gus Duhon, ? Brady, and two unidentified. The sugar refinery operated on three eight-hour work shifts, and a refinery whistle sounded daily at 8:00 a.m., 4:00 p.m., and midnight to begin each shift. (Courtesy of Shirley Casseigne Terrio.)

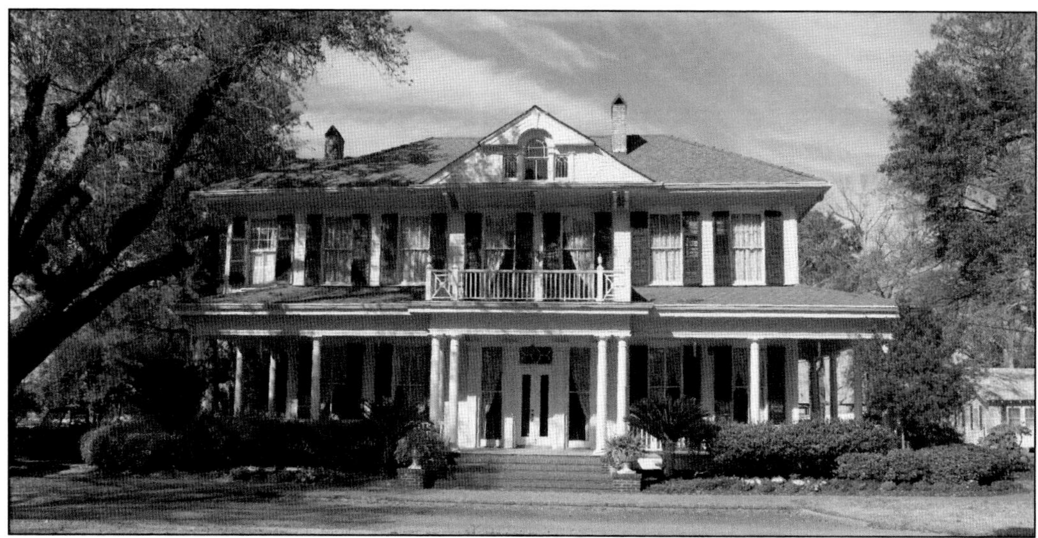

The Godchaux Sugar Refinery guesthouse was built in 1917. Members of the Godchaux family, who had taken up residence in New Orleans, were frequent guests for the Fourth of July fairs in Reserve. In the 1960s, the house was completely renovated by Julio Lobo and National Sugars. During their period of refinery ownership, the Hunt brothers stayed in the guesthouse. Today, the house is owned by the Port of South Louisiana. (Courtesy of Shirley Casseigne Terrio.)

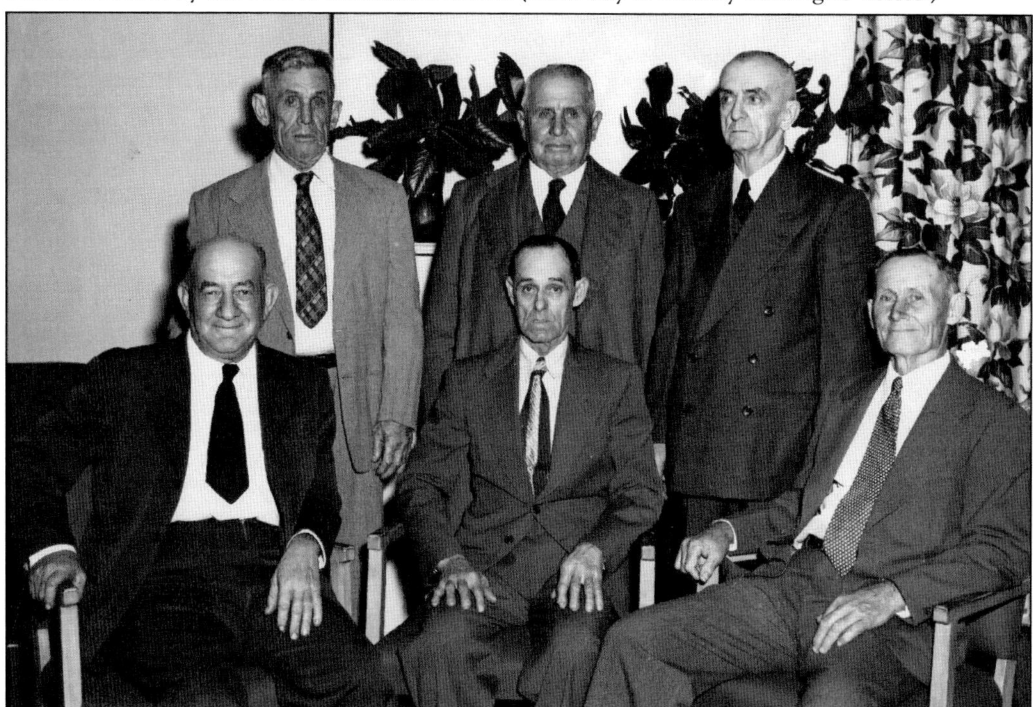

Godchaux Sugar Refinery employees posed for a retirement picture on October 1, 1963. From left to right are (seated, first row) Dantes Keller, Moise Jacob, and George Jacob; (standing, second row) E.P. Jacob, Numa Jacob, and Louis Cambre. At age 76, George Jacob retired with 63 years of service, and Dantes Keller worked 61 years at Godchaux. During a cash flow problem, Numa Jacob contributed money to fund a Godchaux payroll. (Courtesy of Shirley Casseigne Terrio.)

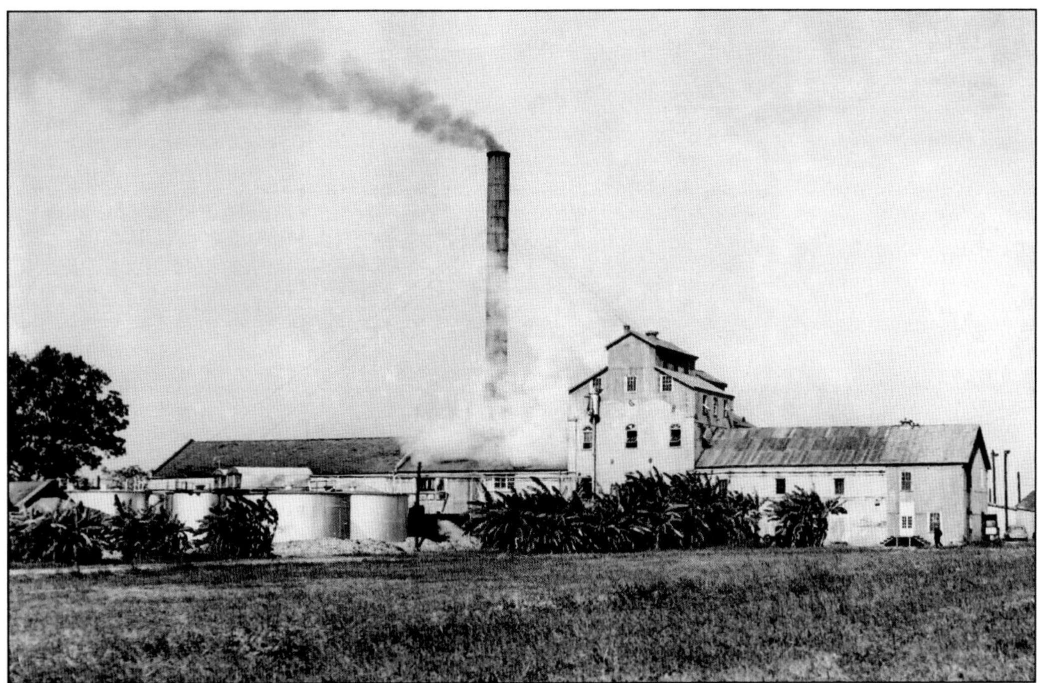

In the 1930s, the San Francisco Planting and Manufacturing Company, Ltd., in Lions specialized in the manufacturing of granulated sugar, high-grade molasses, and syrup. It was purchased by the Levet and Ory families in 1904, and Sidney J. Levet Sr. served as president. As the sugar economy worsened, production at the site stopped in the 1970s and machinery was sold off to buyers in Panama. (Courtesy of Carl L. Levet and family.)

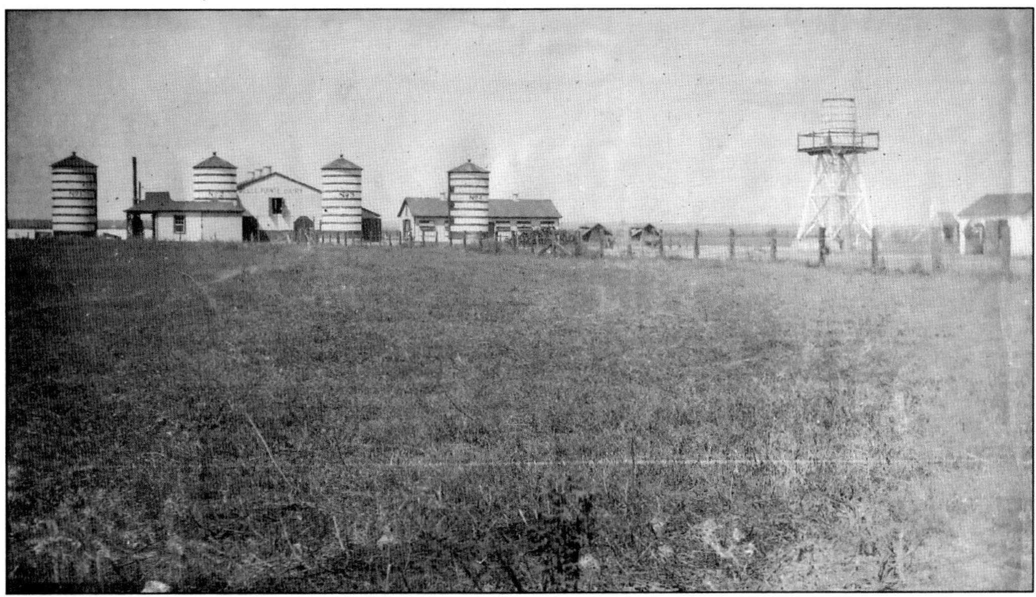

The Godchaux family utilized the Belle Point Plantation site for a milk dairy from 1914 until 1948. C.W. Davis managed the dairy, and each cow had a special diet. The dairy was considered one of the finest in the South, and the Godchaux family, sparing no cost, purchased quality cows. Milk was sold to area residents and to New Orleans hospitals. (Courtesy of Joy Donaldson McGraw.)

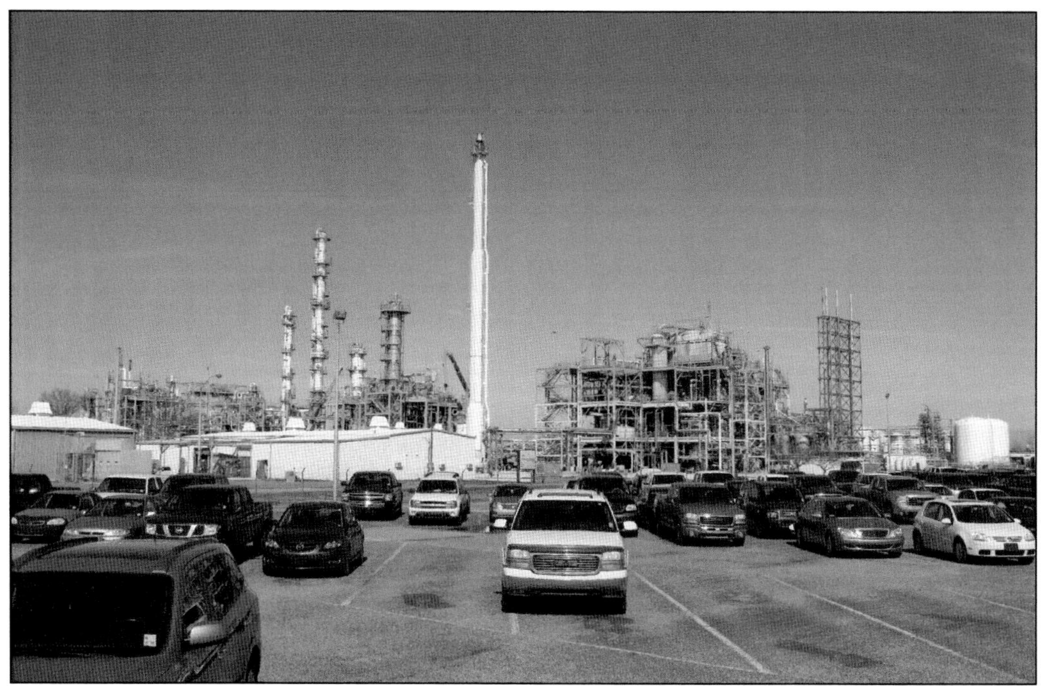

E.I. DuPont purchased the Belle Pointe Plantation site in 1957 and opened a plant in 1962. As one of its products, DuPont produced neoprene, used in the making of Kevlar, which is a substance pivotal in bulletproof vests. (Picture by Peter Forest.)

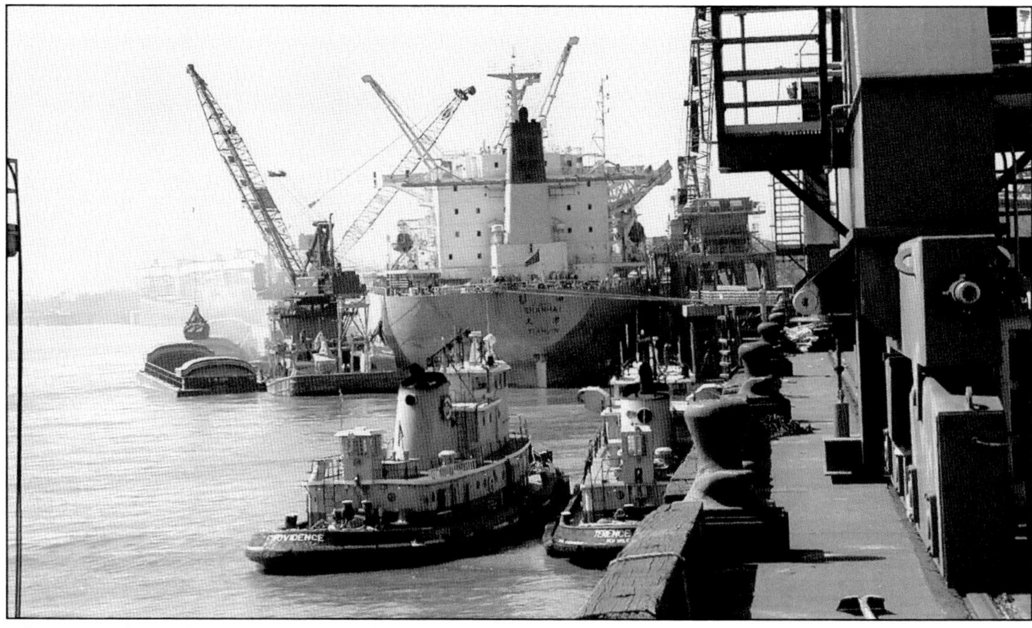

The port of South Louisiana—and this portion of the Globalplex terminal in Reserve—spans a 54-mile corridor of the Mississippi River. Together with the neighboring ports of New Orleans, Baton Rouge, St. Bernard, and Plaquemines, the region has become the world's largest port district responsible for about one-fifth of all US and foreign maritime commercial traffic. (Photograph by Peter Forest.)

Three

Social Life and Celebration

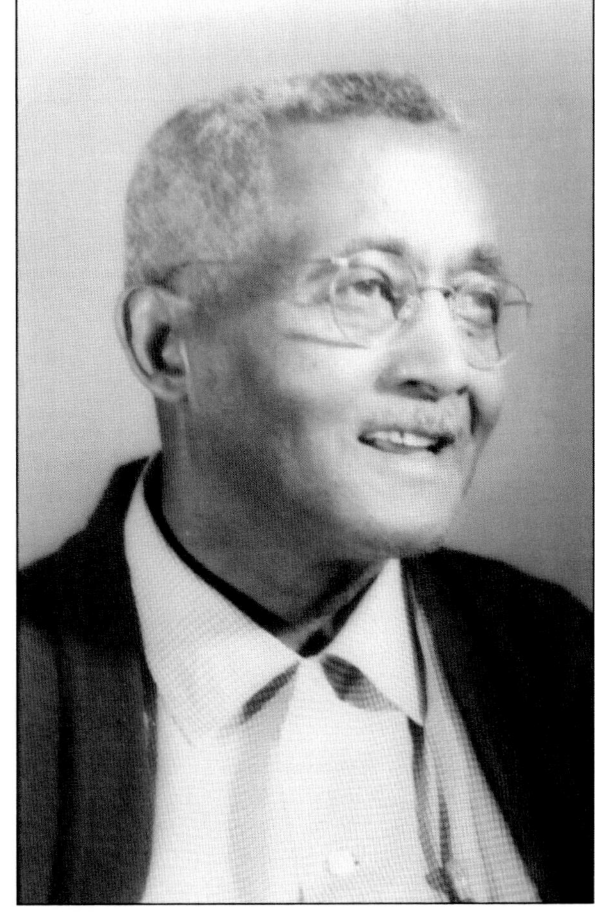

At age 12 or 13, the very versatile Marshall Lawrence began playing with Dejean Alexander's band, and upon Alexander's sudden death, Lawrence took over the Club Pine band and played weekly at the Reserve Community Club and Maurin's Liberty Park. In 1936, the band took a nine-state tour that lasted three months; their performances were sent back home by radio and heard nationwide. Marshall Lawrence's life was full of accomplishments as he could play any musical instrument and was known for being able to fix anything. He first worked as a blacksmith for the Lyons Lumber Company in Garyville, Louisiana, and later worked on the Guidry, C.I. James, and Montegut Plantations. In 1942, Lawrence taught a National Youth Administration training class in automobile mechanics and welding. He then went to Southern University, earned a degree, and taught at Fifth Ward High School. Lawrence's story is of an individual who truly gave himself to his community—and he lived to be 100 years old. (Courtesy of Kathleen Stewart.)

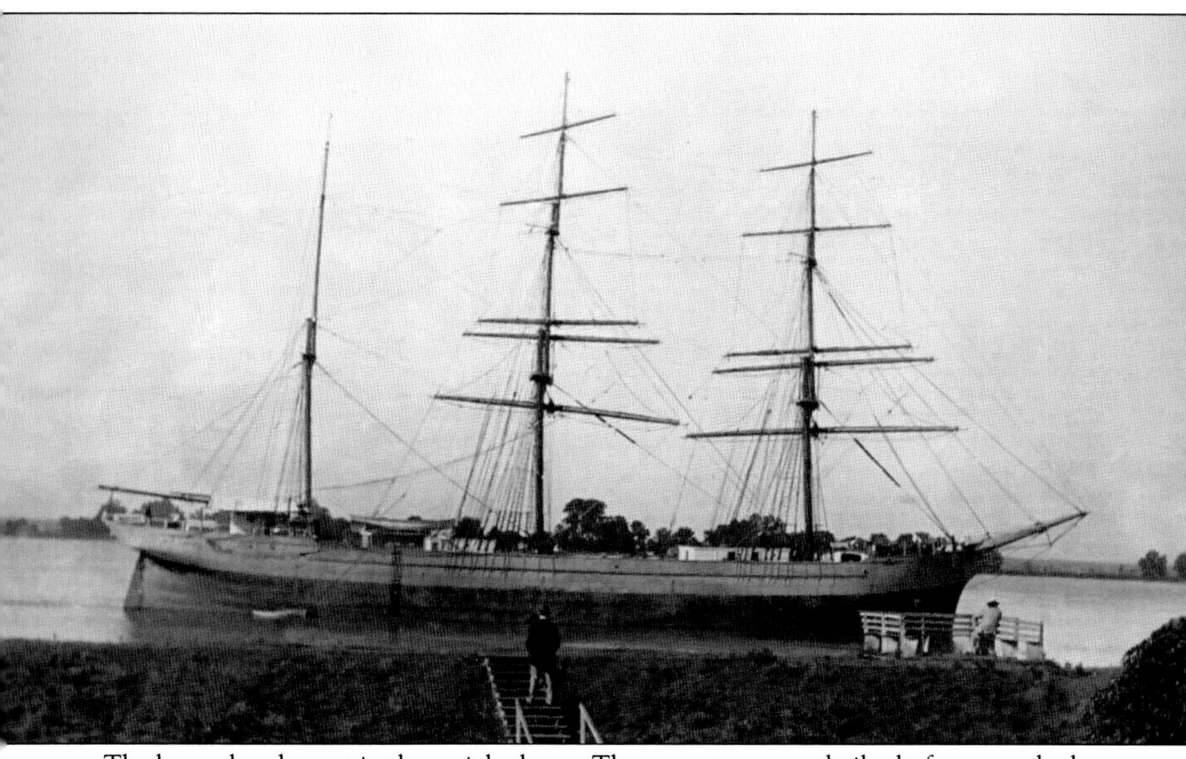

The levee played a part in the social scheme. The property owners built platforms on the levee, extending riverward, with benches and railing on three sides. There, every afternoon at sundown during the mild season, the family sat, breathing *le bon air du fleuve* and enjoying the soft breeze. Often, the neighbors would join the group, and the old folks sat and talked while the young ladies and gentlemen paired off and walked along the levee. The smaller children romped in the grass, had clover fights, or slid on the levee incline on sleds made of three or four barrel staves held together and reinforced with a strip of wood at each end. The arrival of mosquitoes announced that the "airing" was over. Pictured is Dr. L.T. Donaldson, overlooking a boat docked near his home. (Courtesy of Joy Donaldson McGraw.)

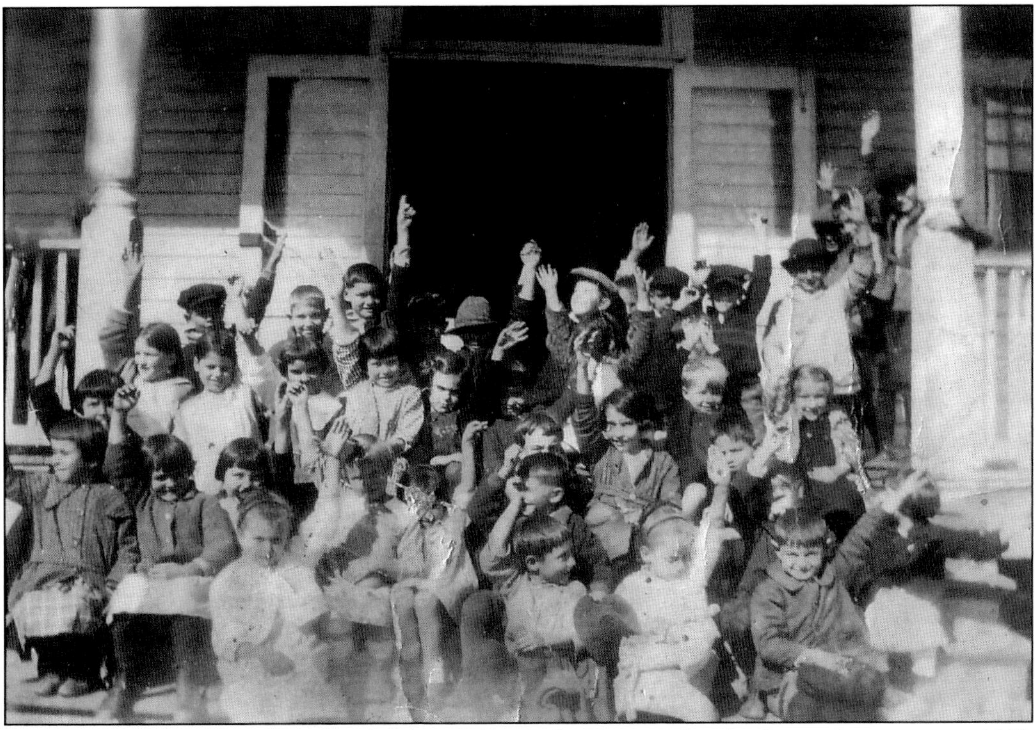

The St. John the Baptist Parish School Board built the Frisco School in Lions, Louisiana, in 1915. Pictured are students gathered for a school photograph. The school remained open until 1935, when it closed and students were transferred to Leon Godchaux Grammar School. (Courtesy of Carl L. Levet and family.)

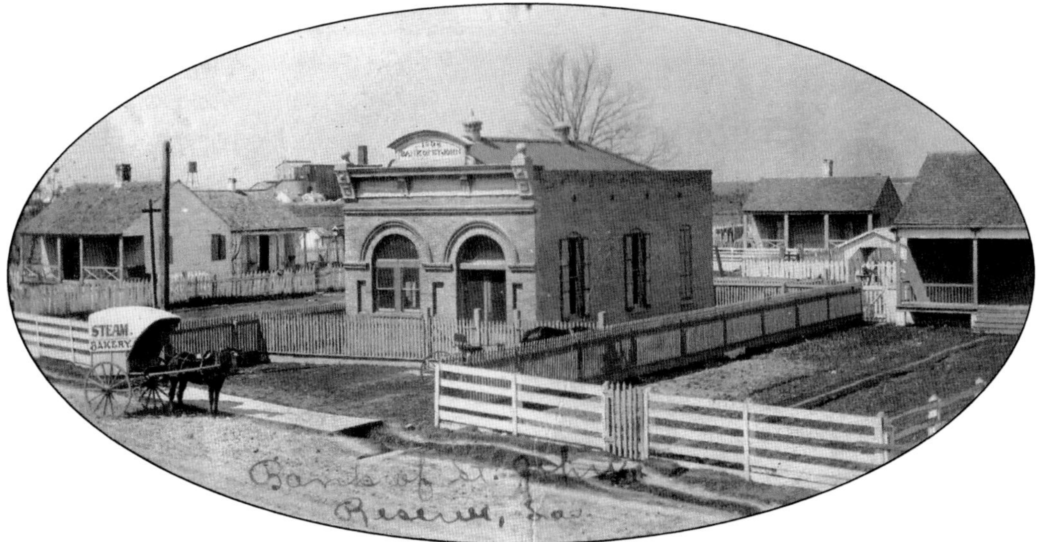

Local farmers and businessmen in St. John the Baptist Parish opened the Bank of St. John in 1904. Through time, the bank was enlarged, and the original portion of the bank was converted into an office that was occupied by former Louisiana state representative and attorney Daniel Elmore Becnel Sr. Today, the bank building is now a part of the Capital One branch in Reserve. (Courtesy of Joy Donaldson McGraw.)

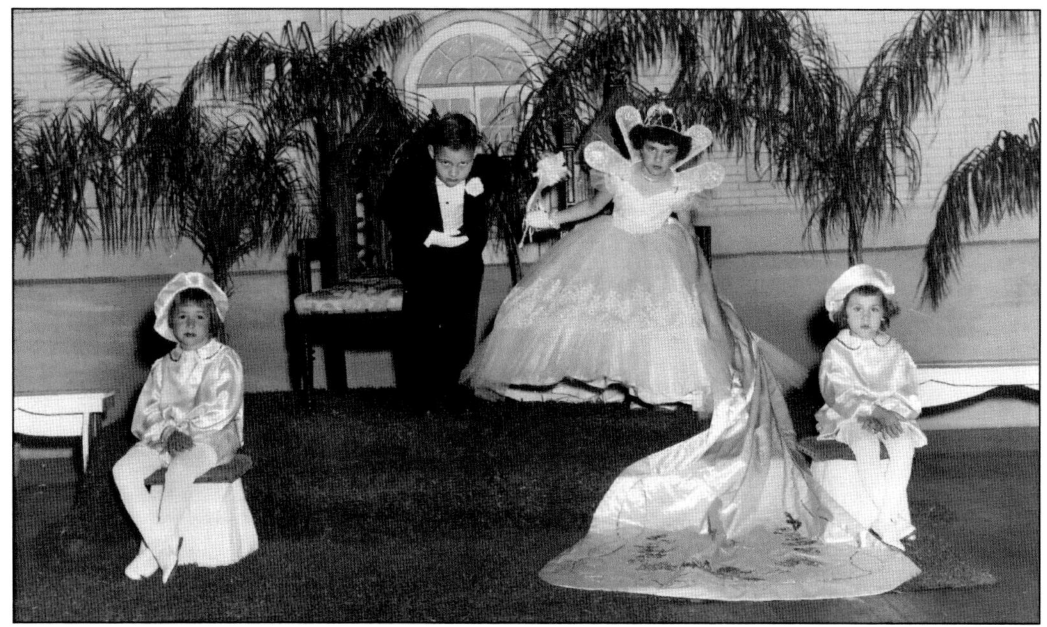

St. Peter Parochial School held a May spring festival. Reigning over the 1959 junior court and bowing are king Jeff Luminais and queen Suzanne Millet. Pages are Amie Berthelot, left, and Susie Bienvenu. The annual event, held at Leon Godchaux High School, was a fundraiser for the school, and the senior court held its event the next day, with king Wallace Hymel and queen Natalie Cali reigning. (Courtesy of Jill Luminais Bordelon.)

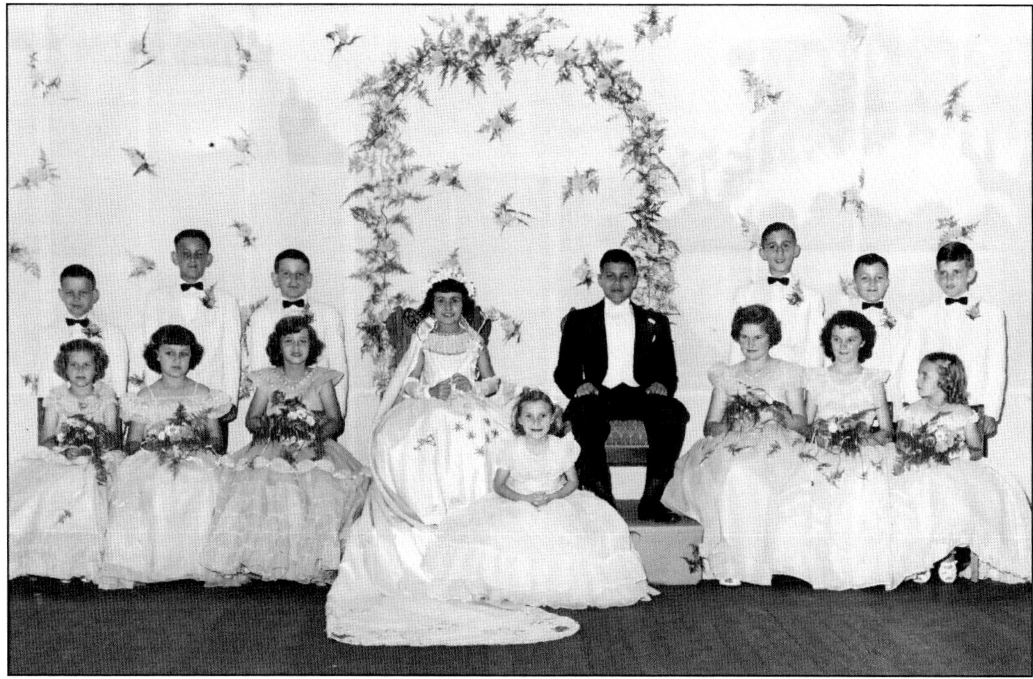

Pictured in 1950 are Leon Godchaux Grammar Spring Festival queen Olga Haik Porteous and king Webby Gauthreaux. The festival, a school fundraiser and popular event, was produced by school principal Edna Bouititon and attracted great crowds. (Courtesy of Phil Breaux.)

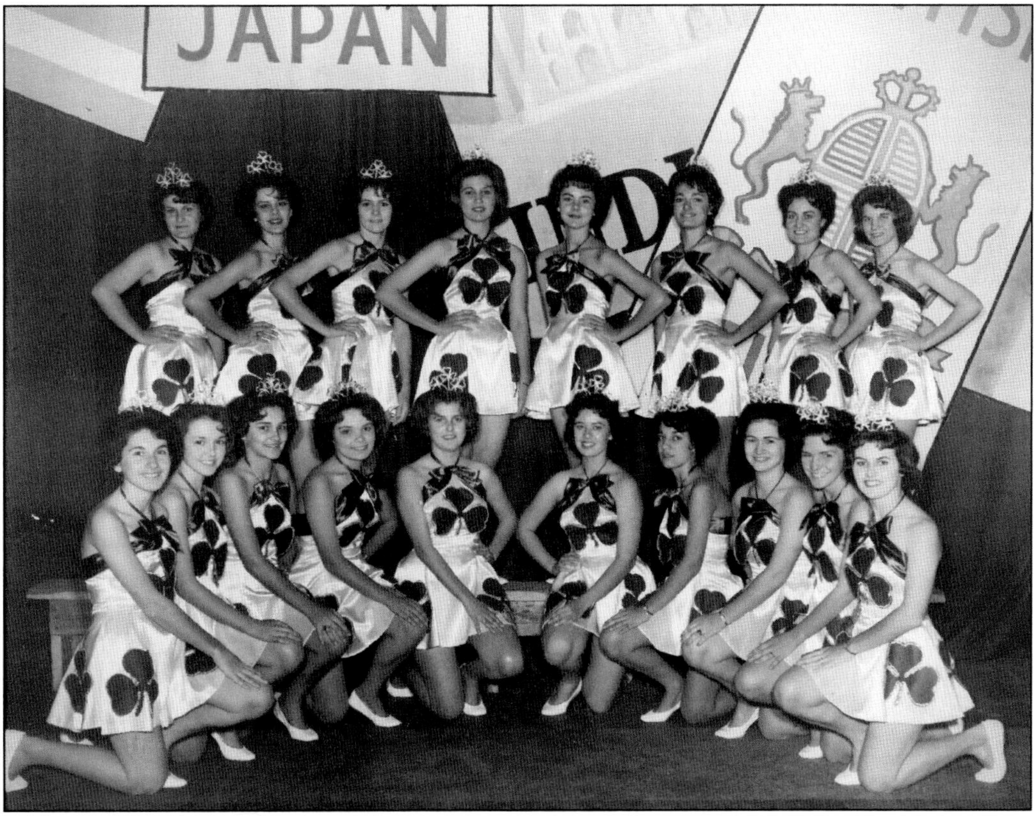

In 1962, ladies from Leon Godchaux High School posed for a photograph during the school's Carnival ball event. The event drew large crowds from the River Parishes and started in the late 1940s. One of the featured bands to perform was Dave Bartholomew, of Edgard, Louisiana, who cowrote songs for rock-and-roll legends Antoine "Fats" Domino, Lloyd Price, and Shirley and Lee. (Courtesy of Amy Brady Williams.)

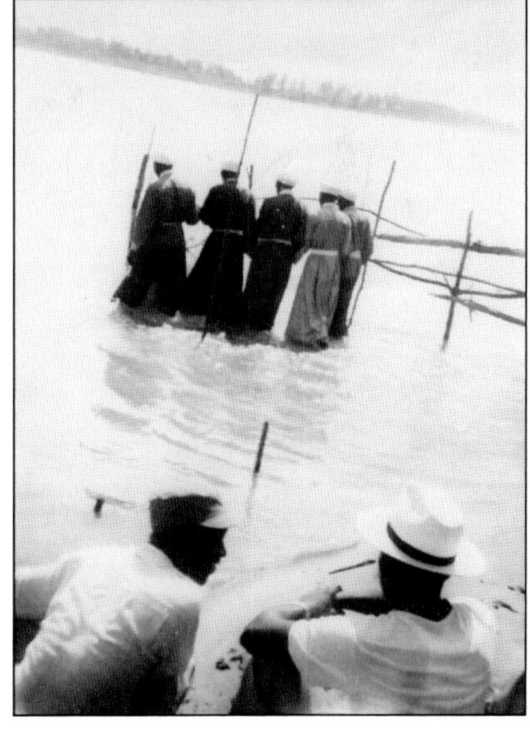

In the 1950s, religion played a major role in the growth and development of the white and African American communities. Pictured is a Mississippi River baptismal. Sandbars along the Mississippi River allowed people to walk out in shallow waters for such activities. Freddie Young is seated at left. (Courtesy of Dionne Lapeyrolerie.)

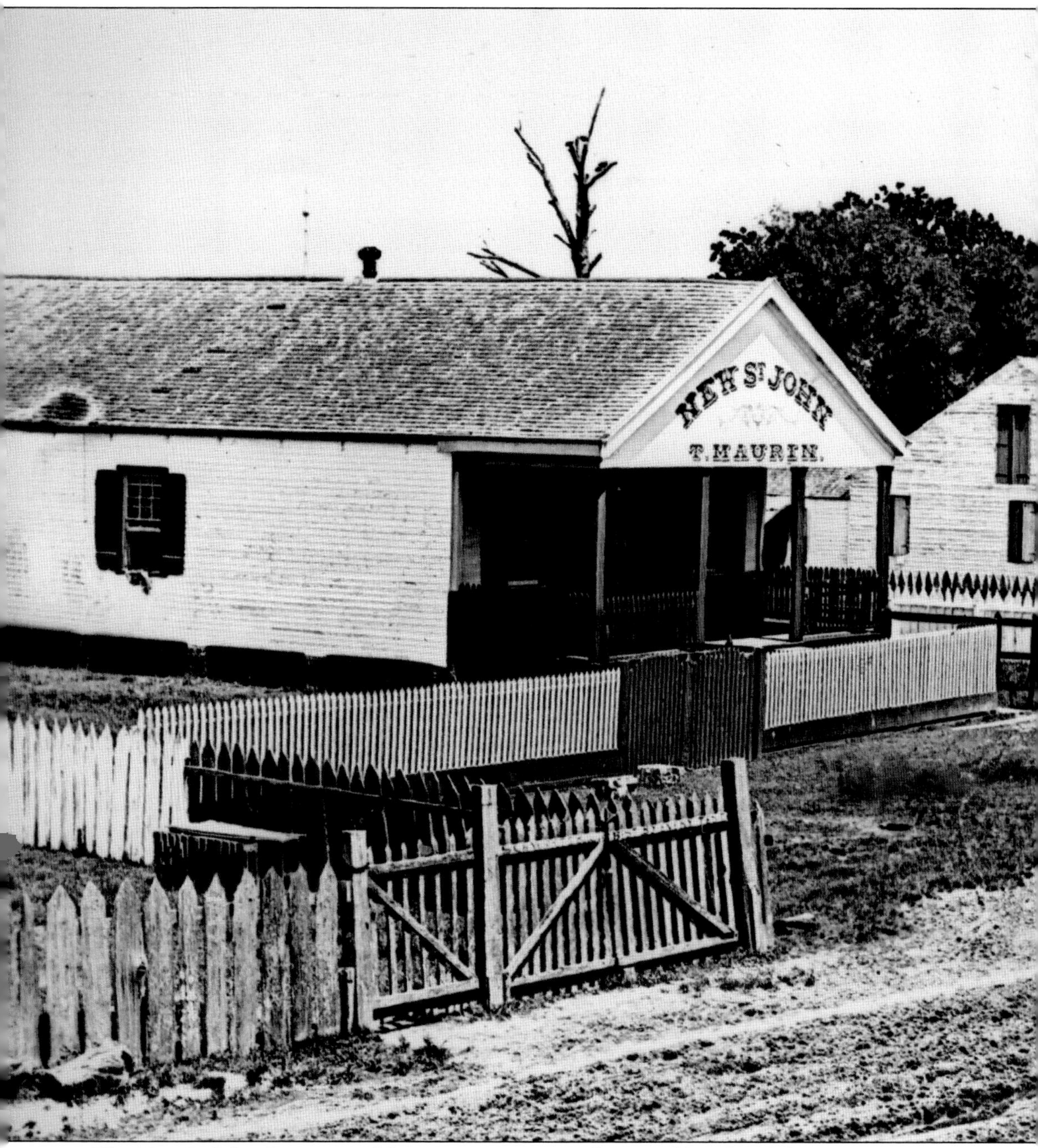

The New St. John Store, near Silvertown, was originally owned by Theodule Maurin. Like many small stores, the New St. John Store served the immediate area. These stores were within walking distance and provided the basic needs for everyday life: bread, eggs, milk, beans, sausage, and so on. The New St. John Store was purchased by Johnny Troxler after the death of Maurin. In time, Troxler owned five stores in Reserve and Mt. Airy, Louisiana, and renamed his stores Live and Let Live. Troxler's brothers Lucien and Clifford helped in the general operation of the Live

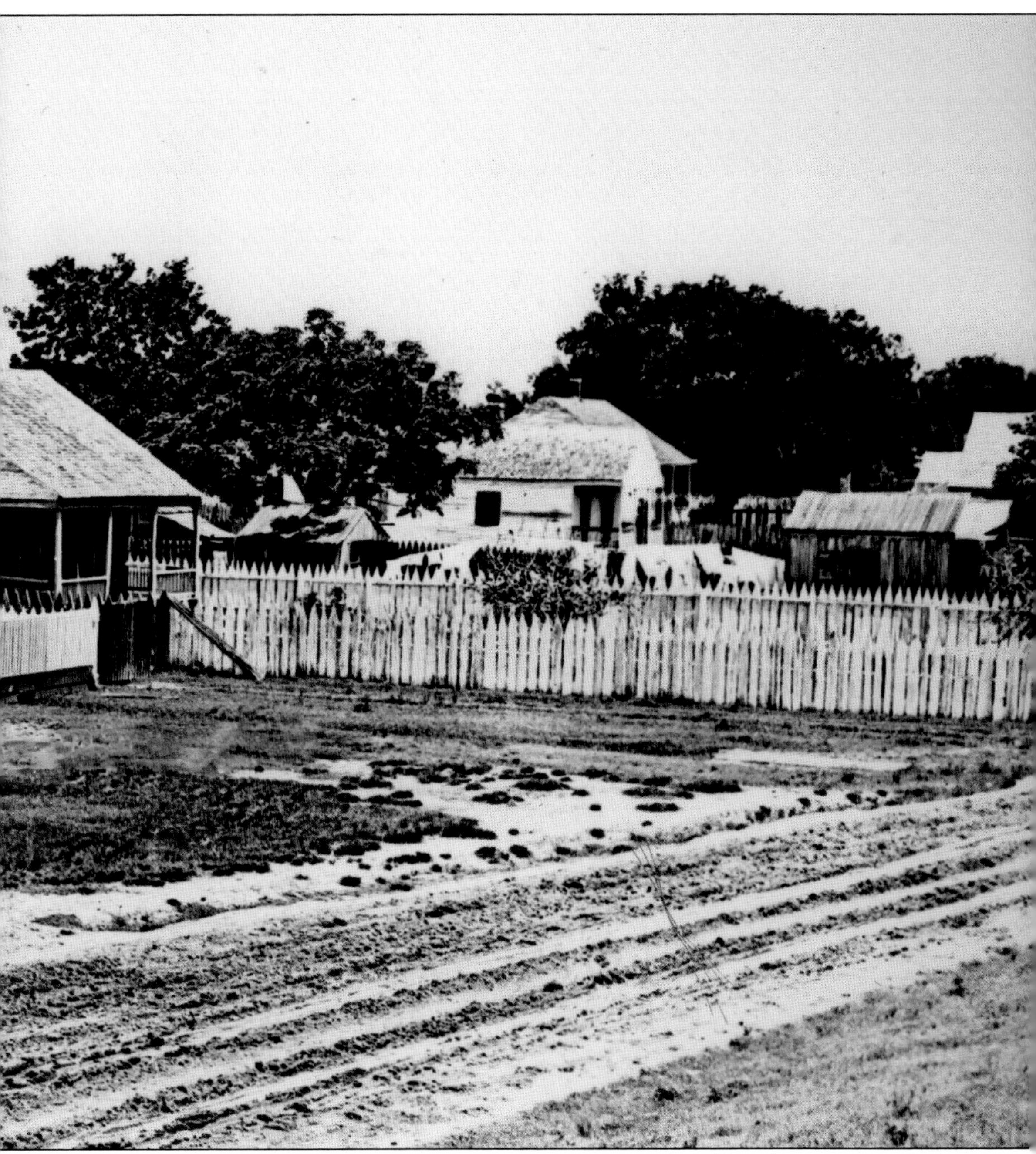

and Let Live stores. Many store owners gave their customers and children *lagniappe*, or a little extra. It was common for the owner to give the customer a few more apples or give the children of the customer a candy bar with their purchases. This practice continued until the late 1960s, when many small stores closed because of the competition of chain supermarkets. (Courtesy of Marion Donaldson.)

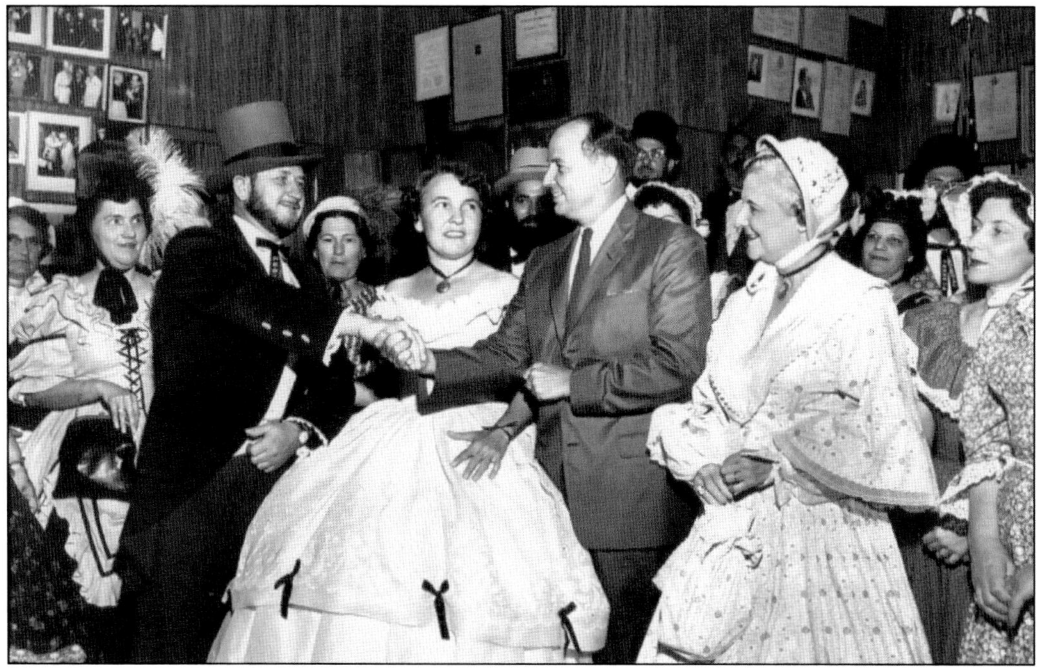

A highlight of the 1960 Reserve Centennial was a trip to New Orleans by centennial king Norman "Shot" Weber, left with hat, and his wife, Doris, the centennial queen. The centennial king and queen were selected from 11 nominees by pulling names out of a hat. Eight maids were also selected to serve on the centennial court. Pictured are centennial supporters in their 1860 clothing as they met with New Orleans mayor Chet Morrison, center. (Courtesy of Blanche Hotard.)

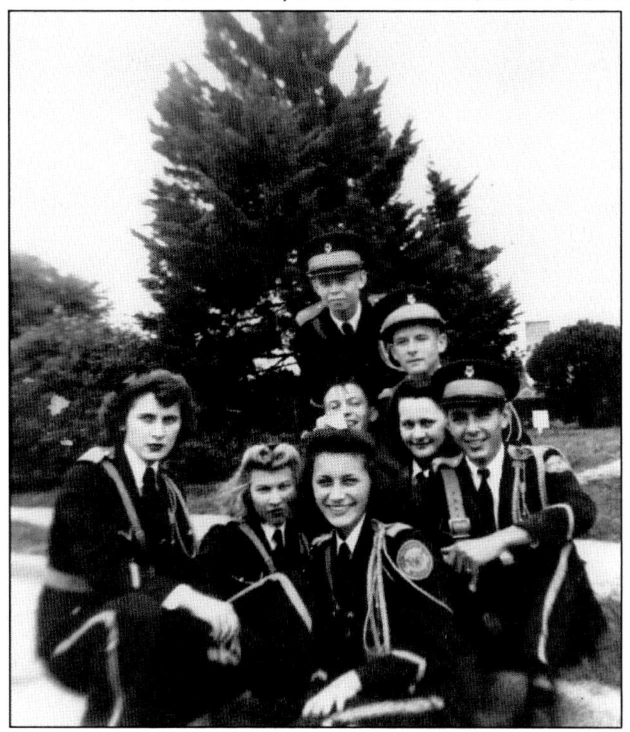

In about 1941, members of the Leon Godchaux High School band pose for a photograph after a halftime performance at a football game. Pictured from left to right are Juanita Jacob, Maxine Aucoin Millet, Inez Madere Millet, Shirley Casseigne Terrio, and unidentified. Standing is Harold "Peanut" Vicknair. The band was under the leadership of Louis Chemay, who later became the principal at John L. Ory Elementary School in LaPlace. (Courtesy of Betty Brown Vicknair.)

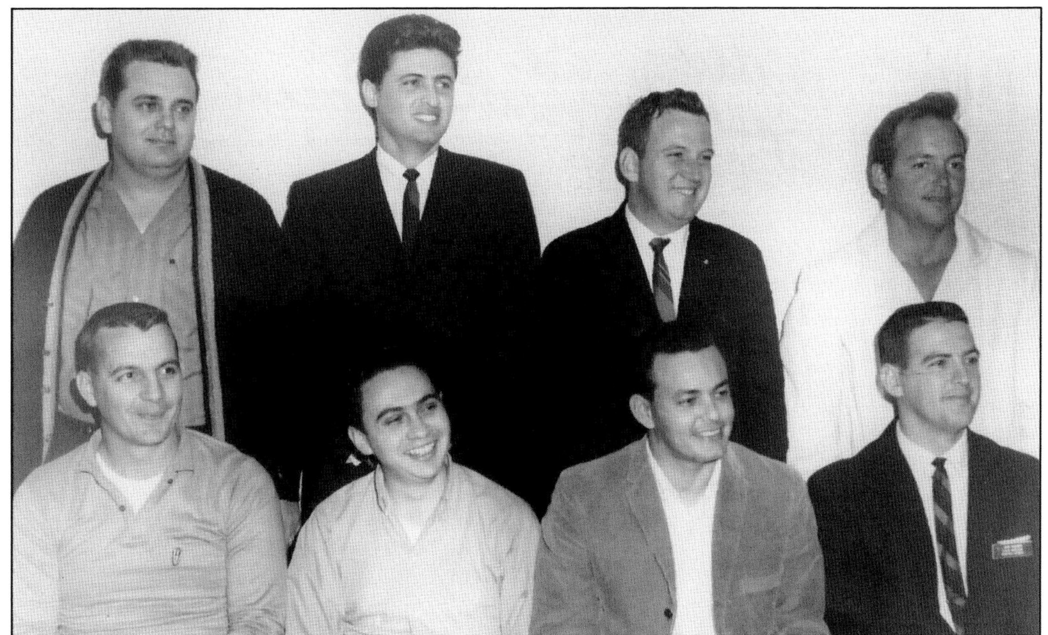

In 1968, the Reserve Jaycees board of directors and office staff posed for a picture during the installation of officers. Pictured from left to right are (first row) Gerald Klibert, Milton Roussel, David Gauthe, and president Donald Madere; (second row) Brian Duhe, Michael Jaubert, Ed Verrett, and Robert Breaux. The Reserve Jaycees was a civic organization for young men from 18 to 35 years of age. (Photographed by Jim Lilly.)

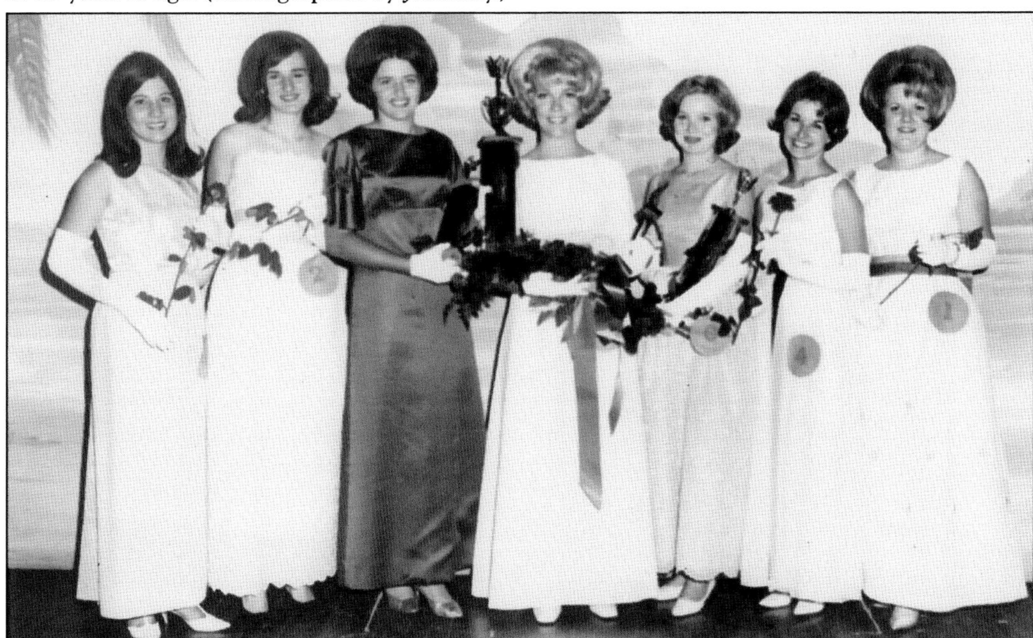

In 1969, the Reserve Jaycees Junior Miss Pageant was held at Leon Godchaux High School. Contestants were judged on an interview and talent. Those pictured are, from left to right, Dawn Falgoust Dottolo, Vickie Smith, Yvette Madere, Betty Rogers (who won the title of Junior Miss), Cindy LeBlanc, Norma Lehman, and Beverly Johnson Jacob. (Courtesy of *L'Observateur*.)

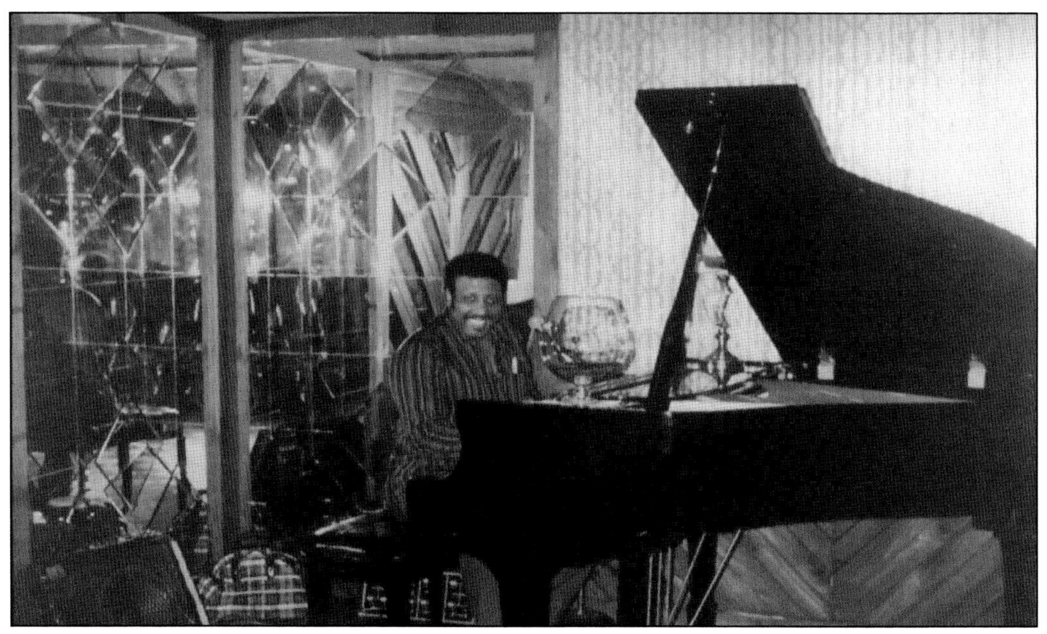

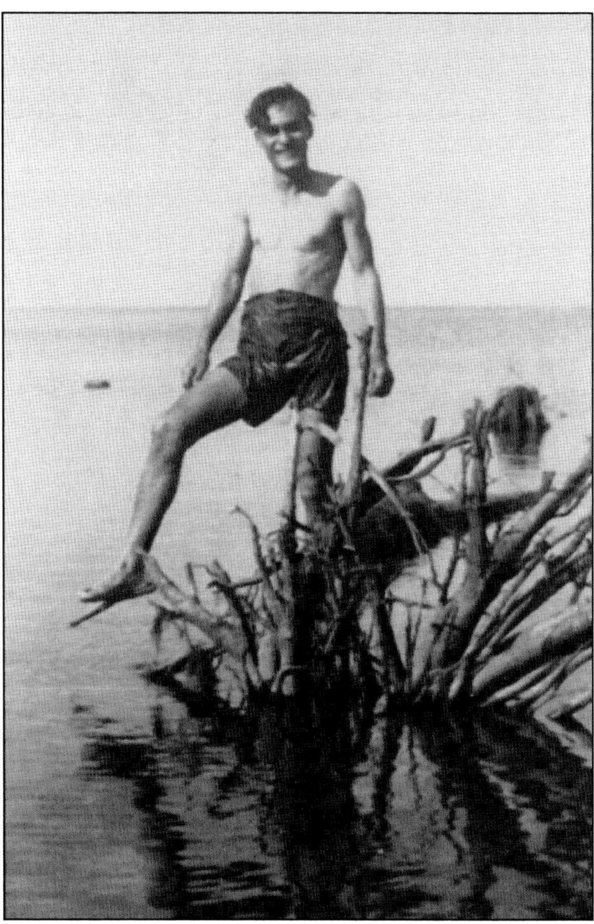

Joseph Ferdinand Valentine, pictured at the piano, knew music was something he loved. At age 16, he performed with the legendary Ray Charles and other greats, including Chuck Berry, Jackie Wilson, Johnny Taylor, Joe Tex, Eddie Floyd, and Joey Hilton. He is a member of the Texas Music Hall of Fame. Valentine's uncle was Thomas Valentine, commonly known as "Kid Thomas," who played for nearly 30 years at Preservation Hall in New Orleans. (Courtesy of Mary Dorothy Mitchell.)

During the 1930s, in an era of staunch segregation, African Americans were excluded from public swimming pools. Pictured is Raymond Tregre, who posed for a photograph while swimming in the Mississippi River near Our Lady of Grace Church. Frenier Beach in LaPlace, Louisiana, was a favorite weekend spot for African Americans as the waters of Lake Pontchartrain were suitable for swimming, and the area made a great picnic spot. (Courtesy of Lisa Tregre.)

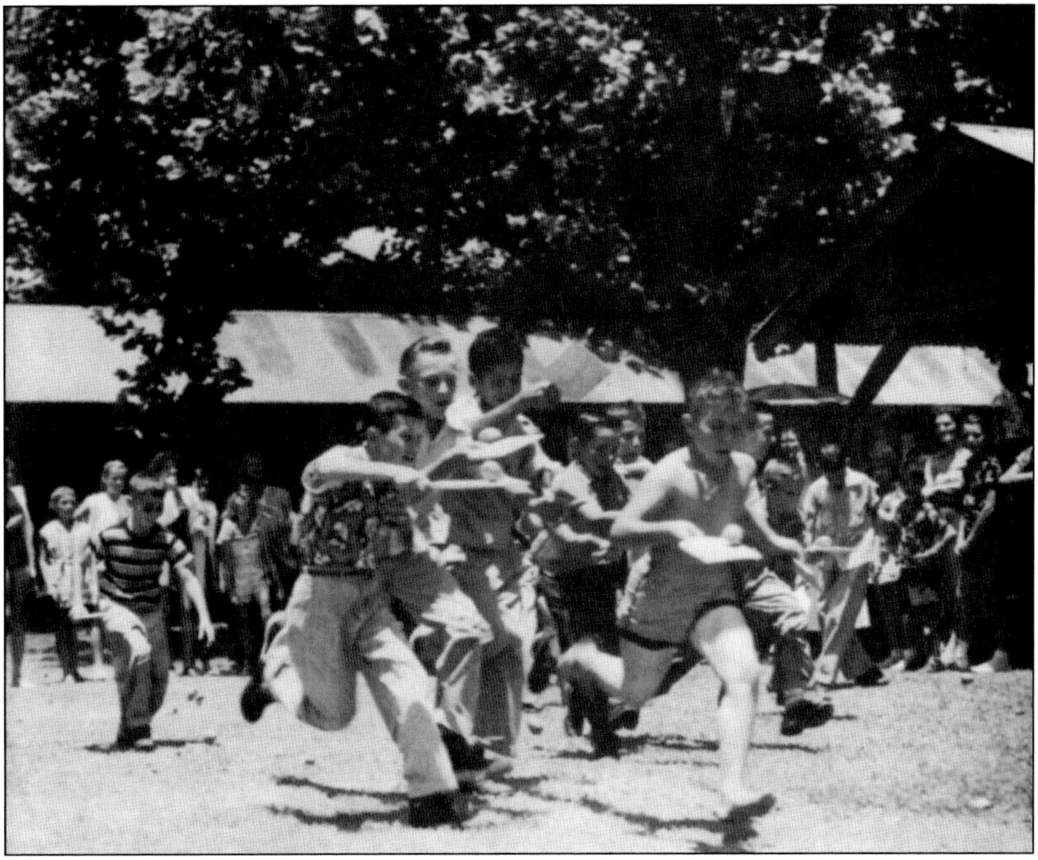

The Godchaux Sugar Refinery's Fourth of July fairs drew crowds of nearly 10,000 visitors to the grounds of the Reserve Community Club. Busses brought workers and families from other Godchaux Sugar refineries and from the Godchaux New Orleans clothing store. Shown above is the boys' egg race and below is the ladies' sack race. The event included swimming races, a diving contest, softball tournament, and a fireworks display. (Courtesy of *Blue Band*.)

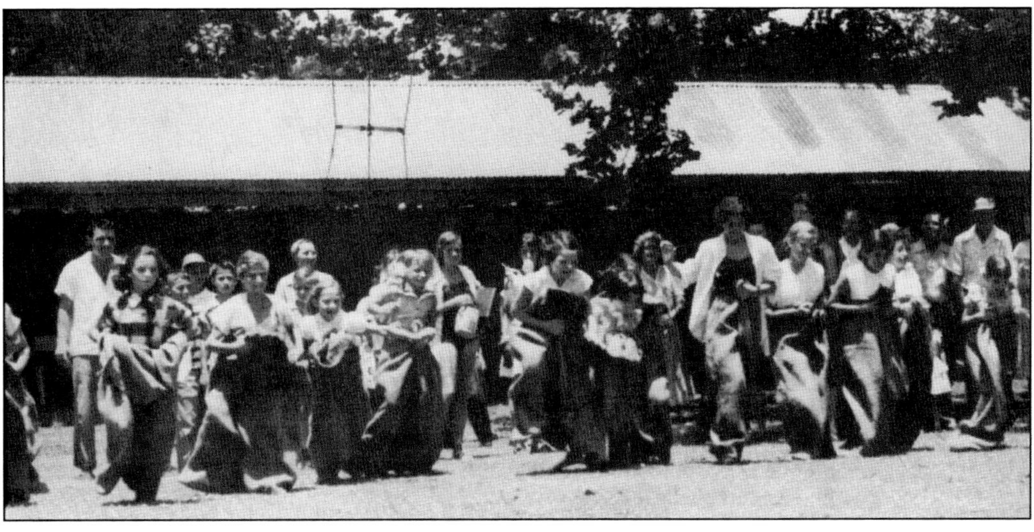

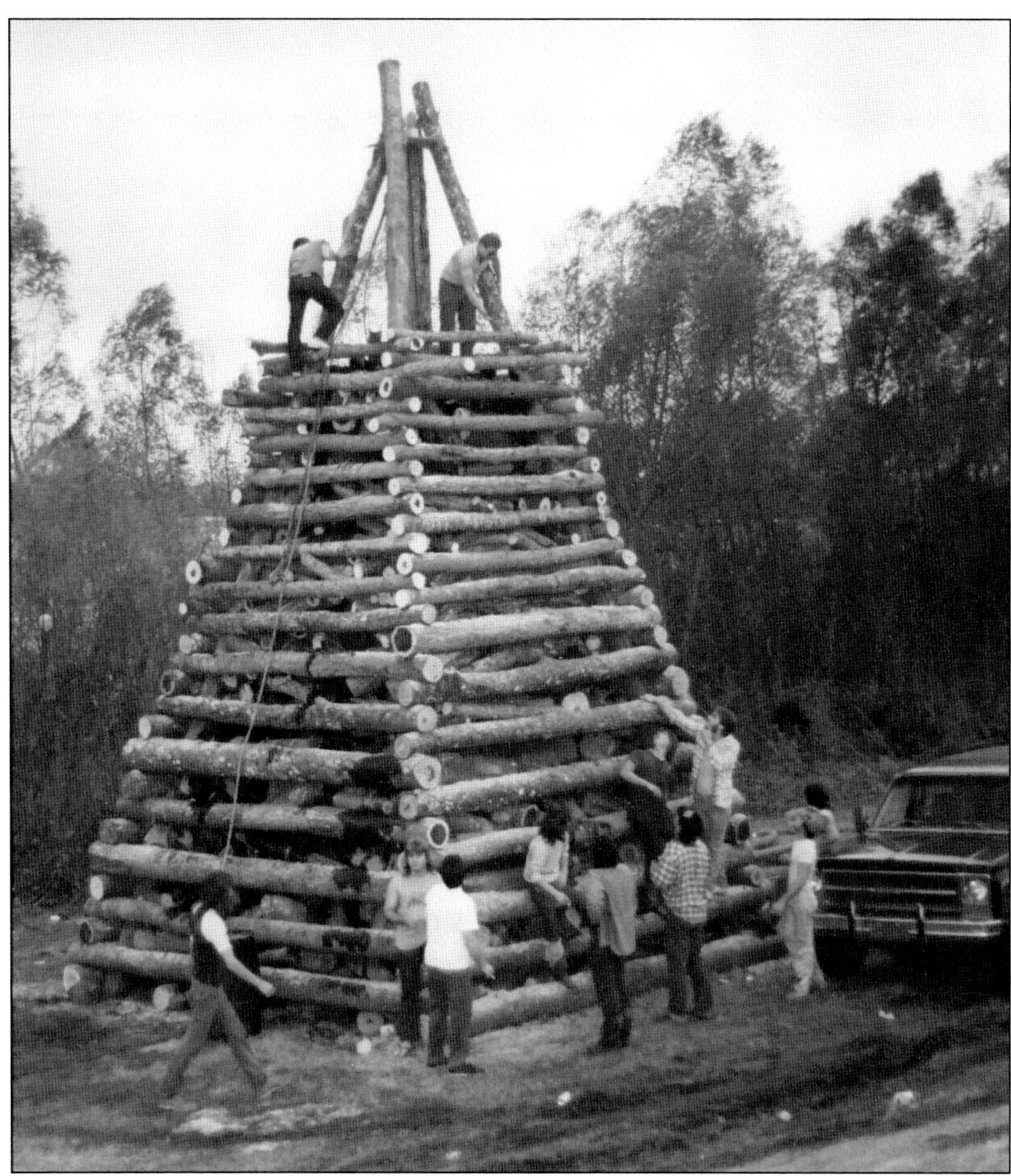

After dark on Christmas Eve, huge bonfires are lit along the levees of the Mississippi River in the Louisiana parishes of St. John the Baptist and St. James. The spirit of bonfire building originated with the early French and German settlers, who "lit the way for Papa Noel" to travel down the Mississippi River. Many leave their bonfires to attend midnight mass at St. Peter Catholic Church. Smaller bonfires are also found in isolated neighborhoods and backyards. These are usually built of logs, cane reed, and bamboo, and created the effect of spectacular fireworks. Today, chainsaws have replaced axes, hatches, and handsaws, and logs are transported by pickup trucks to the levee. The structures have maintained the traditional teepee shape, but with precisely cut logs, designers have become more creative. Nontraditional bonfires gradually emerged in the shape of plantation homes, riverboats, airplanes, boats, cars, and so on. This 1977 bonfire, built on the Mississippi River batture near St. Peter Catholic Church, measured 85 feet tall and 25 feet wide. (Courtesy of Willie Robert.)

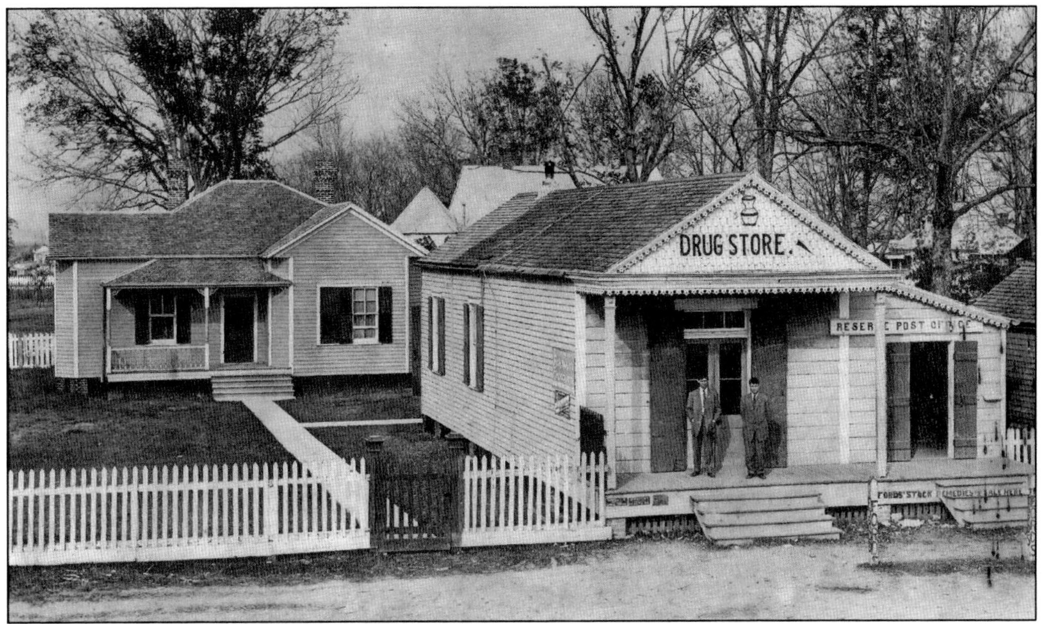

Donaldson's Drug Store served the community for more than 75 years. Built by Dr. Louis T. Donaldson in 1904, Henry A. Donaldson, left, joined his father in 1907. Henry was appointed postmaster at the adjoining Reserve Post Office until 1932. Henry lived in the house on the left. His son Malcolm J. Donaldson took over the store when his father died and continued the family business until 1982. (Courtesy of Marion Donaldson.)

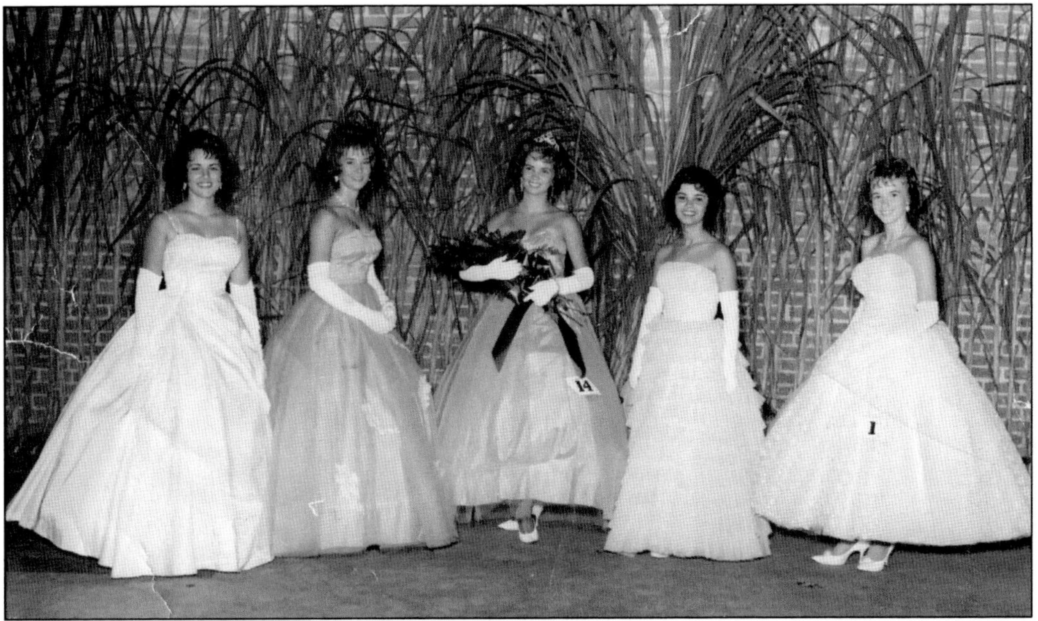

Contestants in the 1961 Reserve Lions Club Sugar Queen Pageant included, from left to right, Cheryl Michel Keller, Suzanne Laiche, Reserve Sugar Queen Debbie Duhe Pearce, unidentified, and Sherrie Triche. The Reserve Sugar Queen would later participate in the state sugar queen pageant held in New Iberia. Over the year, the pageant was organized by Malcolm Donaldson, Richard Oubre, Quincy Montz, and Danielle Madere Boudreaux. (Courtesy of Cheryl Michel Keller.)

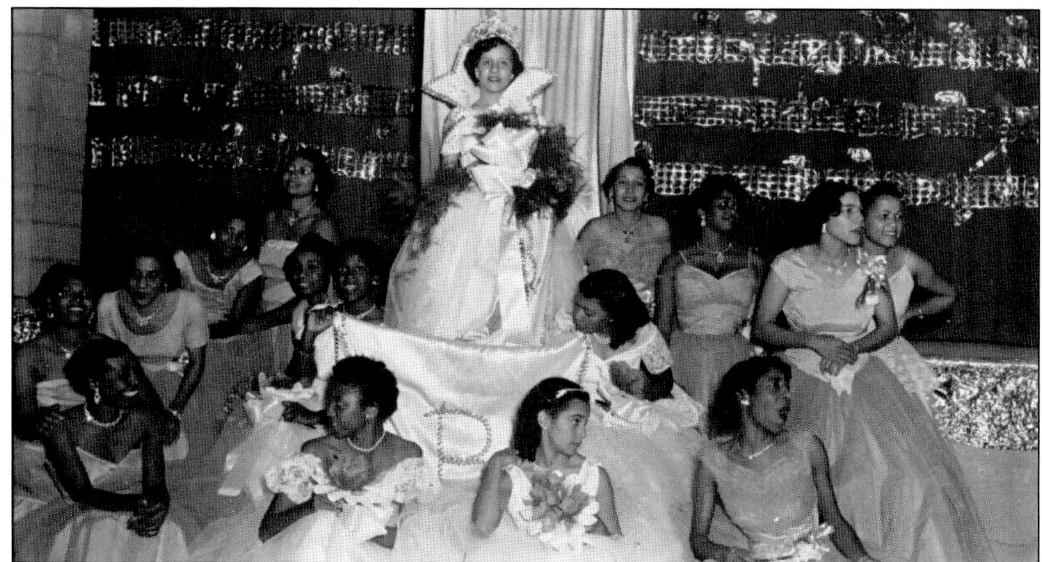

In 1955, the PBS Club sponsored a debutante ball at Our Lady of Grace Gymnasium. Shown at the front center in white dresses are debutantes Gail Clark (left) and Loyce Sorina. Seated behind them are Rosemary Sanders (left), Vivian August (holding banner), and unidentified (holding banner). In the center is queen Shirley Brown Gauff. The girls surrounding them are, from front to back, (left side) Gertrude Cook, Dolores Dorsey, Elma Lapeyrolerie, Rosemary Toney, and Wilhelmina Armour; (right side) Melva Gerard, Adele Lapeyrolerie, Dorothy Lapeyrolerie, Annabella Dunn, and Leona Washington. (Courtesy of Fr. Rodney Joseph.)

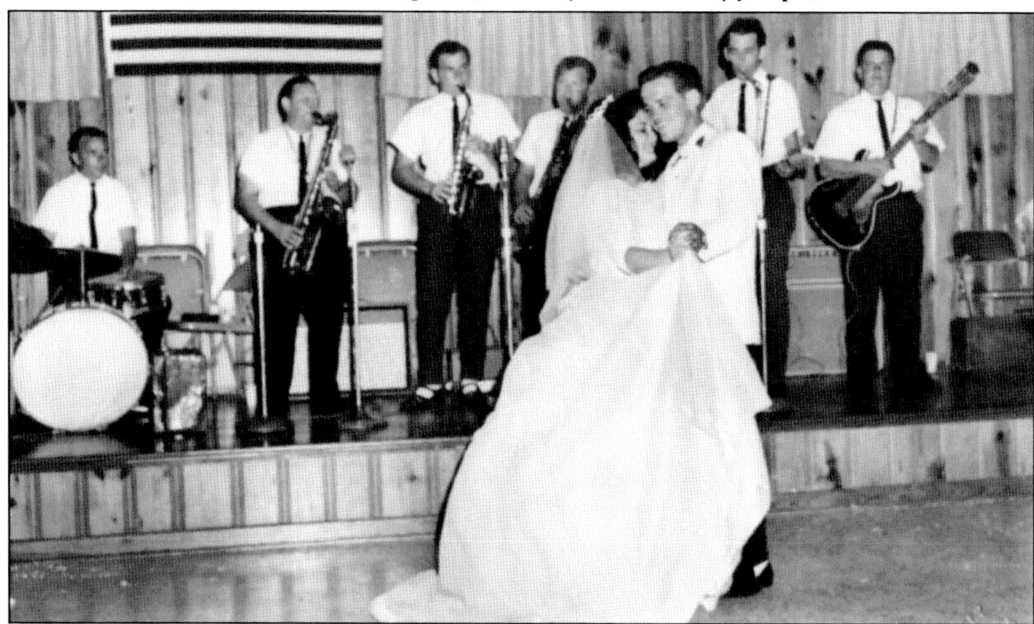

Rhythm Six was a local band that performed at weddings, church fairs, and every Friday night for nearly a decade. They also played at the student dances at Leon Godchaux High School. Band members pictured include, from left to right, Bobby Ayme, Harold "Peanut" Vicknair, Harold Ayme, Bobby Ayme, Manton "Slim" Duhe, and Wilbert Breaud. The wedding couple is Arthur Delaneuville and Frankie Tarullo. (Courtesy of Betty Brown Vicknair.)

In 1966, during the era of the civil rights movement, young African American women broke the color barrier in business and industry. Women received training in business skills from Loyola University. Pictured from left to right are (first row) Dolores Williams, Cynthia Dixon, and Peggy Jackson; (second row) Joyce Johnson, Carolyn Dugas, Vivian August, and Mary Dorothy Mitchell; (third row) Cindy Tregre, Eula Mitchell, Mabel Glover, Kathleen Stewart, instructor Bette Bergman, Ethel Della, and Joan Markey. (Courtesy of Mary Dorothy Mitchell.)

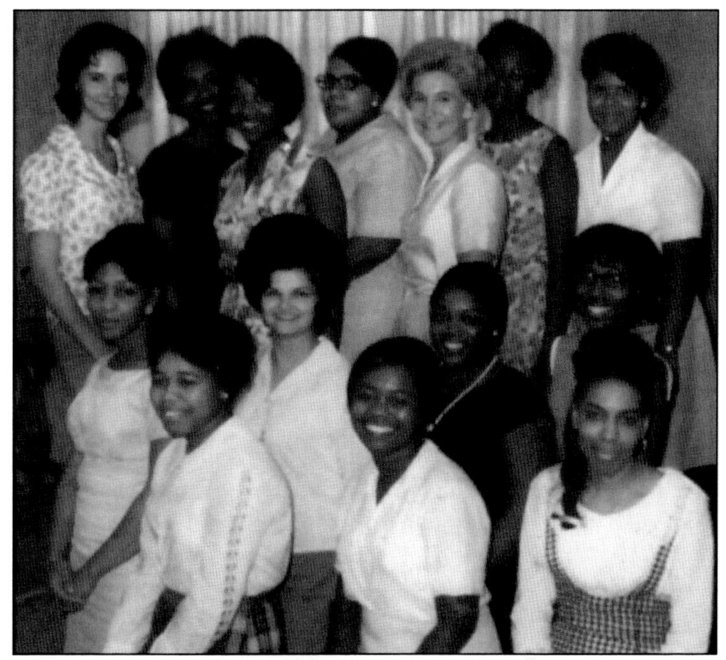

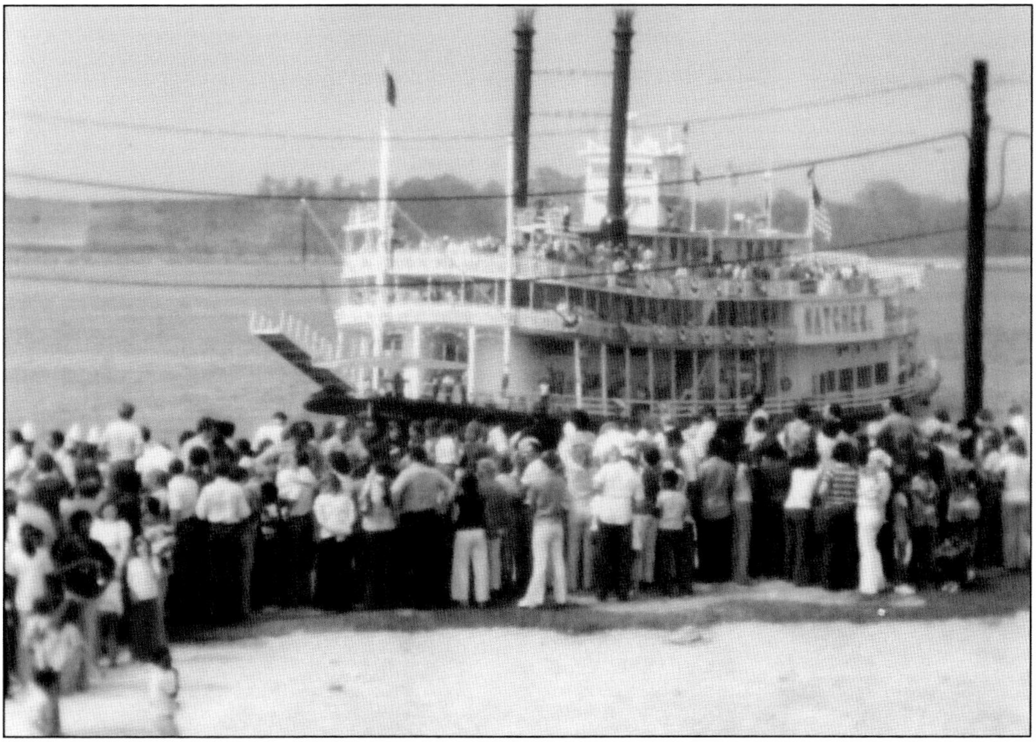

On Saturday, September 25, 1976, Pres. Gerald R. Ford stopped to greet a crowd of more than 3,000 at the Reserve ferry landing on a historic Mississippi River cruise to New Orleans, Louisiana. President Ford addressed the crowd from the SS *Natchez* and later walked through the crowd shaking hands. He also made stops at the Lutcher-Vacherie Ferry Landing and the Destrehan Ferry Landing. (Courtesy of Callan Jacob.)

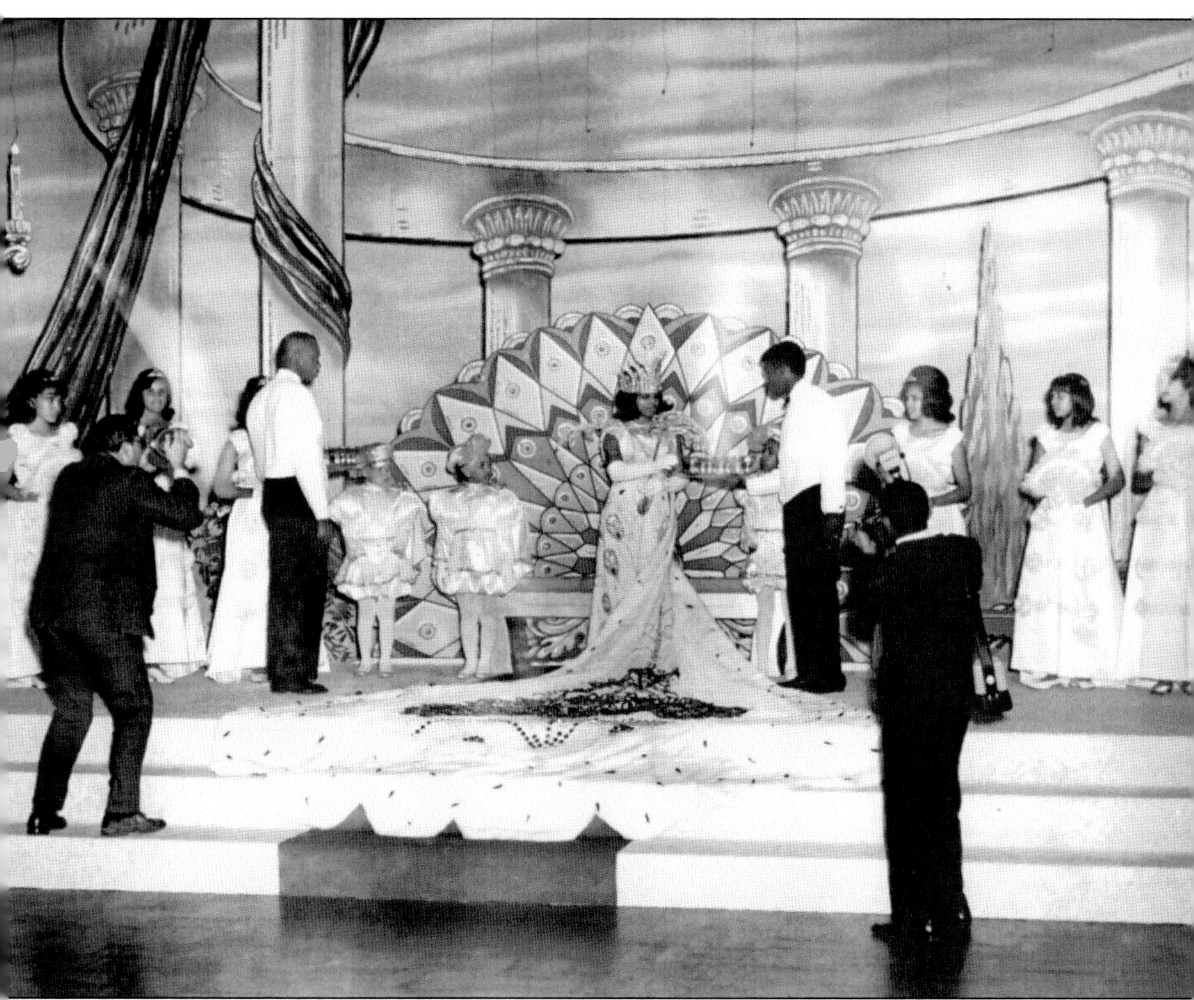

Splendid regalia, elegant gowns, and stylish mementos depict a more exclusive realm of Carnival balls held during the Mardi Gras season. Today's balls vary in scope, extravagance, and level of formality. Although masquerade balls were popular during the Colonial period, it was not until the latter half of the 19th century that organizations known as "krewes" began developing the elaborate protocol. Social events associated with specific groups emerged. The late 19th century witnessed the first African American krewes. The most prestigious of these, formed in 1895, has continued to this day and is now divided into two groups, the Young Men's Illinois Club and the Original Illinois Club. In the 1960s, Dr. Karen Becnel Moore (center) was crowned Mardi Gras queen of the Young Men's Illinois Club Mardi Gras Ball, held at the New Orleans Municipal Hall. She is escorted by her father, Dr. Milton Becnel. Her mother was Enola Tregre Becnel, a lifelong St. John the Baptist Parish educator and school principal. (Courtesy of Lisa Tregre Wilder.)

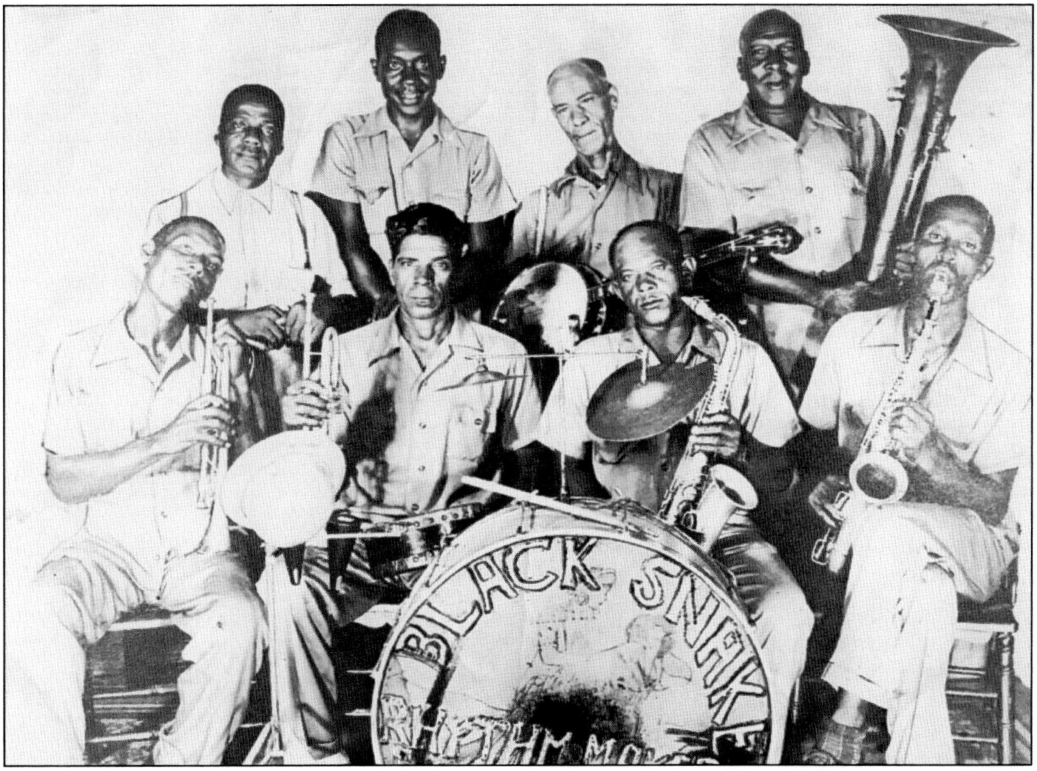

The Black Snake Rhythm Makers, a popular musical group in the 1940s, was named for its leader and drummer Woodrow Wilson "Black Snake" Mitchell. Band members include, from left to right, (first row) Edward Duhe, Felman Duhe, George Lawrence, and Jules "Gold Mine" Duhe; (second row) unidentified, ? Mitchell, Raoul Poche, and James Stewart. Mitchell acquired the nickname as he struck out baseball batters with a "snakelike" curve ball. (Courtesy of Mary Dorothy Mitchell.)

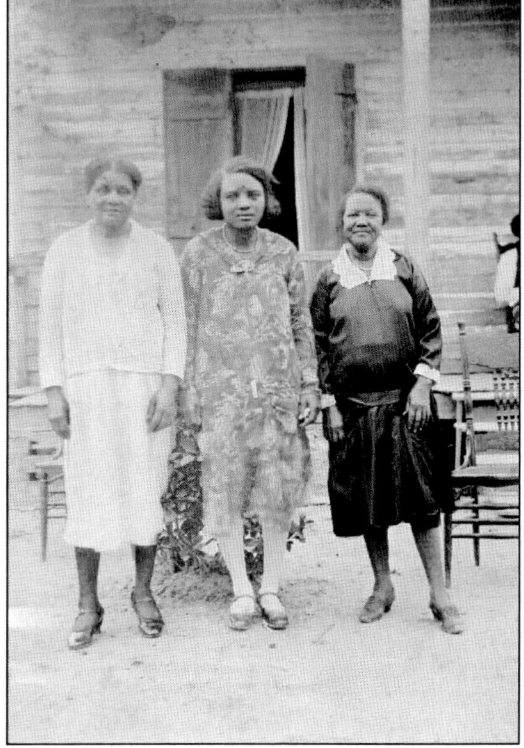

Several Reserve ladies take time out on a Sunday afternoon to pose for a picture. From left to right are Mary Fleming Nicholson, Sedonia Peters, and Julia Fleming (Mary's sister). (Courtesy of Ethelene Nicholson.)

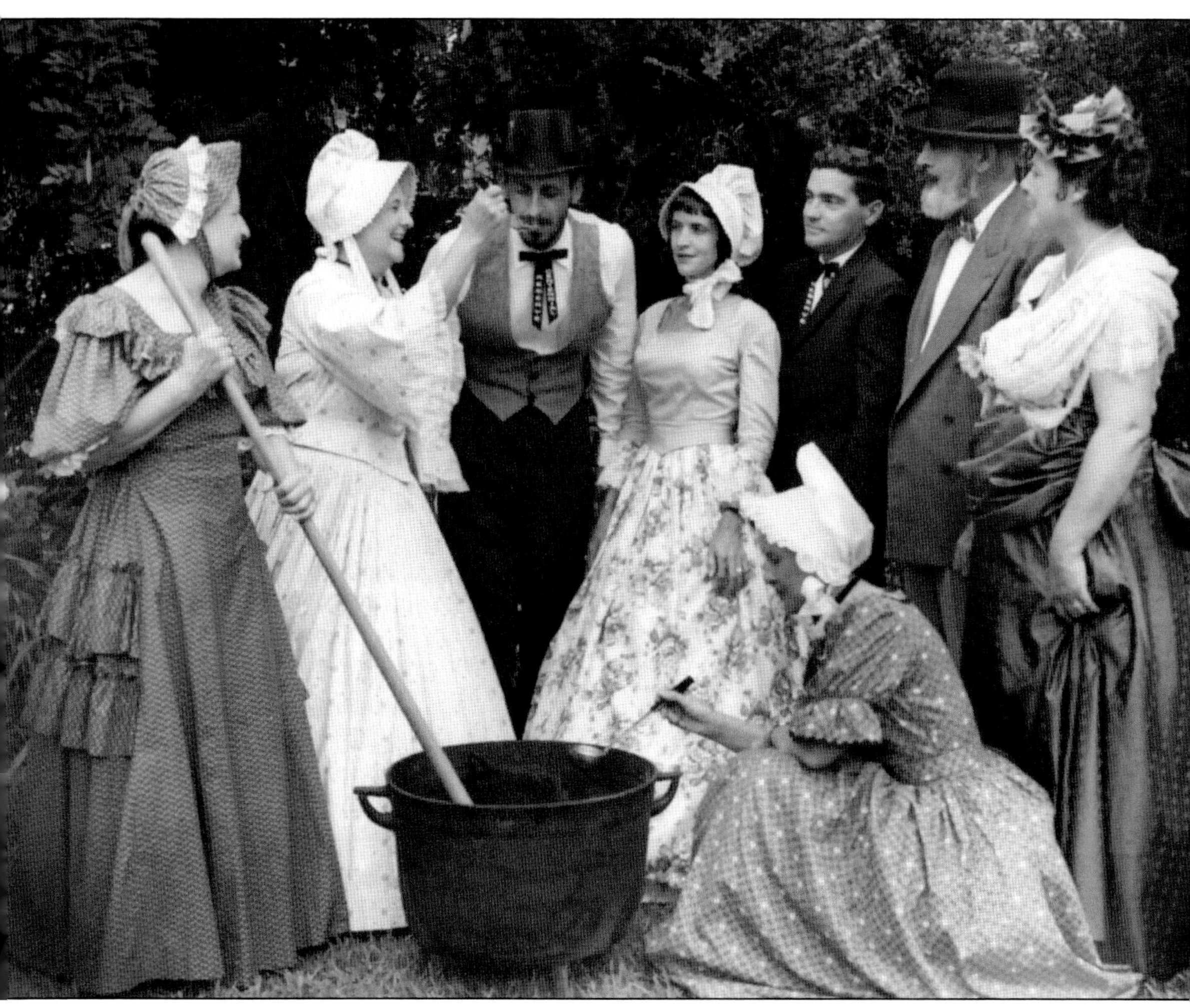

Reserve celebrated its 100th anniversary in 1960. Posing for a picture at the San Francisco Plantation in Lions, Louisiana, are, from left to right, Edna Boutiton, Marguerite Donaldson, Eldridge Gendron, Harold Maurin, Marcel Montegut, and Mrs. W.F. Middleton. Kneeling is Beatrice Lasseigne. Harold Becnel was chosen Mr. Reserve in a bodybuilding contest sponsored by the Reserve Centennial Committee. Alvin Stein and Kendall Cambre were runner-ups. (Courtesy of Blanche Hotard.)

In 1977, a significant piece of history was lost as the Voison House was torn down. Built in 1785, the antebellum house was one of the oldest houses in the Mississippi Valley. Hurricane Betsy tore the roof from the neglected building in 1965; this led to extensive deterioration and, finally, the demise of the house. (Courtesy of Louisiana State Museum.)

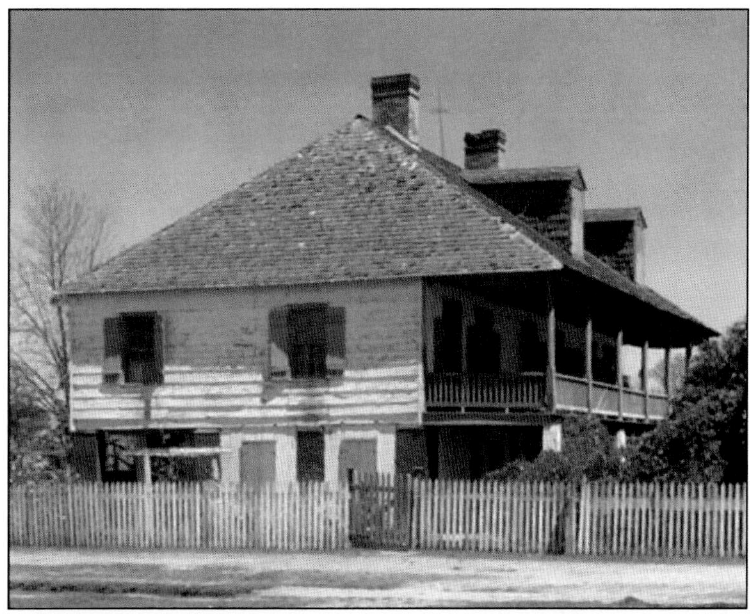

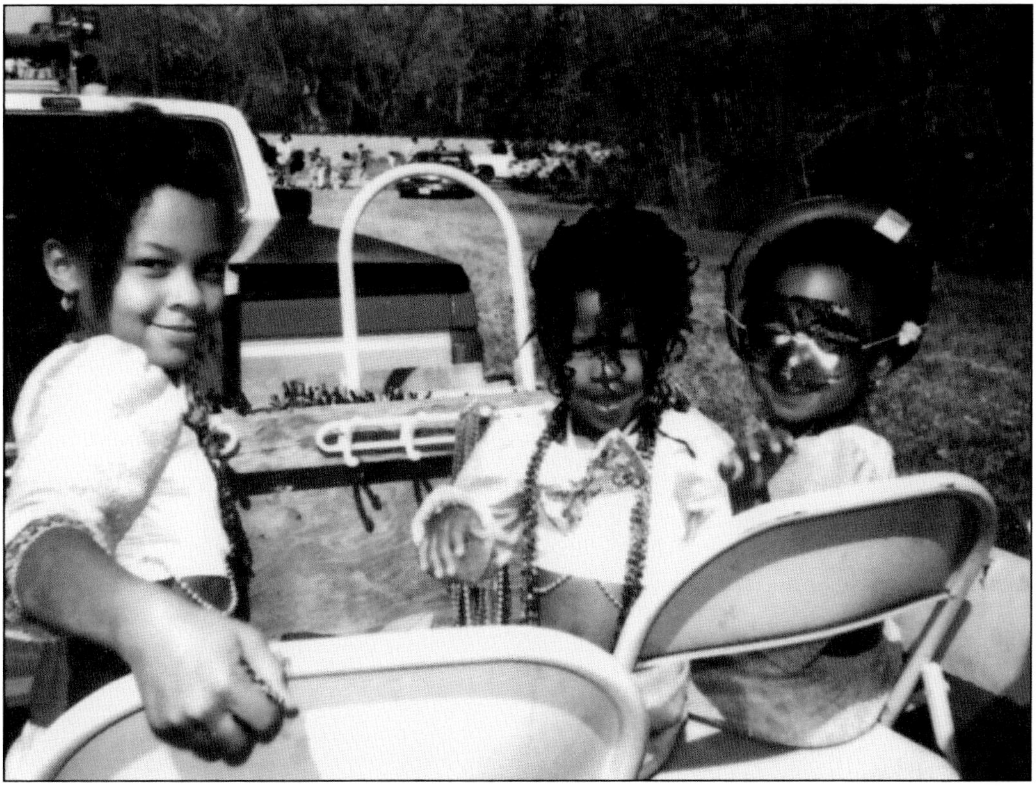

The krewe of Towahpasah rolls through Reserve, open to anyone who wishes to participate. It is celebrated the Saturday before Mardi Gras and features a variety of vehicles; each entrant is designed by the individual owners. Riders choose their own selection of throws, which usually includes beads, cups, and an assortment of stuffed animals. Pictured from left to right are Kai Thomas, Niya Stevens, and Da'Janae Mason. (Courtesy of Albertha "Pinky" Henderson.)

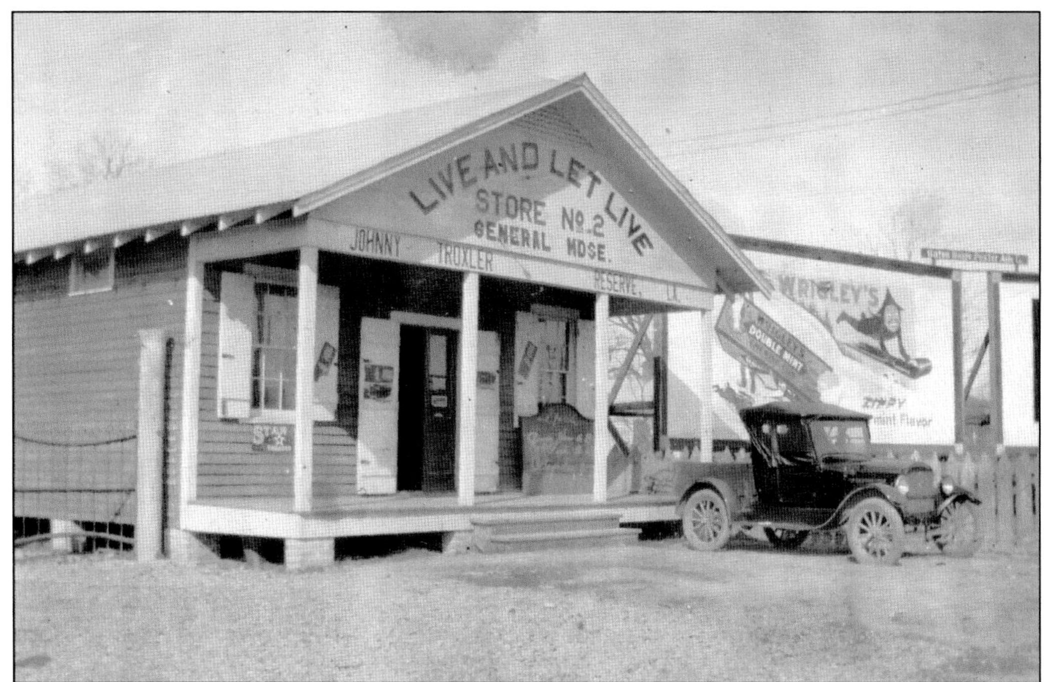

The Live and Let Live Store was owned by Johnny Troxler and located near St. Peter Catholic Church on West Seventh Street. Troxler also owned a Live and Let Live Store No. 2. The Live and Let Live building is still in the area and is currently used for storage. Small stores could be found in every neighborhood. The most-remembered neighborhood store in Reserve was probably Eddie "Dool" Vicknair's on West Ninth Street. (Courtesy of Helen Waguespack Klilbert.)

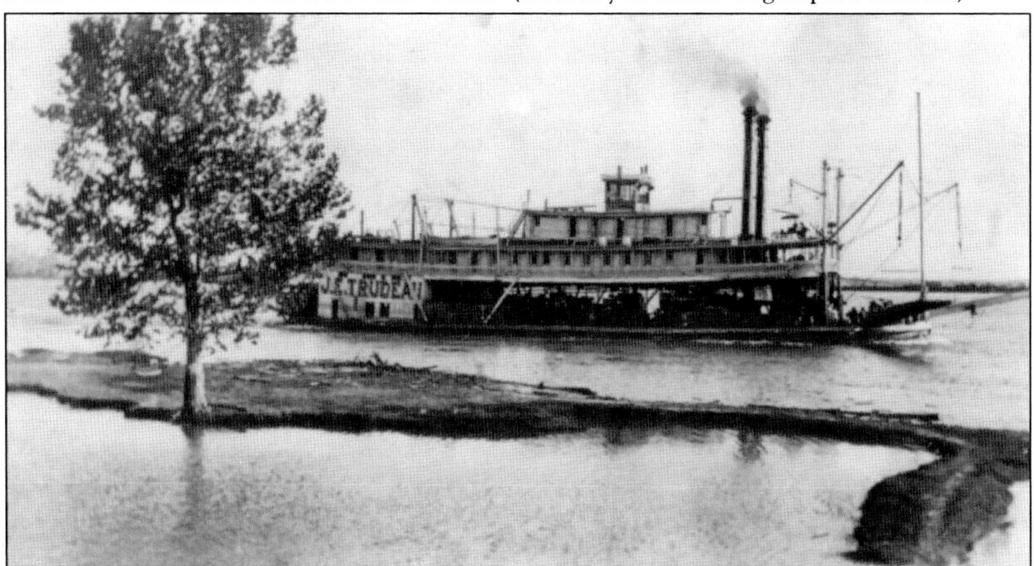

Pictured is the *J.E. Trudeau* backing out from the Acorn Landing batture after delivering merchandise, groceries, wine, and any other orders from New Orleans to residents and grocers near the landing. Because people relied on iceboxes to refrigerate milk and meat products, 100-pound blocks of ice were also delivered by the *Imperial*. The ice was later chipped with an ice pick for customer use. (Courtesy of Joy Donaldson McGraw.)

Displaying their football uniforms and carrying signs for their favorite college teams are brothers Harold (left) and Mark Keller. Both served their parish as public servants when they were elected to political offices. Harold served as a Louisiana state representative from 1964 to 1968, and Mark served as a St. John the Baptist Parish police juror. (Courtesy of Judy Keller Duhon and Ronnie Keller Michel.)

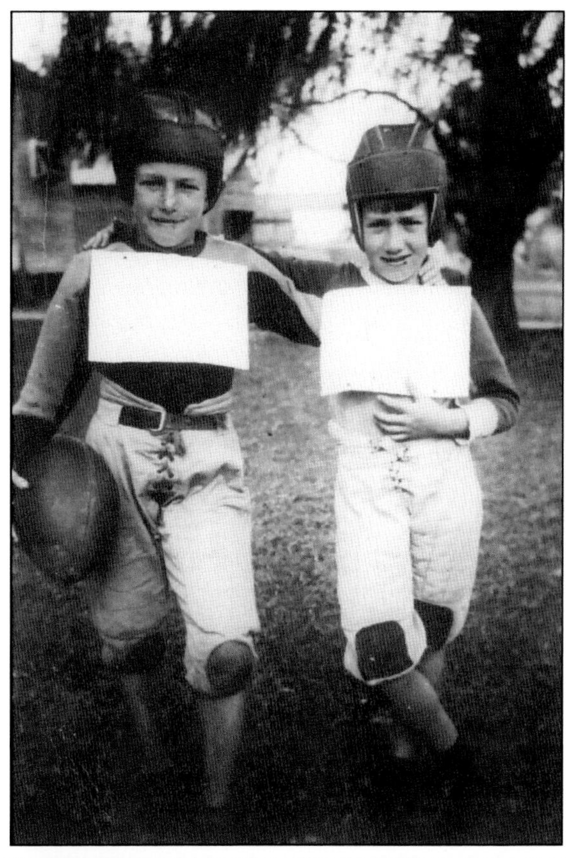

The Leader was a clothing store located along River Road in Reserve. Pictured are the two brothers—Alex and Tewfix Haik—who managed the operation of the store. The Haik family immigrated to the United States from Beirut, Lebanon, in the early 1900s. The store would later be called Haik Store and two sisters-in-law, Evelyn and Waddad, managed the operation. (Courtesy of Donna Lynn Donaldson Fulton.)

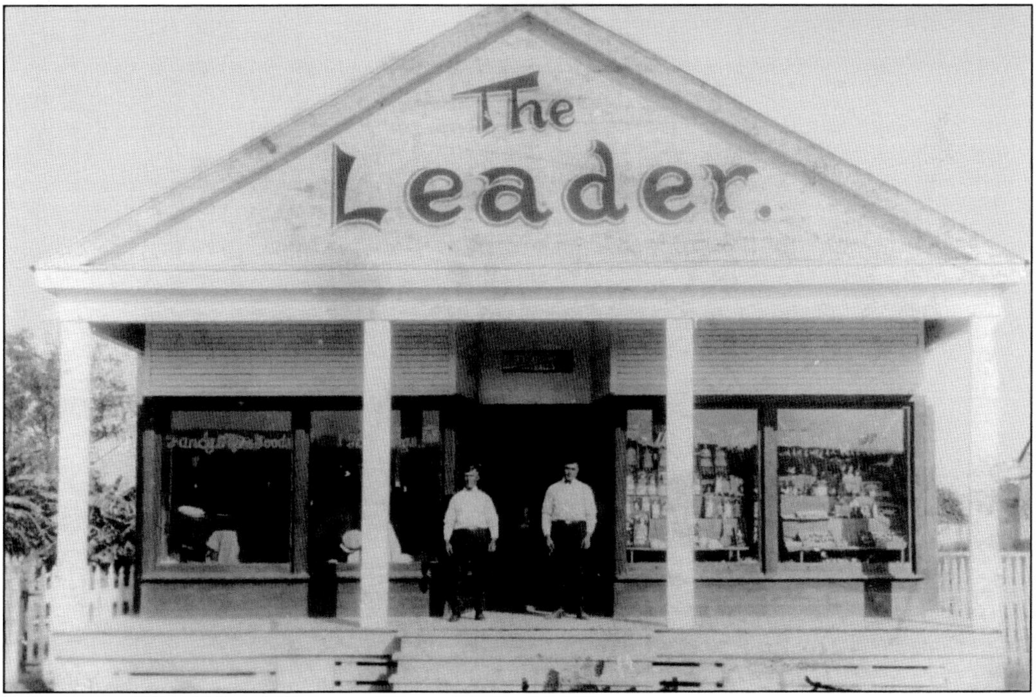

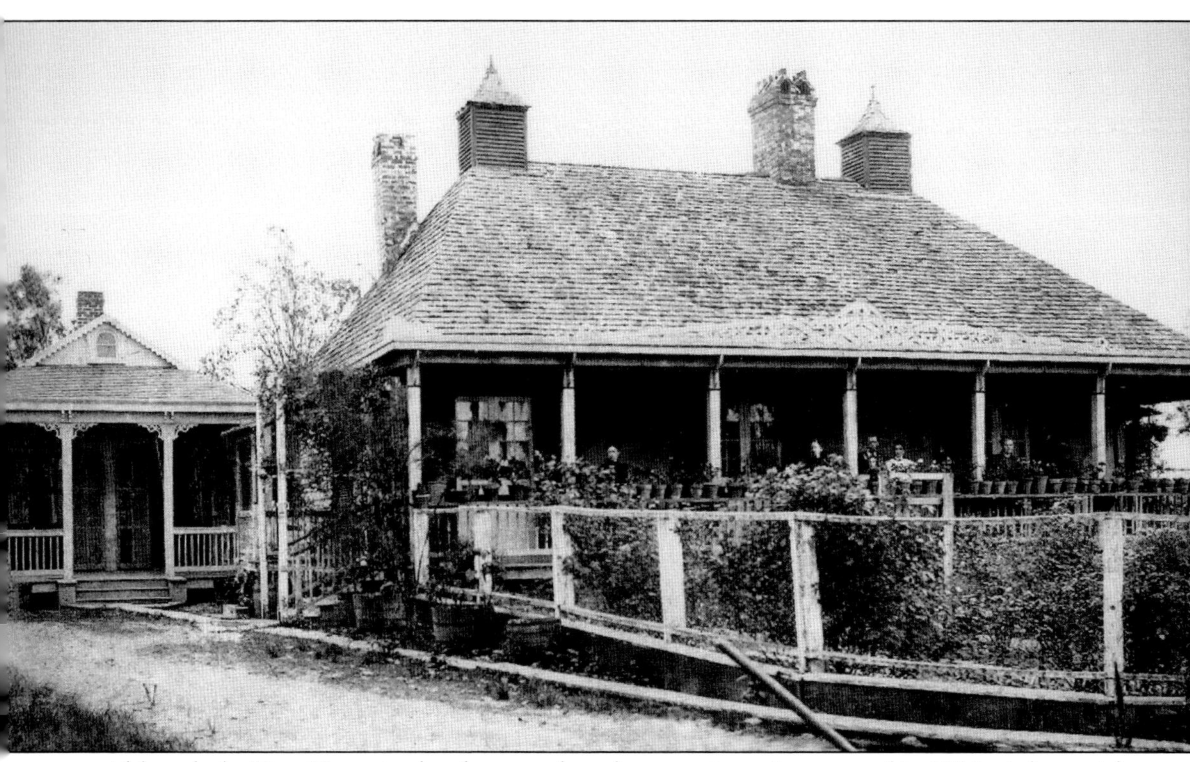

Although the Hart House in the photograph no longer exists—it was razed in 1964—it has a rich history. It was built by the Marmillion family before the Civil War, with mud and sticks covered with clapboard and plaster. The land ran from the Mississippi River to Lake Maurepas and was mostly planted with sugarcane. The Marmillion family lived on the property until 1860, when the property and house were sold to Dr. William J. Hart. After Hart's death, Noelie Hart and her sister Lucille, both unmarried, inherited the house. While they owned the house, Noelie and Lucille took in boarders (school teachers, railroad workers, and government employees). Later, the house went to their brother sheriff William "Billy" Hart and his son William "Sweet" Hart. In 1913, the Hart family operated the Hart Canning Factory, which turned out a product line called Rose Villa that included canned okra, corn, beets, beans, peas, blackberries, and strawberries. (Courtesy of Dr. Douglas Perret Starr.)

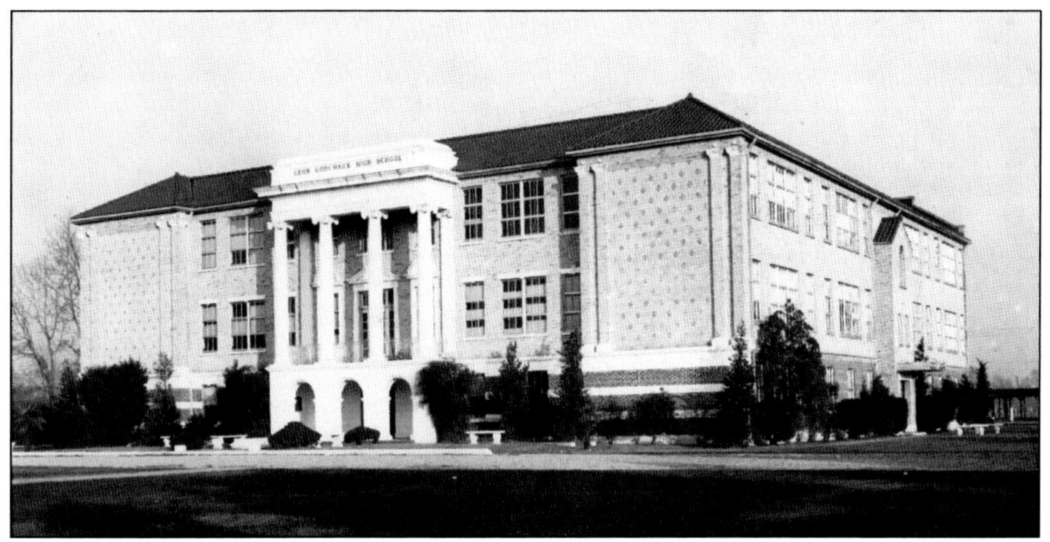

Leon Godchaux High School opened in September 1930 for East Bank students of St. John the Baptist Parish in grades eight through 11. A gymnasium was added in 1939, and the three-story building remained opened until it was destroyed by an arsonist in 1978. The original Leon Godchaux High School, near the Bank of St. John, was renamed Leon Godchaux Grammar School. (Courtesy of Shirley Casseigne Terrio.)

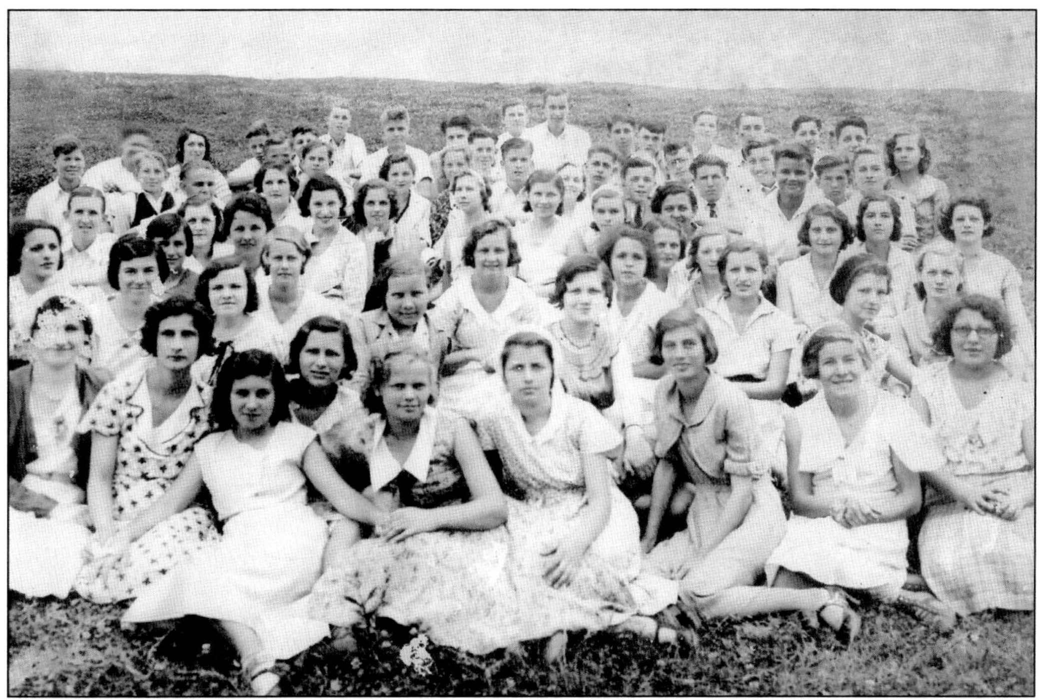

In 1932, graduating students gathered on the Mississippi River levee in front of Leon Godchaux High School to pose for a group picture. During that time, Louisiana seniors graduated in the 11th grade, and eighth grade students were considered freshmen in high school. It was not until 1947 that an extra year was added to Louisiana schools, and students attended a 12th year of school. (Courtesy of Carl L. Levet and family.)

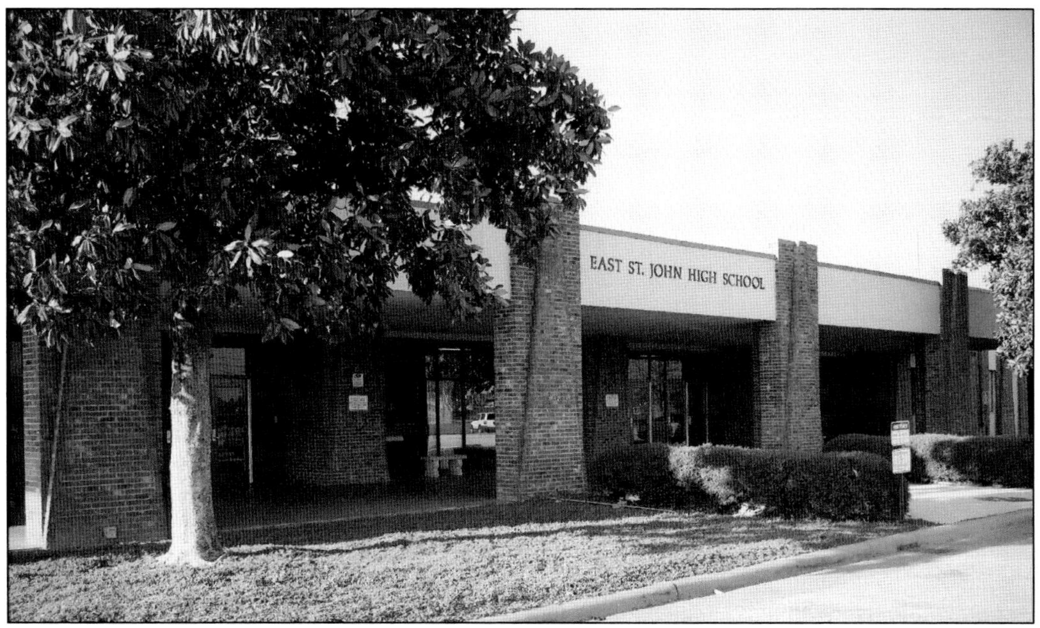

A fire that destroyed Leon Godchaux High School forced the St. John the Baptist Parish School Board to build a new structure for its East Bank students. The new school was completed for the 1976–1977 school session, and the St. John the Baptist Parish School Board named the new school East St. John High School. A ninth grade academy wing was added in the early 2000s, and an athletic field house was rebuilt in 2011. (Courtesy of Gerald Keller.)

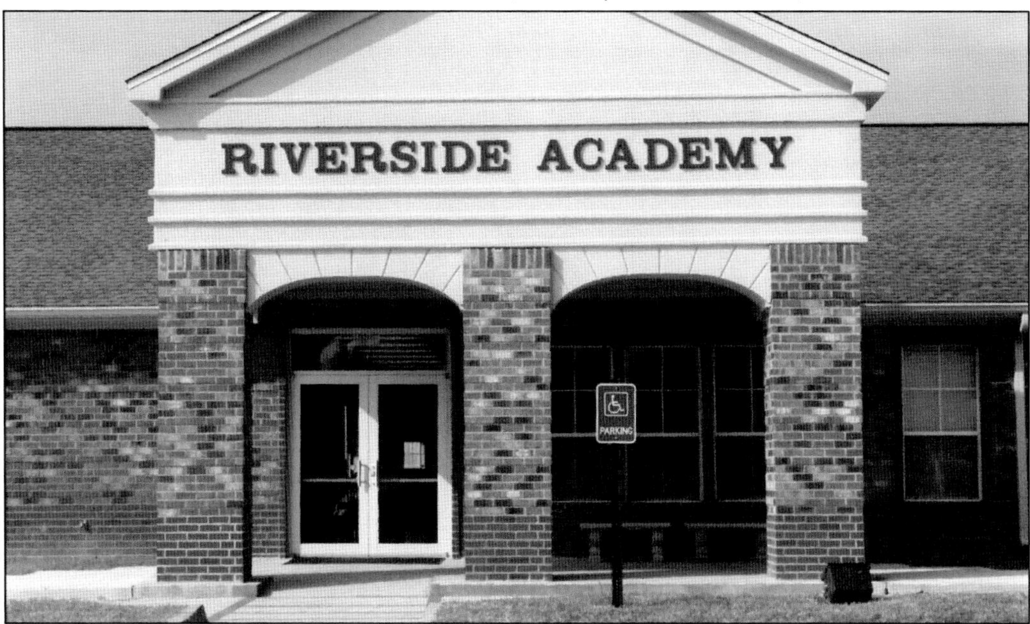

Riverside Academy opened its doors on September 18, 1970. The student body consisted of grades one through 12. Later improvements included a prekindergarten and kindergarten wing. The school geared up for the 21st century with a strong focus on academics. Extracurricular activities include a complete music program (beginning in grade four), a state-of-the-art technology curriculum, and a strong home economics program. (Courtesy of Carrie Turnbull.)

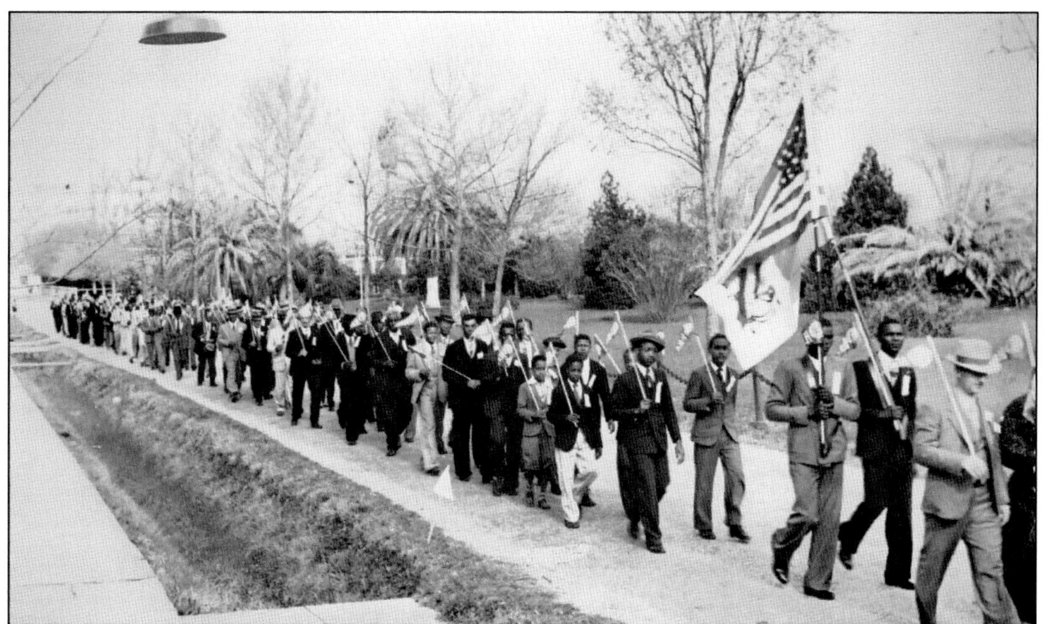

Knights of Peter Claver No. 73 members are marching to services at Our Lady of Grace Catholic Church. The Knights of Peter Claver is the largest historically African American Catholic lay organization in the United States. Its purpose is "to render service to God and His Holy Church, render aid and assistance to the sick and disabled, and promote social and intellectual association among our members." (Courtesy of Our Lady of Grace Church.)

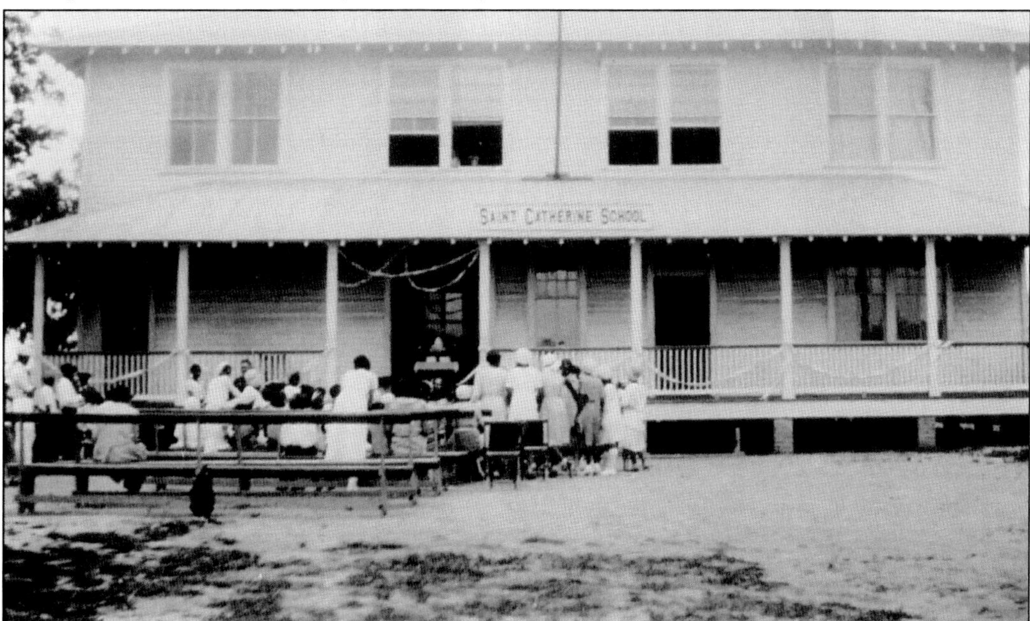

In the 1930s, St. Peter Catholic Church pastor Msgr. Jean Eyraud saw a need for African Americans to receive a Catholic education and opened St. Catherine Catholic School to the rear of the church cemetery in 1931. The school was staffed with lay teachers from Xavier University. St. Catherine was moved in 1937 to Our Lady of Grace Church Parish and renamed Our Lady of Grace. (Courtesy of Our Lady of Grace Catholic Church.)

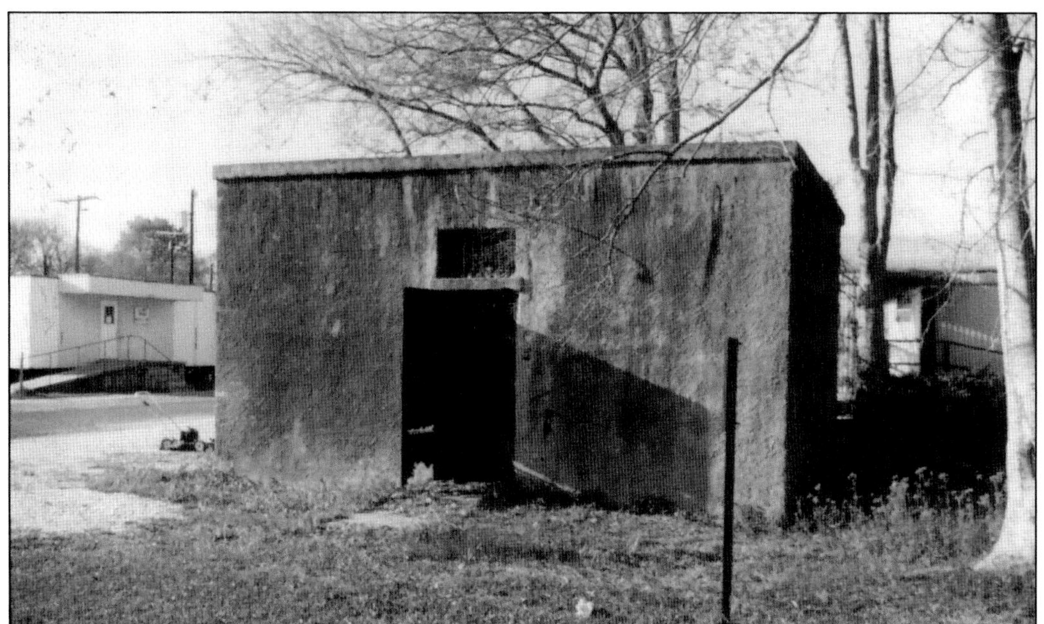

In St. John the Baptist Parish, the sheriff's sweatbox was located across the street from the St. John Theatre on West Fourth Street. Parish law officials used the building as a weekend holding place for drunks and those disturbing the peace. There were the usual violators, who posed no serious threat, and they were usually released by sheriff Percy Hebert early Monday morning. (Courtesy of Shirley Casseigne Terrio.)

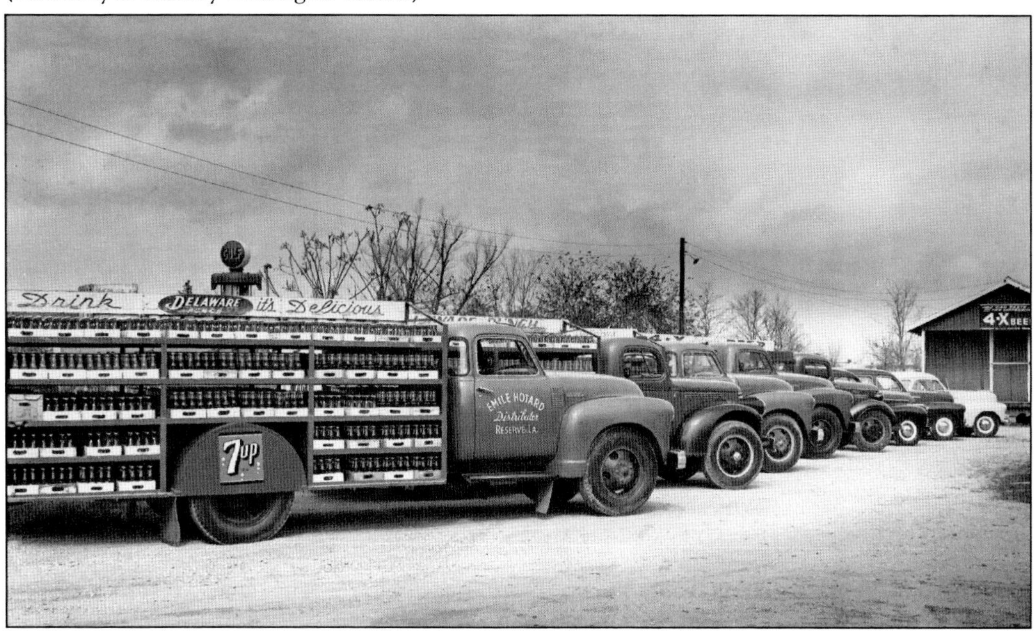

In April 1928, Emile Hotard and his brother-in-law Jules Haydel formed a distributorship with Zetz Bottling Company of New Orleans to serve the River Parishes. Soon, Hotard and his wife became the sole owners of the distributorship, which they operated until their death. The soft drink company was taken over by son Emile Hotard Jr., daughter Jewell Hotard Aucoin, and grandson Randy Aucoin. The distributorship closed in 1989. (Courtesy of Trisha Guidry Aucoin.)

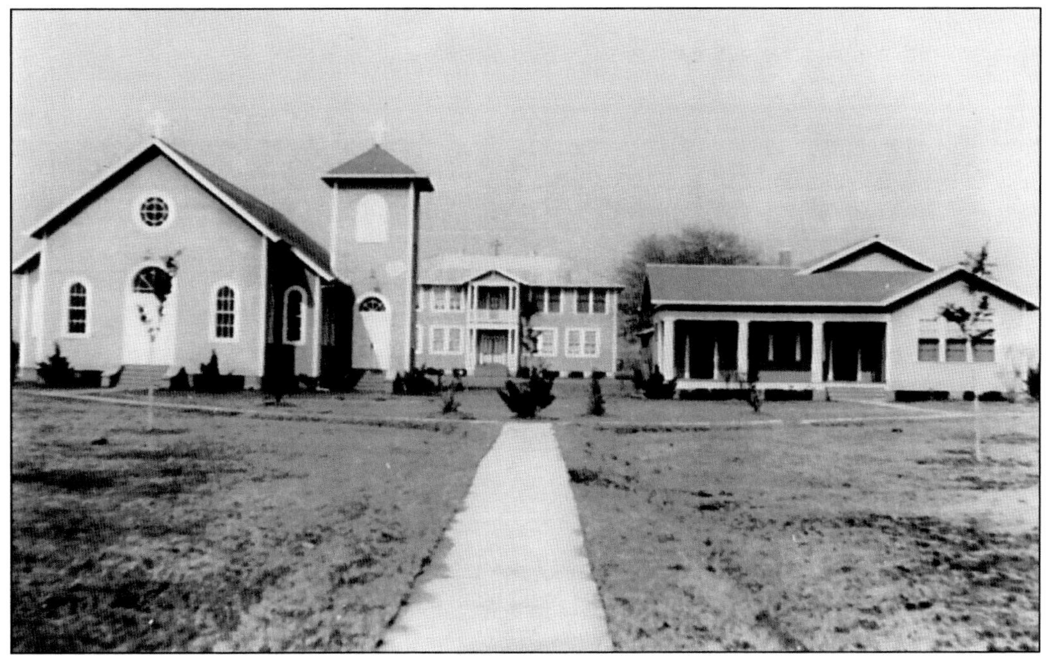

Pictured in the 1950s is the Our Lady of Grace Church school and rectory. The school and facilities were dedicated on June 13, 1937. The church was under the leadership of the Josephite priest and the Sisters of the Holy Family, and lay teachers served the school from 1942 through 1997. The school has been staffed by lay teachers since 1998. (Courtesy of Rev. Joseph Rodney.)

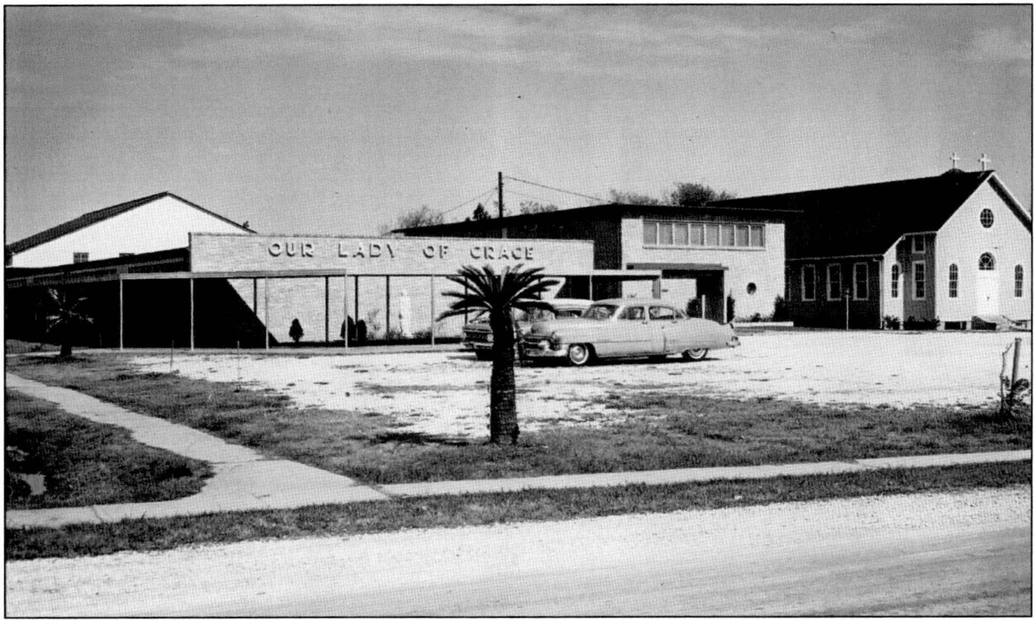

A fire destroyed five classrooms of Our Lady of Grace Elementary School and the Sisters of Holy Family convent on January 29, 1957. Because of the tireless effort of Rev. Joseph LeFrois, the Archdiocese of New Orleans, and generous donations from church parishioners, a new school consisting of eight classrooms and a cafeteria was completed for the opening of school in September 1957. (Courtesy of Rev. Joseph Rodney.)

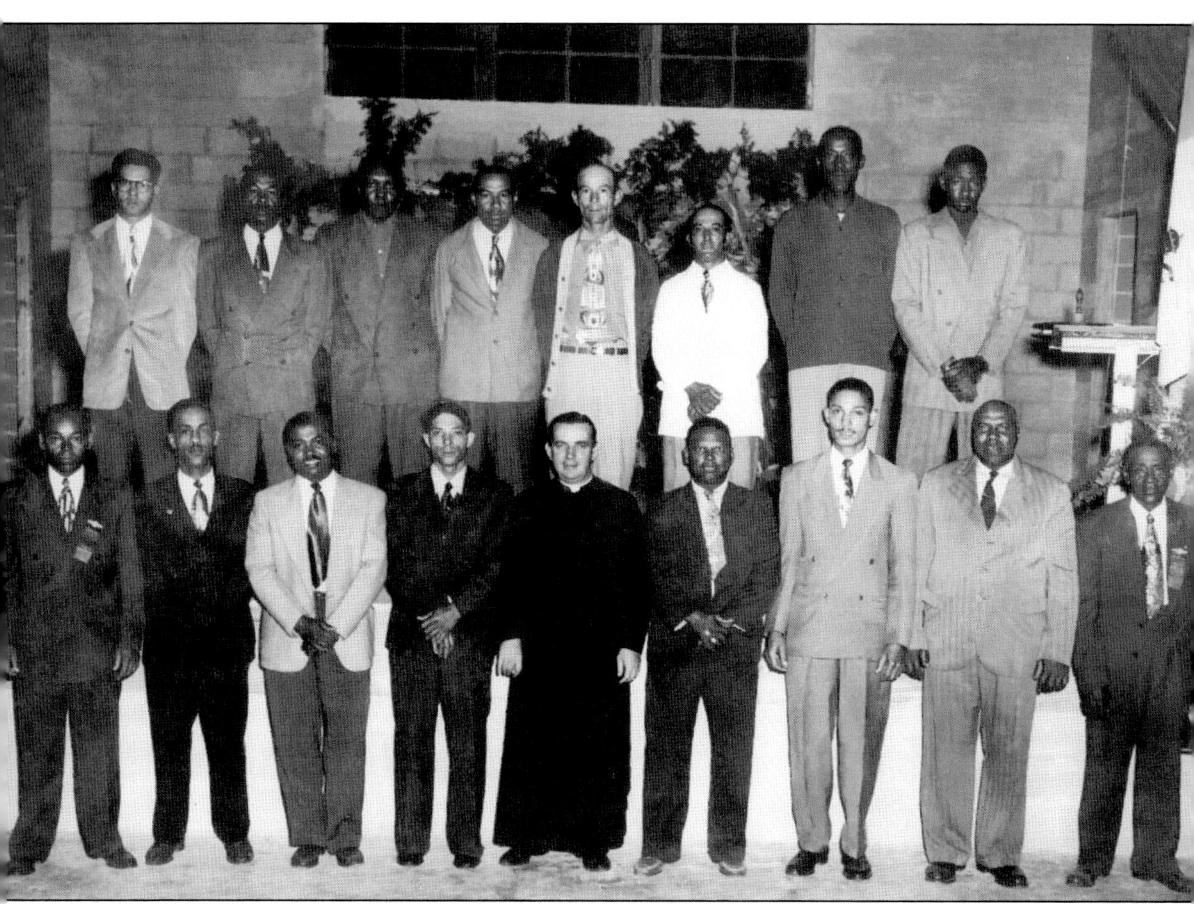

Beginning in 1937, countless men and women parishioners and volunteers throughout Reserve and the River Parishes have contributed their finances, time, and talents and worked tirelessly to build and maintain the quality of Our Lady of Grace's church building, school, gymnasium, rectory, and convent. This 1953 photograph shows some of the planners and construction workers, including, from left to right, (first row) Edward Hall, Alvin Leche, Walter Keller Jr., Rodney Perrilloux, pastor Reverend Turner, contractor Walter Keller Sr., Nolan Perrilloux Sr., Joseph Stewart, and Ursin Toney; (second row) Kim Richard, Lucien Gauff Sr., Clancy Stewart, Valsin Gauff, Benjamin Alexander Sr., Edwin Sorina, Albert Stewart, and Glenzy Cook. The Knights of Peter Claver and the Knights of Peter Claver Auxiliary Court No. 73 have always stepped forward during fundraising events and helped to maintain the alter during times of special events, such as Christmas, Easter, first communions, confirmations, and so on. (Courtesy of Our Lady of Grace.)

Four

Recreation and Athletics

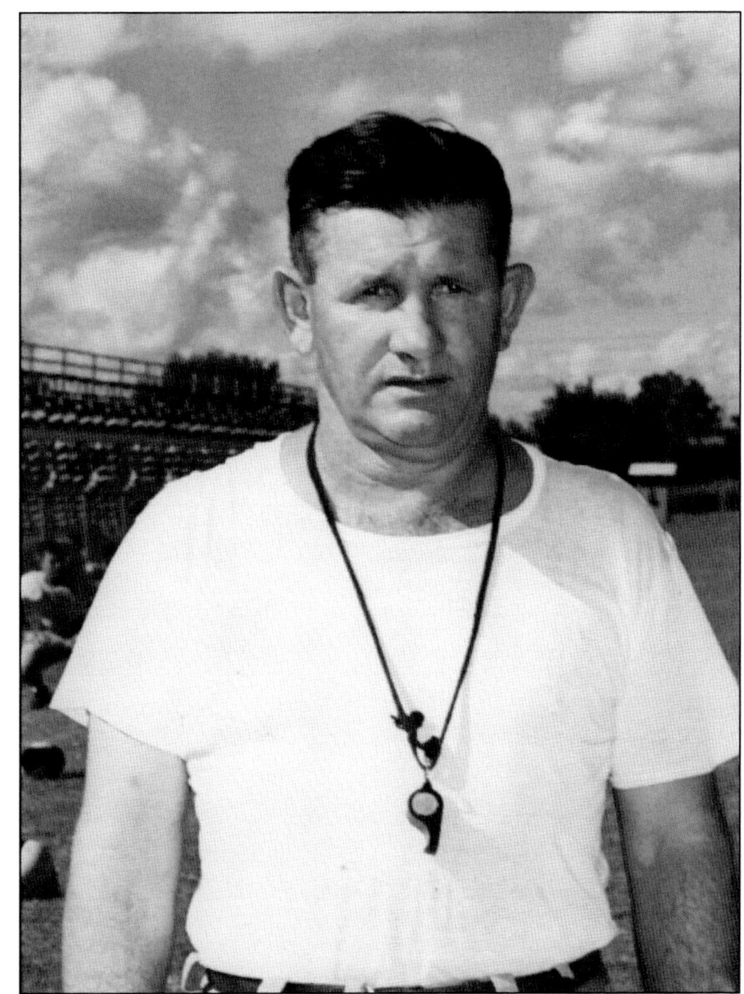

Joseph "Joe" Lucien Keller was the school's first all-state football player. Turning down scholarship offers to Tulane and Loyola Universities, he instead attended Louisiana State University on a football scholarship. He and his fellow football team members were bodyguards to Louisiana governor Huey P. Long. He returned to coach at his alma mater, and his 36 years of coaching earned him a spot in the Louisiana High School Athletic Association Hall of Fame and the Greater New Orleans Sports Hall of Fame. (Courtesy of *L'Observateur*.)

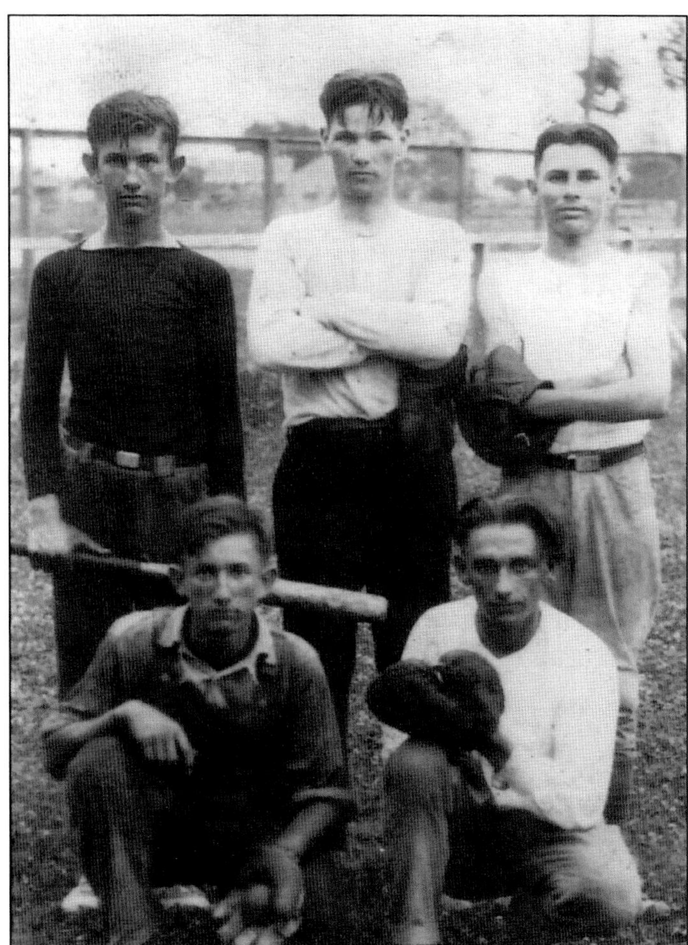

In 1922, like in many small communities around the country, Reserve youths engaged in sandlot baseball games during the summer months. From left to right are (first row) Louis Keller and Sidney Keller; (second row) Joseph Keller, Bill Boudin, and Ernest Madere. (Courtesy of Wanda Lee Madere Clement.)

Football came to Leon Godchaux High School and the River Parishes in 1924. Pictured is the 1925 Leon Godchaux High School football team, which played its home football games at the Godchaux Community Park. Coached by Frank "Spike" Noel (third row, far left), the Wildcats won five games and lost two. The single-wing offense was lead by Joe Keller, John Cox, and Louis Keller. (Courtesy of Roland "Peanut" Williams.)

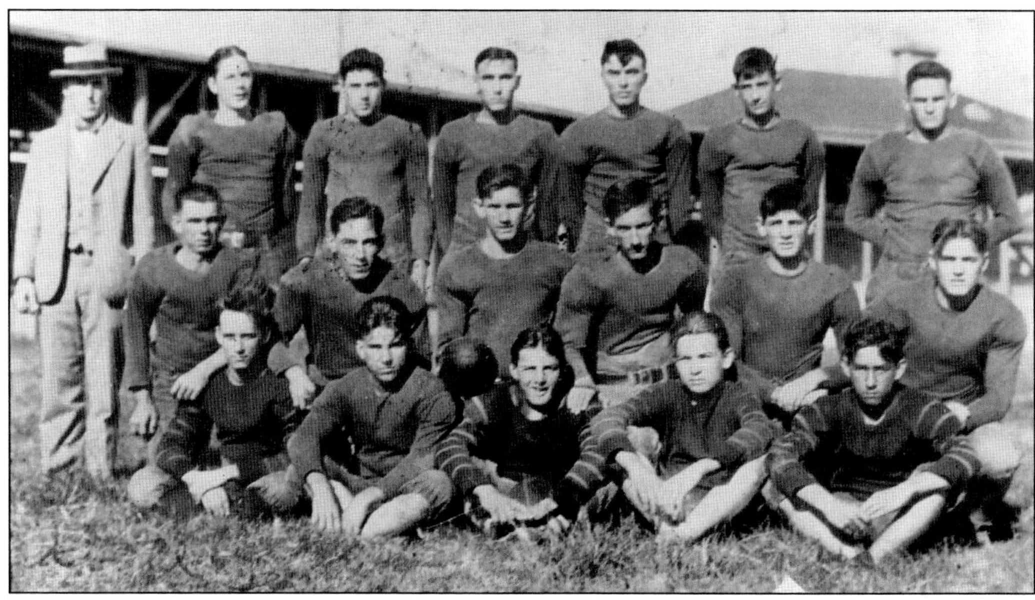

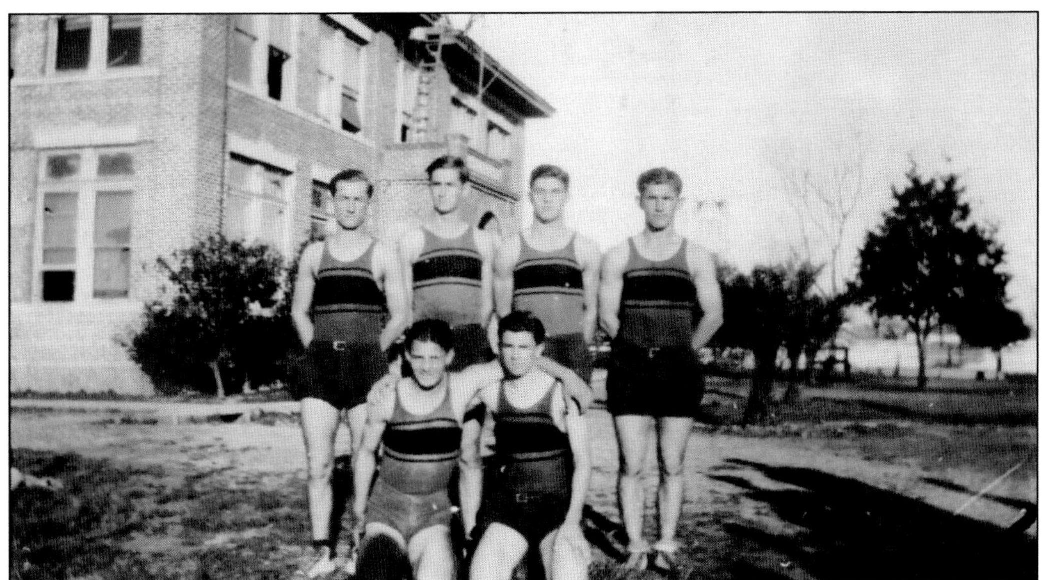

The 1925 Leon Godchaux High School track and field team includes, from left to right, (first row) Eddie Madere and unidentified; (second row) Louis Keller, Joseph "Joe" Duhe, Edwin "Caydell" Vicknair, and Joseph "Joe" Keller. Vicknair, Keller, and Duhe attended the 1925 national high school track meet in Chicago. Vicknair finished fourth in the nation in the shot put. (Courtesy of Marlene Tregre Cambre.)

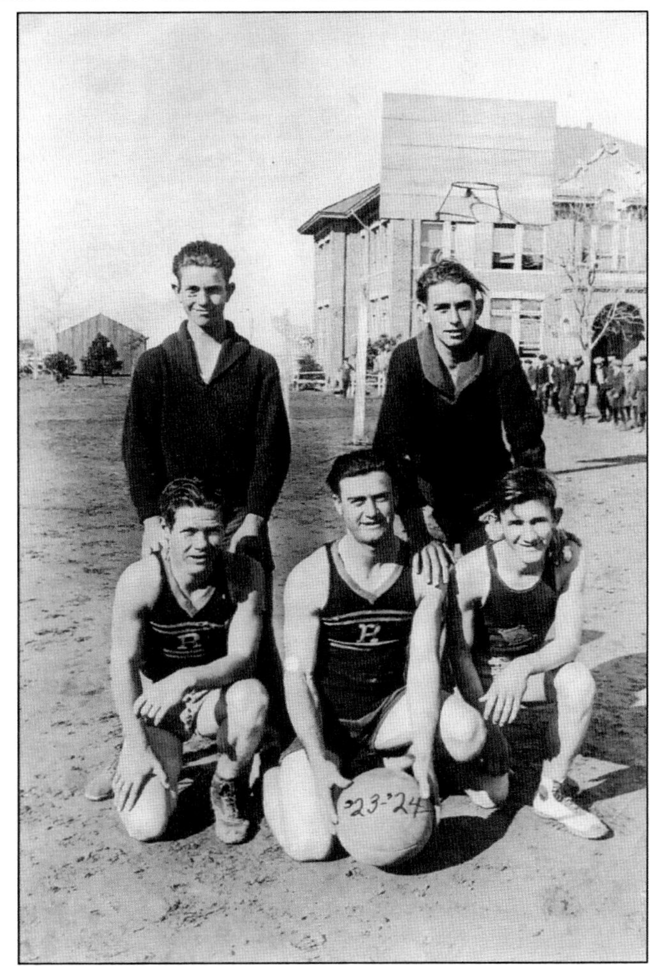

Pictured is the 1923–1924 Leon Godchaux High School basketball team. From left to right are (kneeling) Alonzo Boudin, Roy Tregre, and Joseph Keller. The two gentlemen standing behind them are unidentified. The high school had no indoor facility or gymnasium, and basketball games and practices were played outdoors on a dirt surface. One of the events of that era was an athletic competition at the South Louisiana Fair in Donaldsonville, Louisiana. (Courtesy of Marlene Tregre Cambre.)

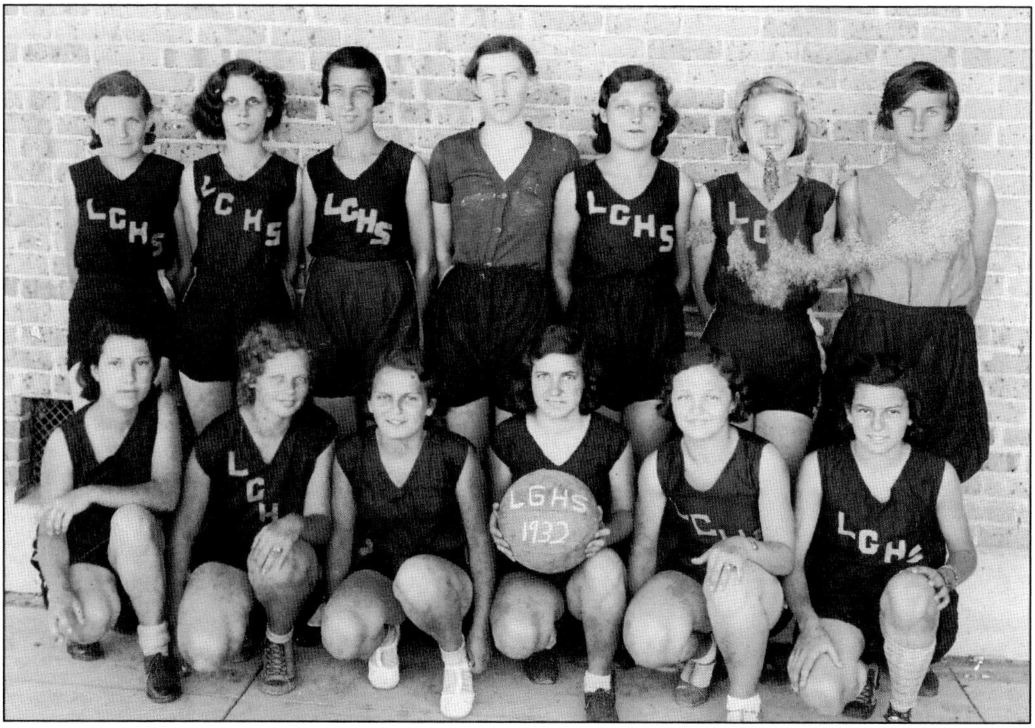

A rare photograph features the 1932 Leon Godchaux High School girls' basketball team. Very few female sporting photographs were maintained by the school, and unfortunately, none of the players in the photograph are identified. A school gymnasium was not built until 1939, and like those of their male counterparts, girls' basketball games and practices were held outdoors. (Courtesy of Shirley Casseigne Terrio.)

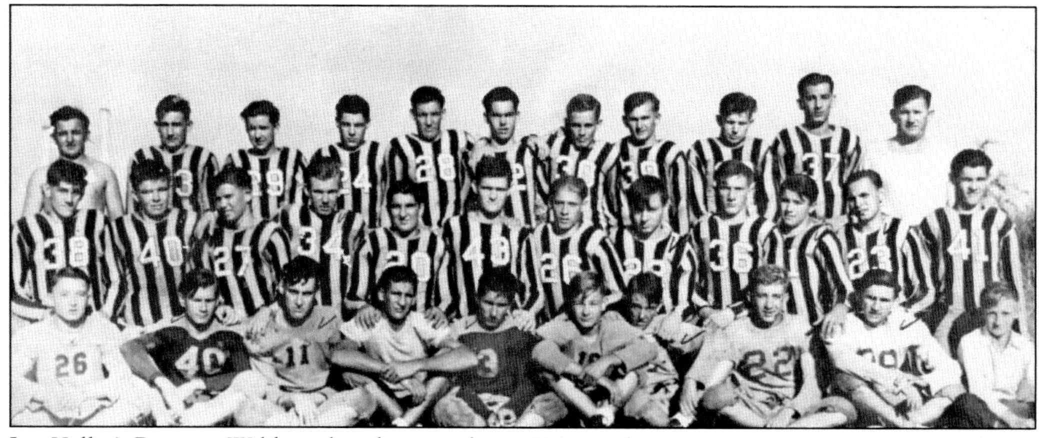

Joe Keller's Reserve Wildcats hit their stride in 1940 as the team's seven wins and three losses earned them a spot in Lutcher High School's fifth Cypress Bowl. The team's workhorse was freshman (eighth-grader) Herman Duhe. Duhe earned all-state honors in 1941, and after a tour of military duty, he turned down a professional football offer from owner and manager George Halas to play with the Chicago Bears. (Courtesy of Maurice Entremont.)

Pictured is Leon Godchaux High School (Reserve) all-state and All-American running back Leroy "Black Stallion" Labat. He continued his gridiron stardom at Louisiana State University and was the team's leading rusher in 1951. Selected as the most valuable player in the 1953 Blue-Gray game, Labat was drafted by the Baltimore Colts. He passed up a professional career and entered the US Marine Corps instead. (Courtesy of *L'Observateur*.)

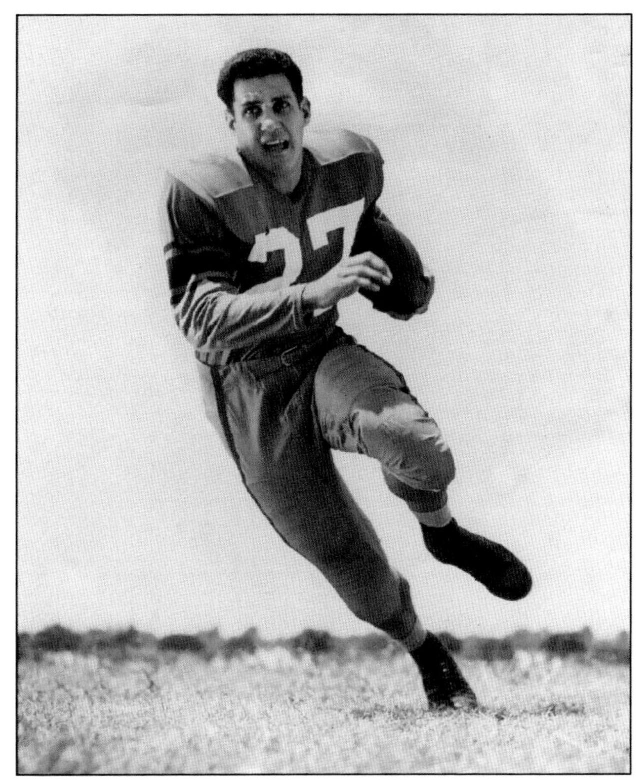

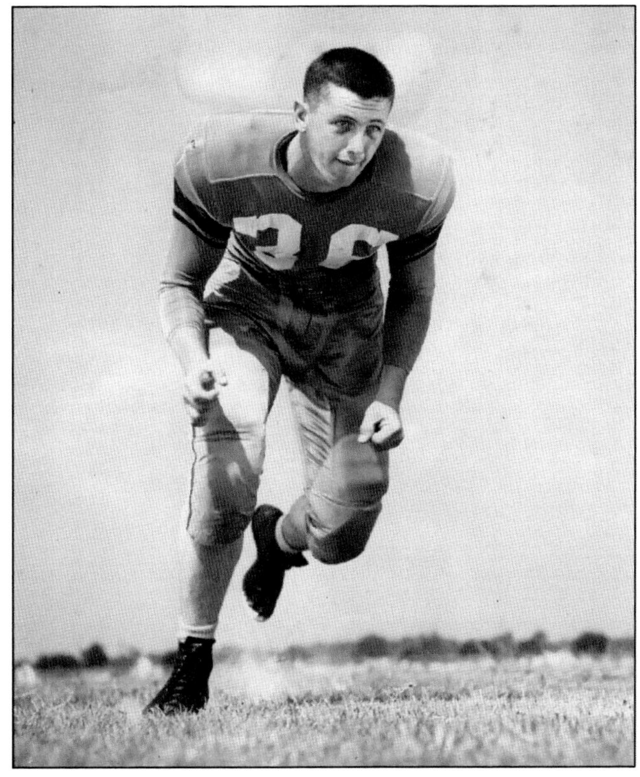

Twice all-state football, baseball, and track star John Oswald Duhe was one of many student athletes to achieve honors in the sports arena at Leon Godchaux High School. Heavily recruited as a football, track, and baseball player, Oswald Duhe ignored a baseball offer from the Pittsburgh Pirates and signed a 1951 football grant-in-aid scholarship to attend Louisiana State University (Courtesy of *L'Observateur*.)

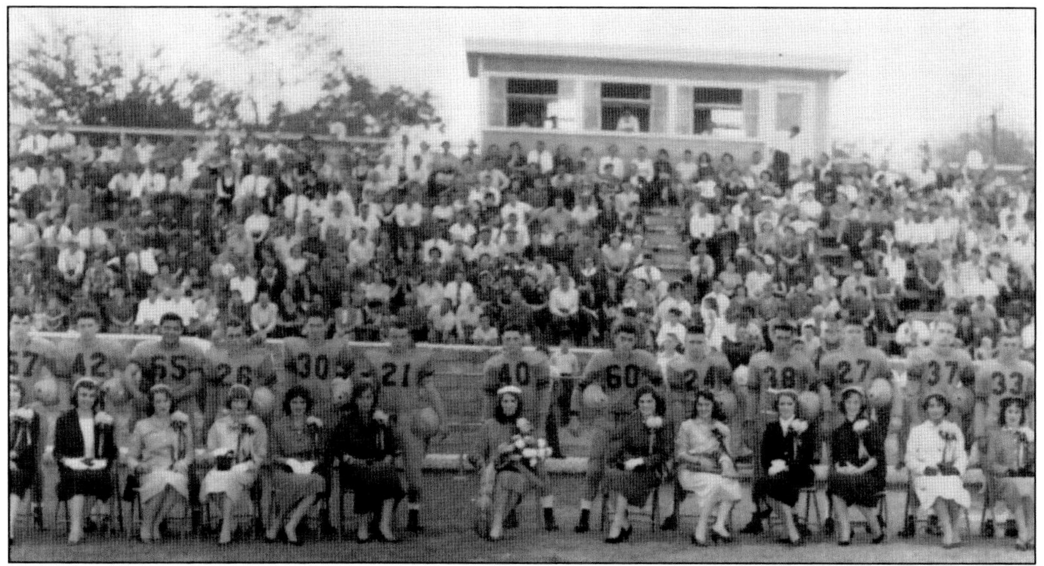

Pictured is the 1955 homecoming scene at Leon Godchaux. The 1955 squad finished as the South Louisiana Champions, losing 27-14 to Neville High School in the state finals in Reserve. Joe Keller's Wildcats finished the season with 12 wins and two losses, and the team was lead by all-state center Kenneth Madere and second-team all-state players quarterback Nemour "Steve" Delaneuville and guard Tommy Reno. (Courtesy of Emile Hotard.)

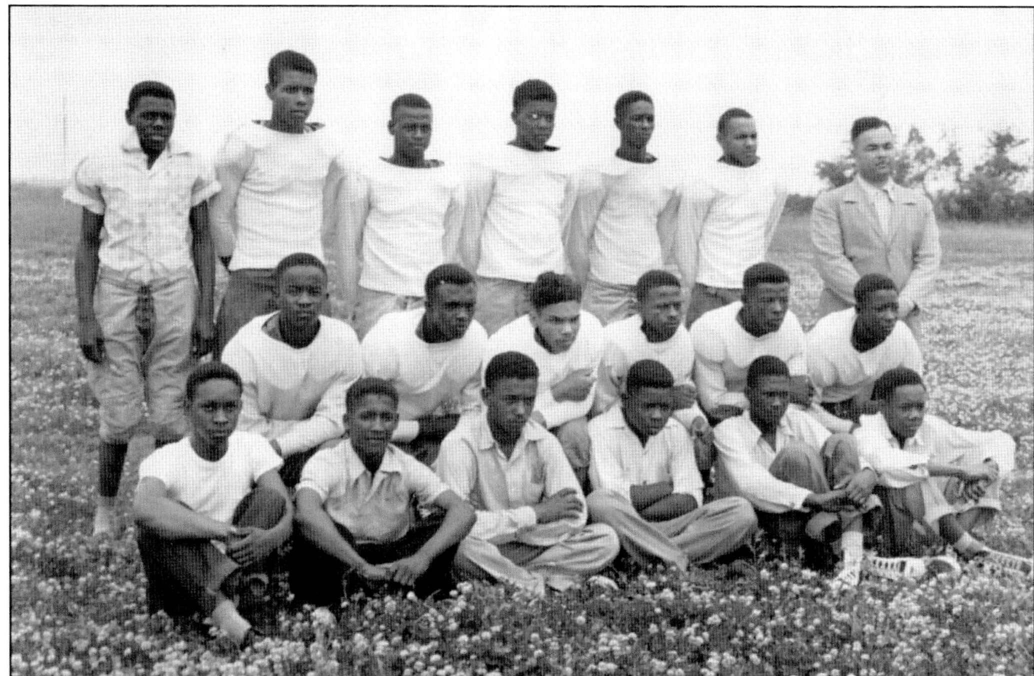

Pictured in the 1950s is Fifth Ward High School's football team. From left to right are (first row) Ferdinand Wallace, Roy Fobb, George Etienne, Lawrence Henderson, Clement Gibson, and Autry Alexis; (second row) Oscar Snyder, Hilton Mitchell Jr., McLouis Robinet, Lucien Madere Jr., Joseph Gregoire, and Ezekiel Jackson Jr.; (third row) Raymond Batiste, Wilfred Bernard Jr., Leroy Keller, Percy Duhe, Edward Caesar, Calvin Keller, and coach Ralph Miller. (Wilhelmina Bernard Armour.)

David "Red" Ayme, son of Bobby and Linda Hotard Ayme, is well known around the International Management Group Academies in Bradenton, Florida, as he has coached some of the game's best professional tennis players, ranging from Boris Becker to Tommy Haas. A graduate of St. Charles Catholic High School in LaPlace, Louisiana, Red was a walk-on tennis player at Nichols State University. (Photograph by International Management Group Academy.)

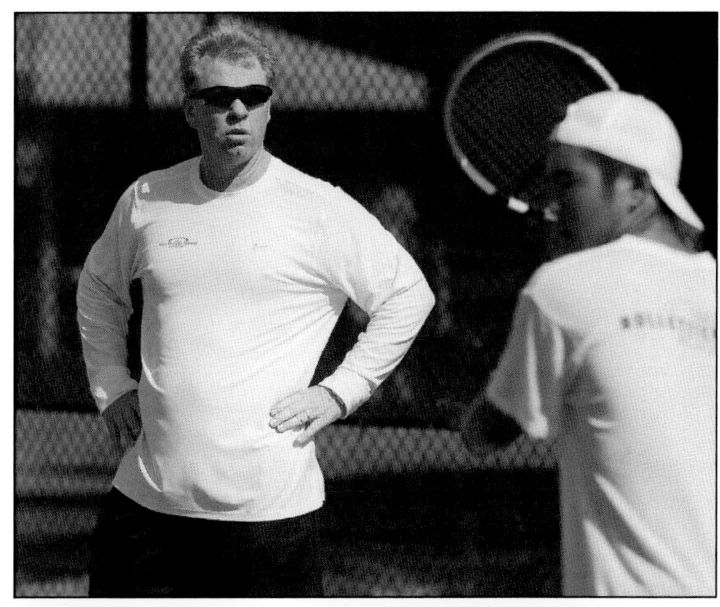

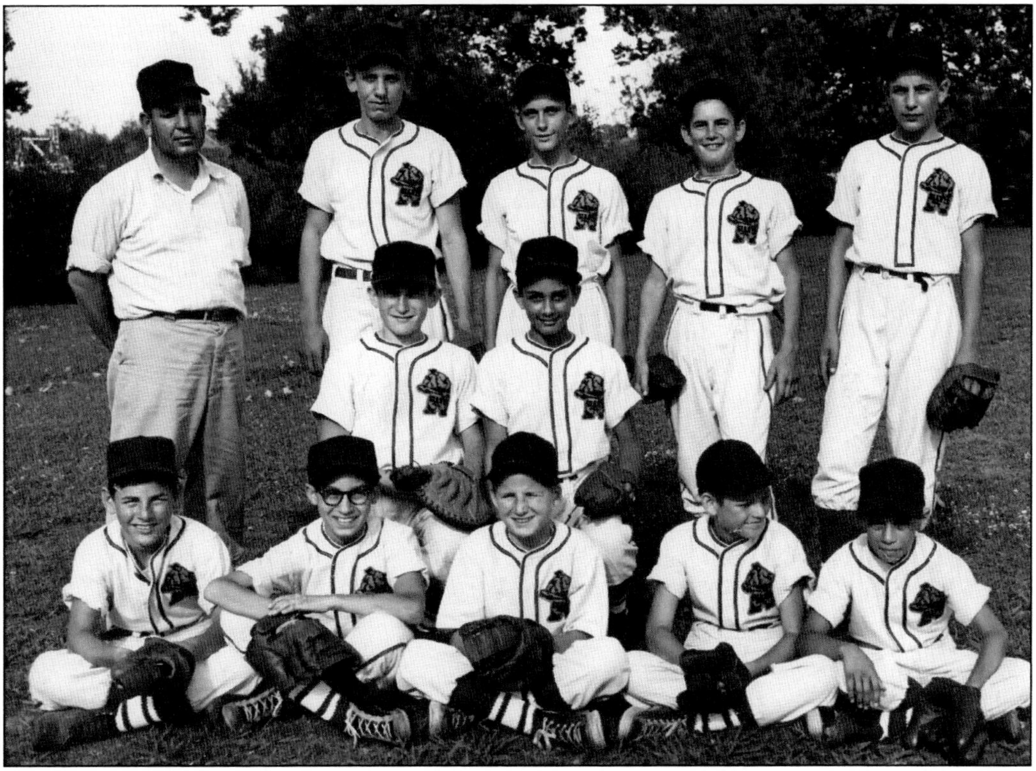

In 1952, the first Reserve Little League baseball program was organized by employees of the Godchaux Sugar Refinery. Games were played at the Reserve Community Park and Lasseigne Park in LaPlace. Pictured are members of the Reserve Giants. From left to right are (first row) Armand Brady, Phil Breaux, ? Broden, Richard Granier, and Ronald Torres; (second row) Joe Montz and Johnny Cicet; (third row) coach Joseph Bossier, Rene Miller, Dorrel Catoire, Farrell Weber, and Gerald Klibert. (Courtesy of Phil Breaux.)

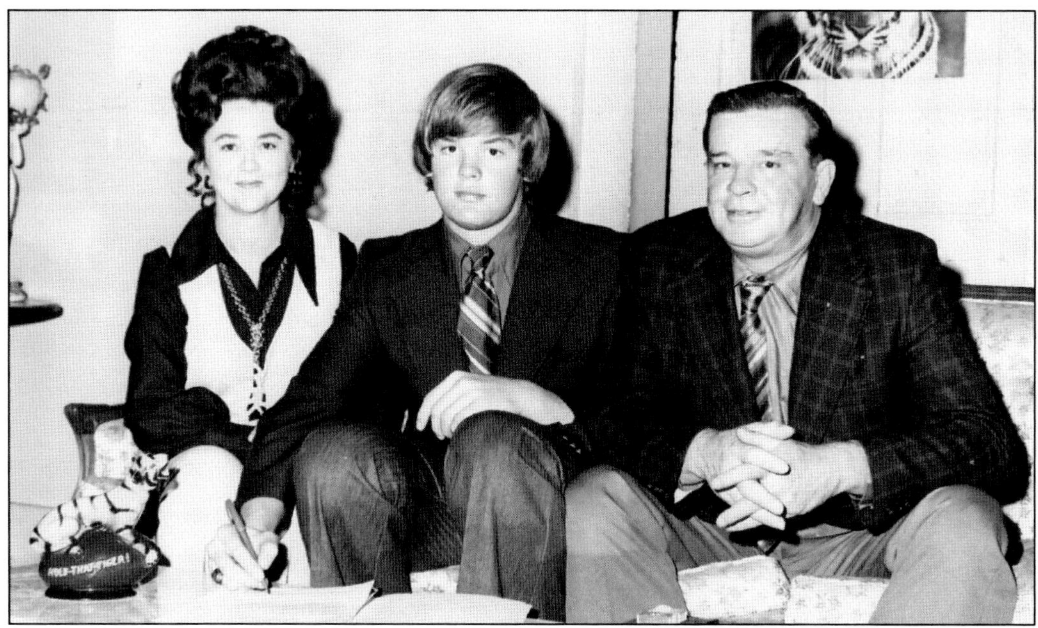

Pictured is Adam Joseph "A.J." Duhe Jr., center, with his parents. He is signing a grant-in-aid scholarship to Louisiana State University. A first-round choice in the 1977 National Football League draft, Duhe played eight seasons for the Miami Dolphins. His three interceptions against the New York Jets sent the Dolphins to Super Bowl XVII. Duhe was named to the Louisiana Sports Writers Hall of Fame in 2001. (Courtesy of Roland "Peanut" Williams.)

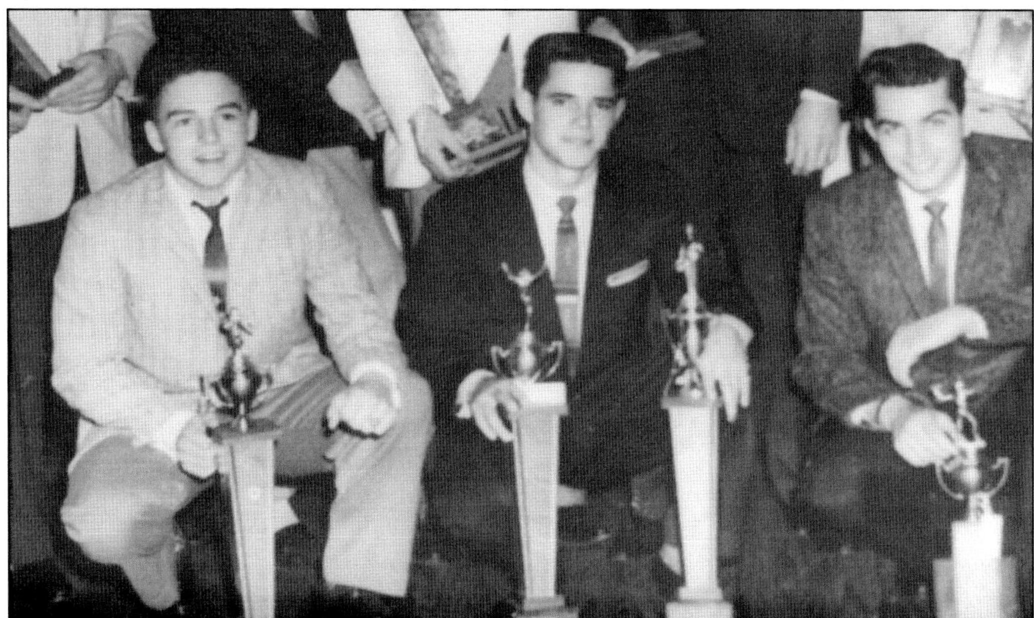

Members of the 1958 Leon Godchaux High School Louisiana High School Football State Championship team included Jimmy Stein (left), Brent Roussel (center), and Neal Prudhomme. The Wildcats defeated Neville High School 25-14, to win the school's first state title. Paced by all-state tackle Henry Catoire and running back Bobby Millet, Joe Keller described his 1958 team as the best-balanced team he had ever coached. (Courtesy of East St. John High School.)

East St. John High School graduate and Grambling State University baseball star Gerald "Ice" Williams played 14 years in the Major League (1992–2005) as an outfielder for the New York Yankees, Milwaukee Brewers, Atlanta Braves, Tampa Bay Devil Rays, and Florida Marlins. He wears a World Series ring as a member of the Atlanta Braves. (Photograph by Tampa Bay Rays.)

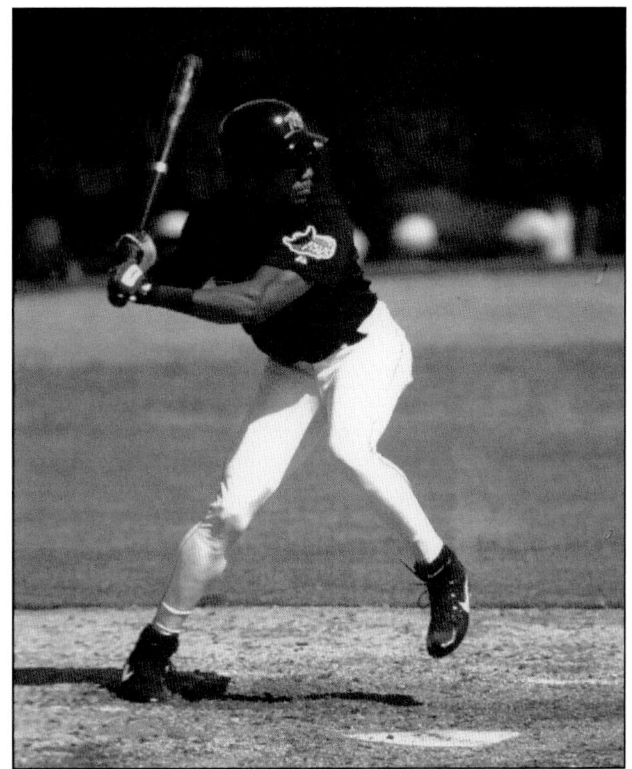

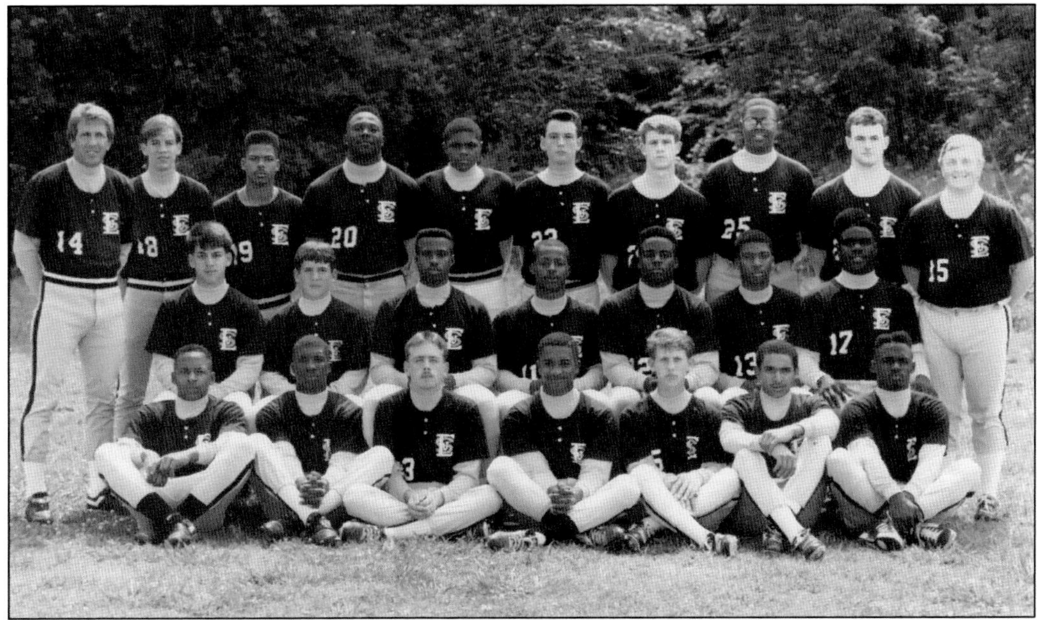

In 1990, coach John Owens and the East St. John High School baseball team accomplished perfection by going undefeated, 28-0, and winning the 4A championship. During the three-game state tournament in Shreveport, Louisiana, the Wildcats scored 44 runs. The team was paced by hitters Leroy Williams and Darrel Nicholas, and the pitching staff was anchored by Courtney Mitchell, who finished with 10 wins and no losses. (Courtesy of East St. John High School.)

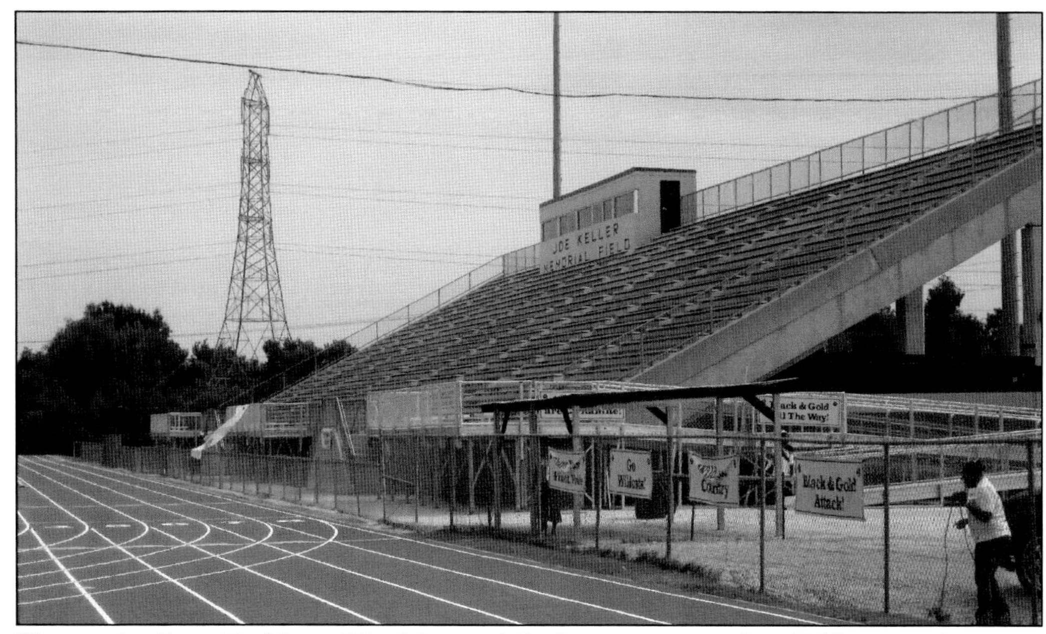

The wooden Leon Godchaux War Memorial Stadium, constructed in 1946, was no longer an adequate football arena for the East St. John High School football team. The St. John the Baptist Parish School Board constructed a new football stadium in the Belle Point subdivision. The new stadium was named after the school's most successful coach, Joseph Keller. The Joe Keller Memorial Stadium was dedicated in 1992. (Courtesy of CSRS.)

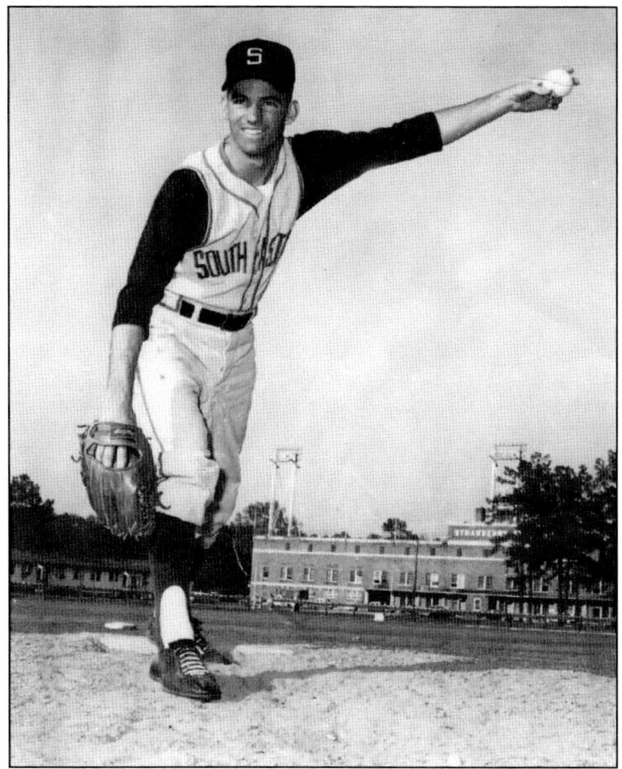

Southpaw pitcher Elton "Pine" Remondet attended DeLaSalle High School in New Orleans, where he earned all-city and all-state honors and lead the DeLaSalle Cavaliers to a state baseball title. He attended Southeastern Louisiana University in Hammond, Louisiana, and won six games without a loss and an earned run average of under one run per game. He was recently elected into DeLaSalle's hall of fame. (Courtesy of Elton "Pine" Remondet.)

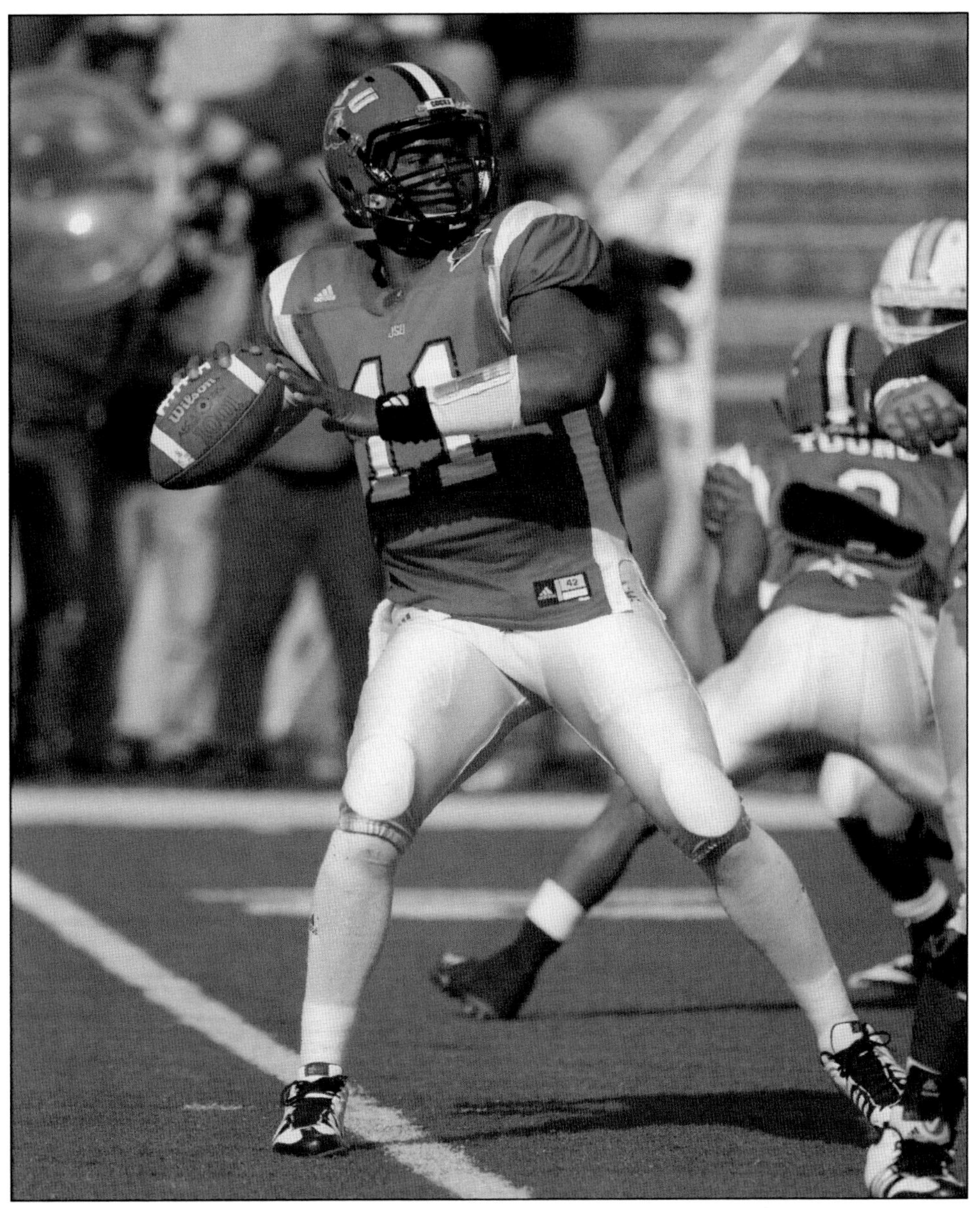

Ryan Perrilloux had one of the most dominating prep careers in Louisiana history at East St. John High School, totaling 12,705 yards of offense, which ranks second all-time offensively. In his four years at East St. John, Perrilloux had a total of 155 touchdowns and racked up a Louisiana High School record of 5,006 yards of offense as a senior. He won the 2004 Hall Trophy as the nation's most outstanding high school football player, was named the Offensive Player of the Year by *USA Today*, Louisiana's Mr. Football, and a *Parade* All-American. He was invited to play in the US Army All-American Bowl. Perrilloux attended Louisiana State University in Baton Rouge and later transferred to Jacksonville State University. After going undrafted in the 2010 National Football League Draft, the Minnesota Vikings invited him to a tryout. He was later signed by the Hartford Colonials, of the United Football League. On January 13, 2011, Perrilloux was signed to a reserve/future contract with the New York Giants of the National Football League. (Photograph by Steve Latham, Jacksonville State University.)

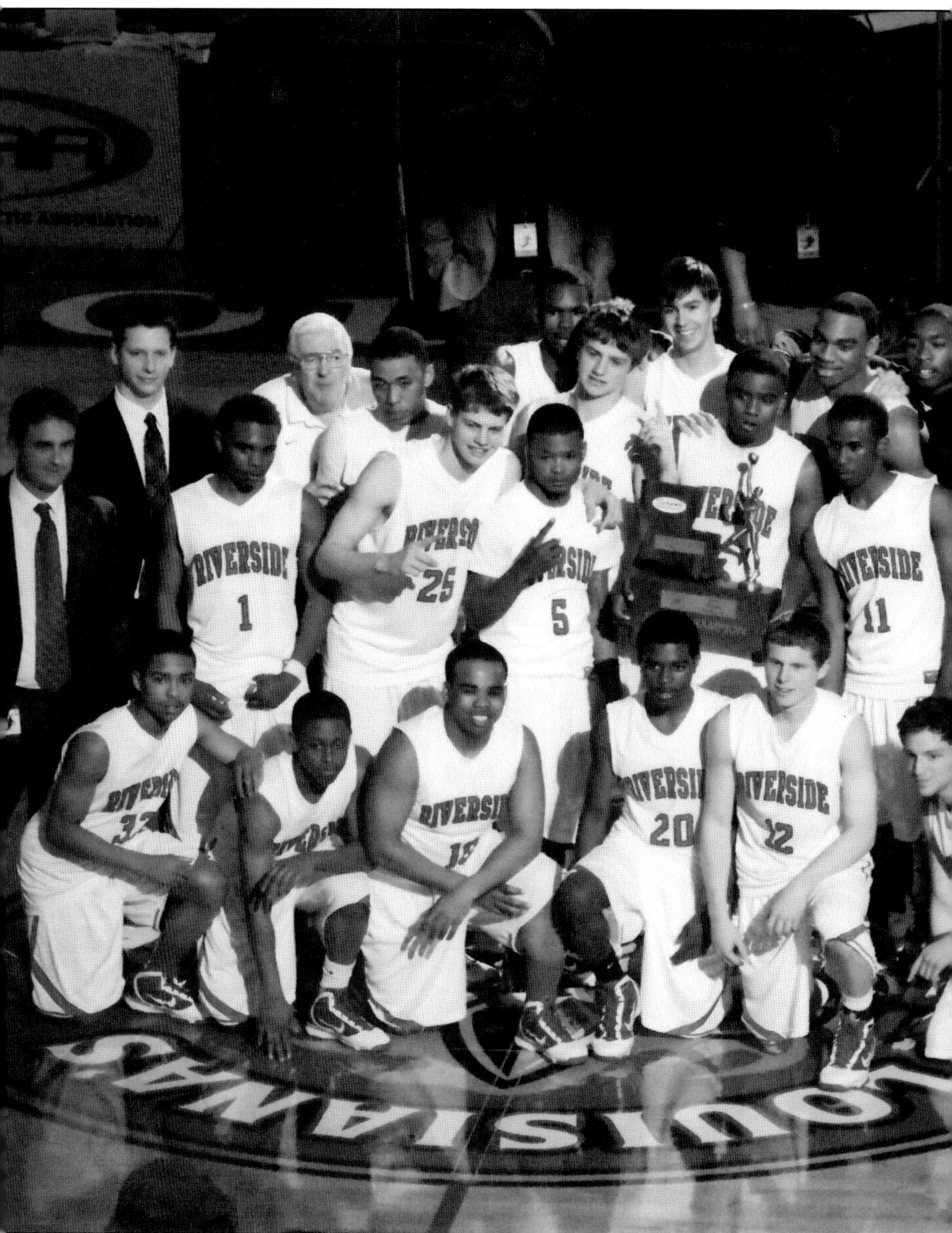
RIVERSIDE
1
25
5
RIVERSIDE
11
RIVERSIDE
20
RIVERSIDE
12

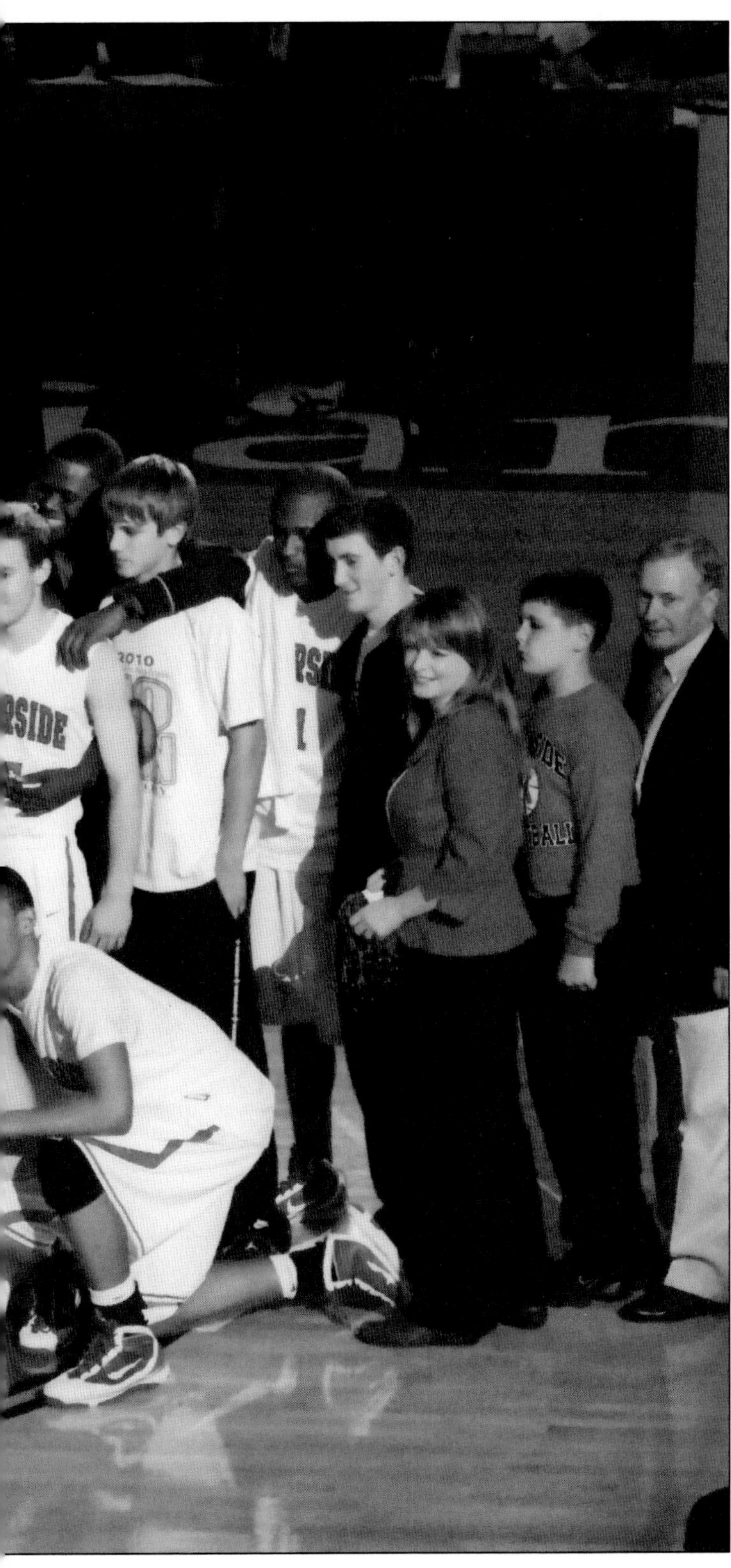

Members of the Riverside Academy 2010 district basketball champions celebrated their 84-61 win over Jonesboro-Hodges to win the Louisiana 2A Basketball Championship at the University of Louisiana Lafayette Cajundome. Coach Timmy Byrd brought his basketball skills from the Reserve Christian School and coached Riverside Academy to its first state basketball championship. The team finished the year with 26 wins and six losses. Ranked as one of America's top basketball teams, the Rebels finished second in the 2011 All-State Sugar Bowl Prep Classical Basketball Tournament, defeated 61-58 by the Dallas Kimball Knights. The school repeated its performance in 2011, defeating Evangel 82-61 at the Cajundome to capture its second state Class 2A basketball title. The Rebels were led by junior Ricardo Gathiers, who was selected as the Louisiana Gatorade Boys Basketball Player of the Year. (Courtesy of Carrie Turnbull.)

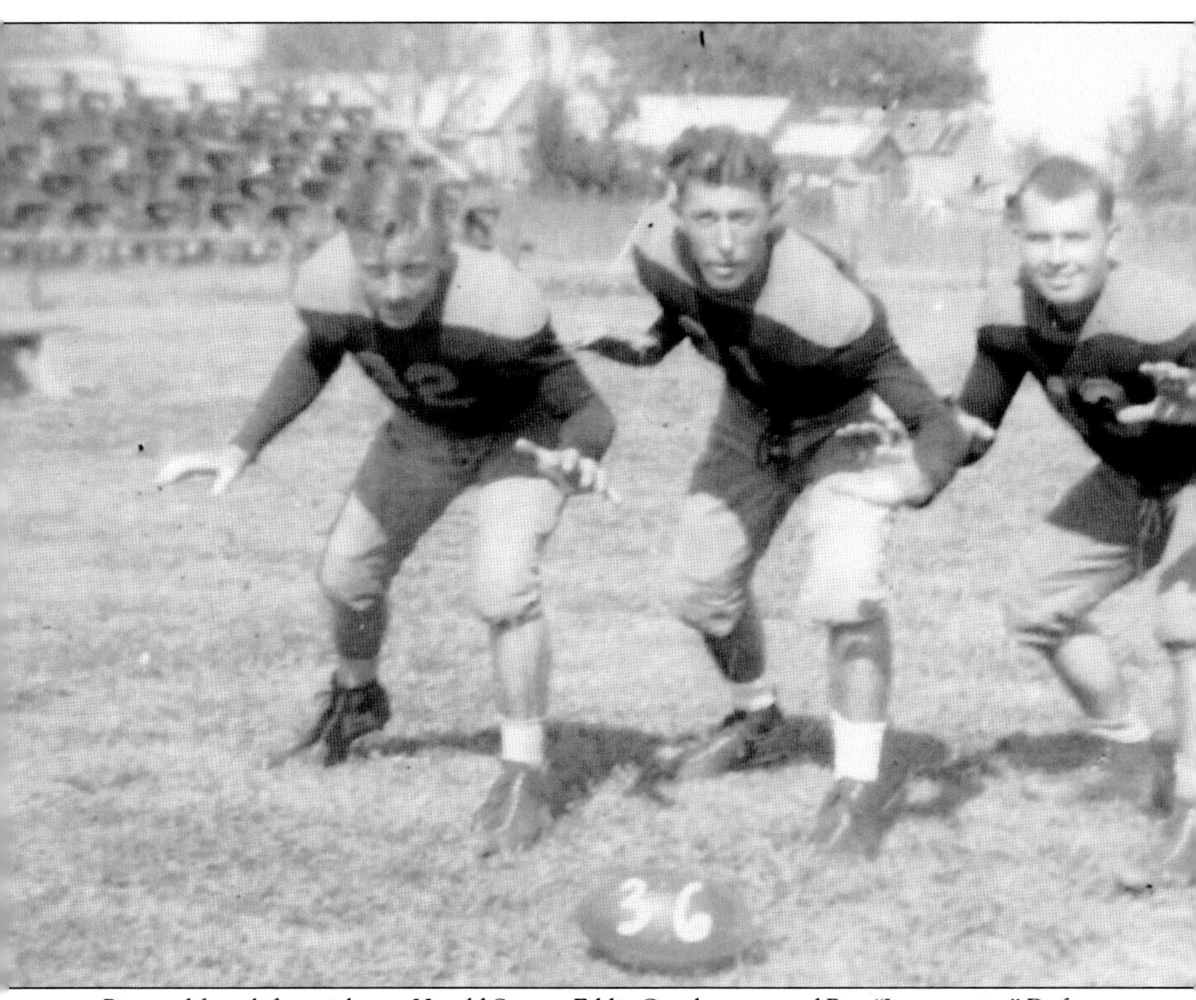

Pictured from left to right are Harold Simon, Eddie Gauthreaux, and Roy "Locomotive" Dufresne, members of the 1936 Leon Godchaux (Reserve) High School Cypess Bowl Champion team. Although, the Wildcats finished their football season with a modest five wins, three losses, and one tie, they earned an invitation to play Lafayette High School in the inaugural Lutcher High School Cypress Bowl on December 5, 1936. The Wildcats prevailed with a 21-7 victory. (Courtesy of Roy "Locomotive" Dufresne.)

Five

Reservians

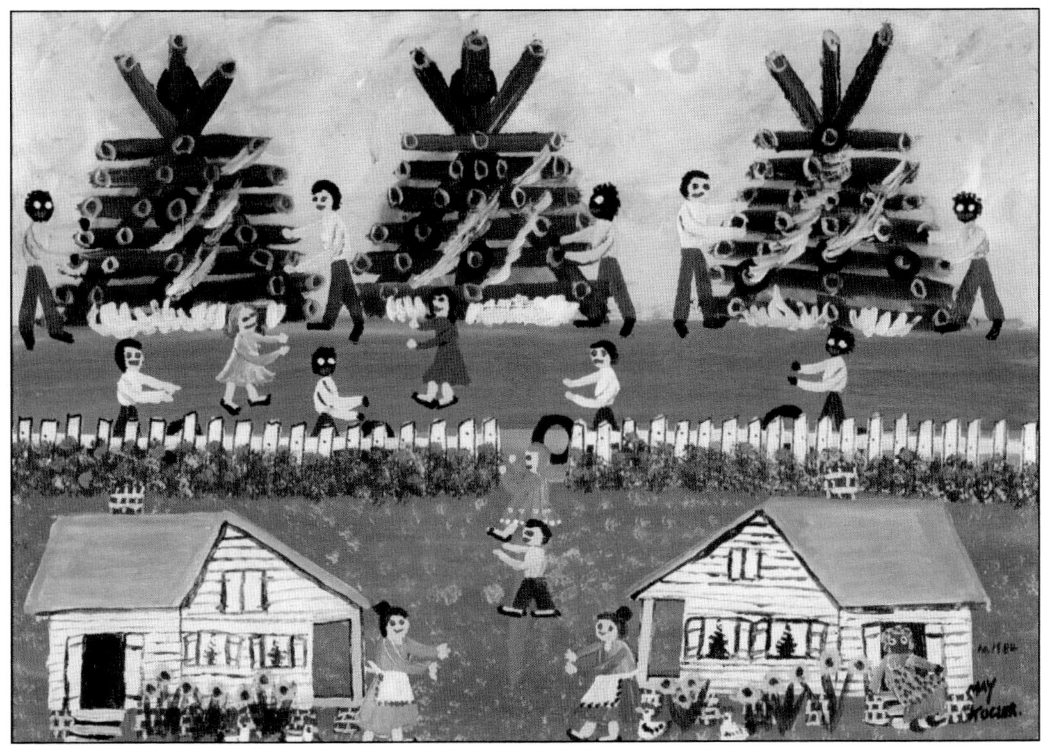

Widely recognized, May Catoire Kugler began drawing during her early years at Leon Godchaux Grammar School. Kugler would develop a style of art known as "pigmy art," and her early recollections of Reserve are exhibited in her artwork. Pictured is a yard scene. A lady in a red dress, who represents her mother, appears in all of her paintings. On the back of the painting Kugler includes a narrative about the abstract. Her artwork has been widely praised and collected. (Courtesy of St. John Industrial Group.)

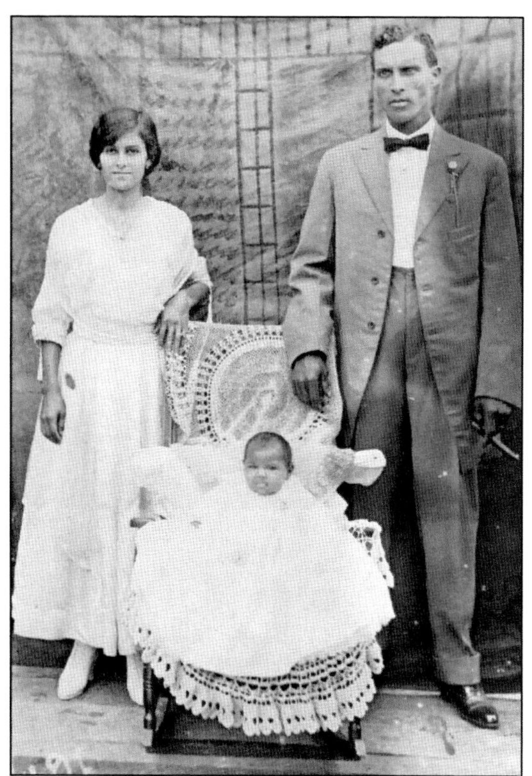

During the 1920s, Viola Soraparu Tregre (left) and her husband, Alfred Tregre Sr. (right), are pictured with their son Alfred Tregre Jr. They are also the parents of Wilbert Tregre Sr. and grandparents of Michael Tregre, the former director of the St. John the Baptist Parish Emergency Preparedness program. (Courtesy of Lisa Tregre Wilder.)

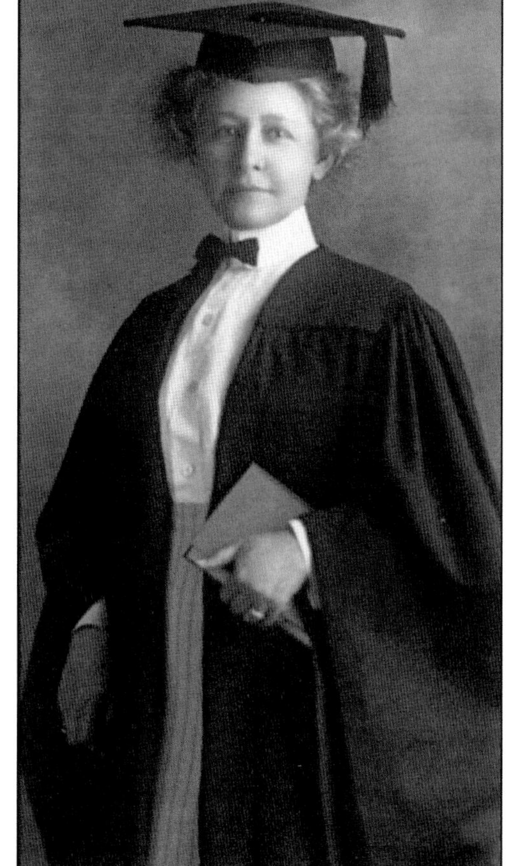

Marie Gabrielle Noelie Hart, the daughter of Dr. William Hart, filled in for her mother as postmistress of the Bonnet Carré Post Office. She began the first public school in the parlor of the San Francisco Plantation house. In 1912, Noelie completed her bachelor of arts degree in French at Louisiana State University and taught French at the University of Texas-Austin. (Courtesy of Dr. Douglas Starr.)

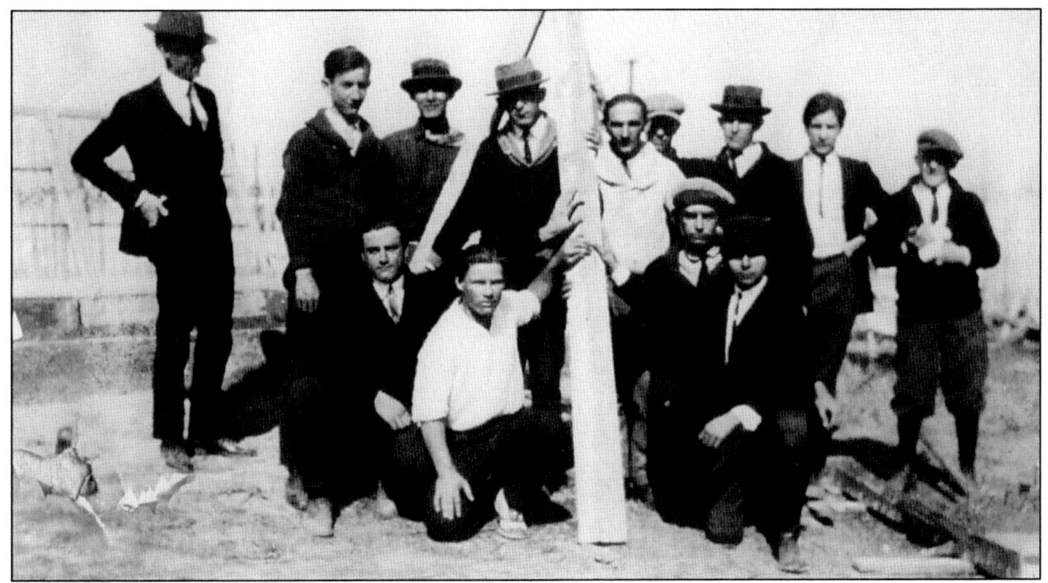

In 1923, Leon Godchaux High School students and school principal J.O. Montegut (top left) planted two palm trees on the high school grounds. Next to Montegut are, from left to right, Louis Keller, Eusebe Cambre, Henry Schmidth, Sidney Keller, Guy Cambre, Ernest Millet, E. Bourgeois, and Ellis Reine. Of the two trees, one died within weeks of the planting, but the second lived a long life before being finally cut down in 2009 for safety reasons. (Courtesy of Marlene Tregre.)

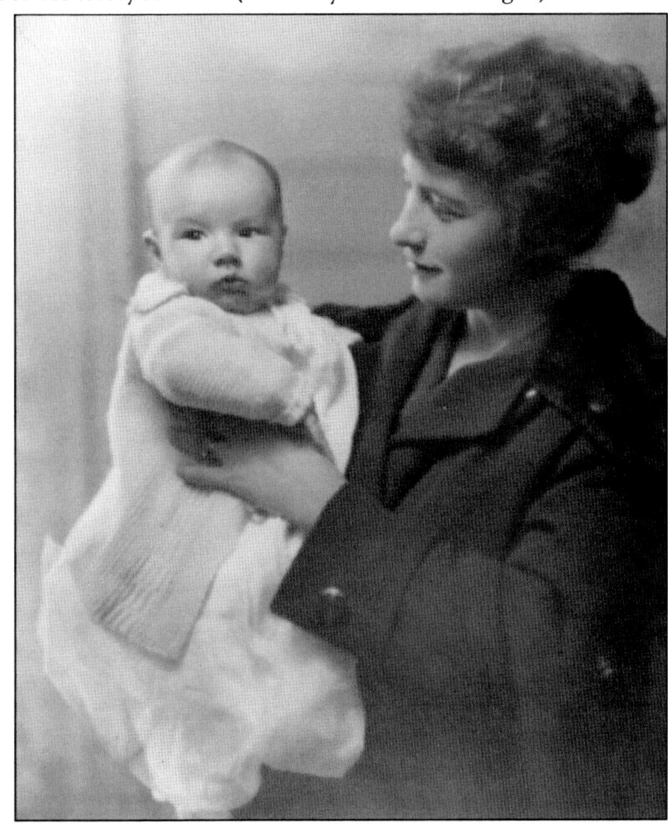

In 1921, Emma Ory Boudreaux, wife of Noah "Preacher" Boudreaux, is pictured with her son Ory Boudreaux. Ory become a commissioned officer during World War II and made bombing raids over North Africa in his B-24 Liberator. He remained in the US Air Force and rose to the rank of colonel. Upon his retirement, Ory moved to Sacramento, California. (Courtesy of Iris Boudreaux Rousse.)

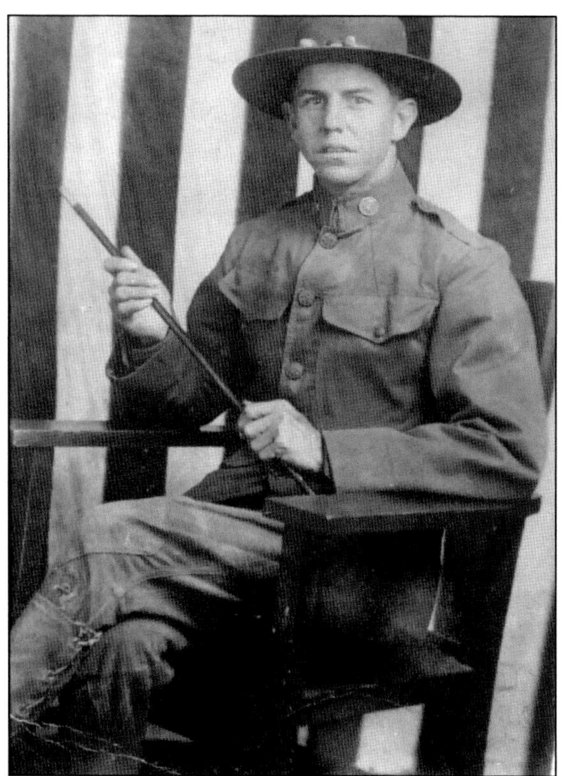

Reserve locals were always early volunteers for military service in time of war. Pictured in about 1919 is Johnny Demarcy, who was waiting to be processed when World War I ended. In all, 570 St. John the Baptist Parish residents were drafted during World War I, with 521 who were inducted into military services. (Courtesy of Earline Weber Jouty.)

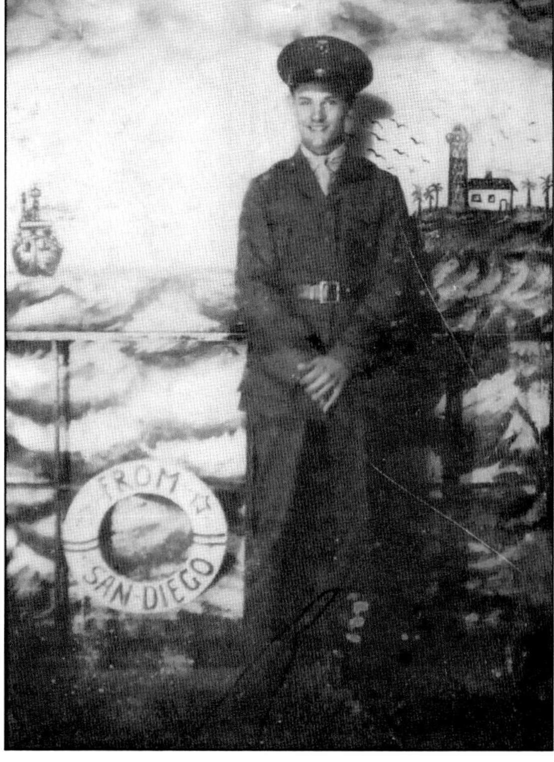

Reserve native Pfc. Marion Phillip Robert, the son of James Thomas Robert and Pearl Marie Zernigue, joined his high school football friends after the attack by Japan on Pearl Harbor and enlisted in the US Marine Corps in January 1942. Robert was killed in action while landing at Tarawa on November 20, 1943. (Courtesy of Bea Robert Maurin.)

E.J. Guidry Jr. was one of several Reserve locals captured as a prisoner of war during the Battle of the Bulge. Wounded and hospitalized in Germany, Guidry escaped his captors by swimming across a river to American lines. Guidry returned home after the war and joined the rest of the Guidry family, growing sugarcane on the Terre Haute Plantation. (Courtesy of Trisha Guidry Aucoin.)

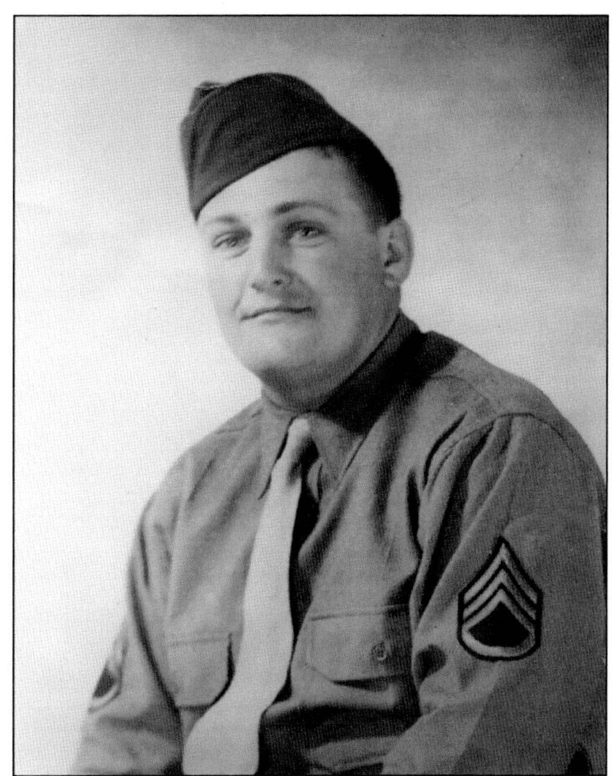

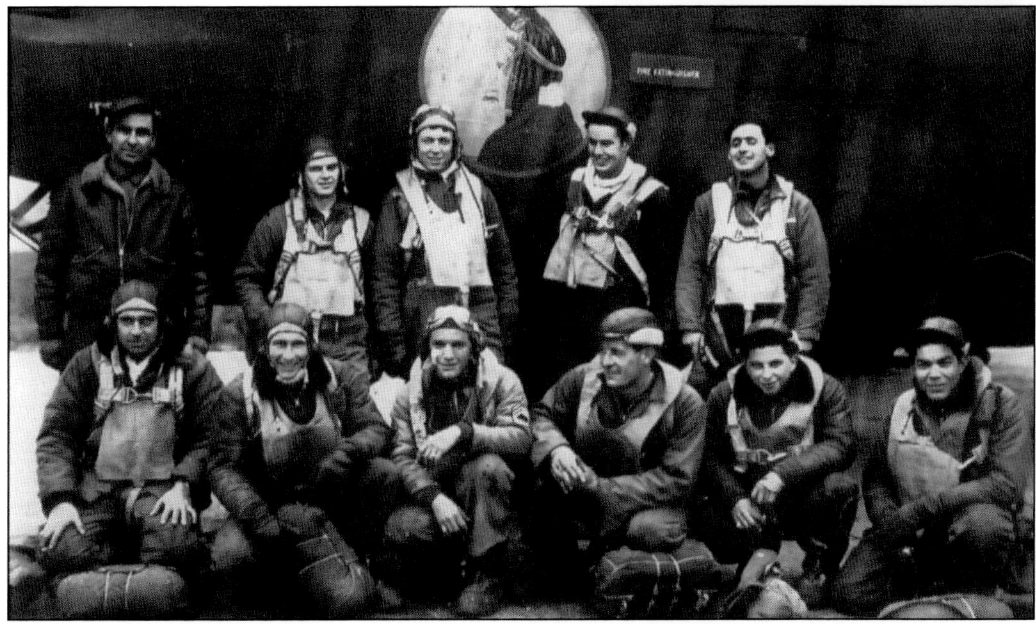

S.Sgt. Joseph LeBouef's (first row, second from left) B-24 bomber was shot down over Brunswick, Germany, on May 8, 1944. For nearly a year, he was imprisoned at Stalag Luft IV, near Gross Tychow, Poland. As the Russians approached the camp, he was part of a forced march that traveled 603 miles in a blinding snowstorm. LeBouef was liberated on April 26, 1945. (Courtesy of Emilie LeBouef Larsen.)

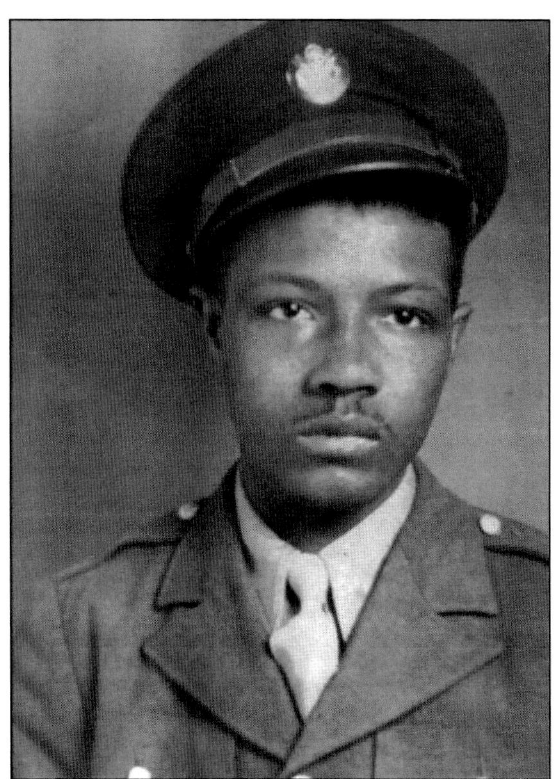

World War II veteran Joseph Roy Keller was inducted into the US Army on March 2, 1943. His Military Occupational Specialties included armor and driver. Keller fought in campaigns, including Normandy and the Ardennes. Missing in action for four days, Keller was honored with seven commendations. Honorably discharged on December 28, 1945, Keller, Technician Fifth Grade, served proudly with the 3433rd Quartermaster Truck Company. (Courtesy of Mary Dorothy Mitchell.)

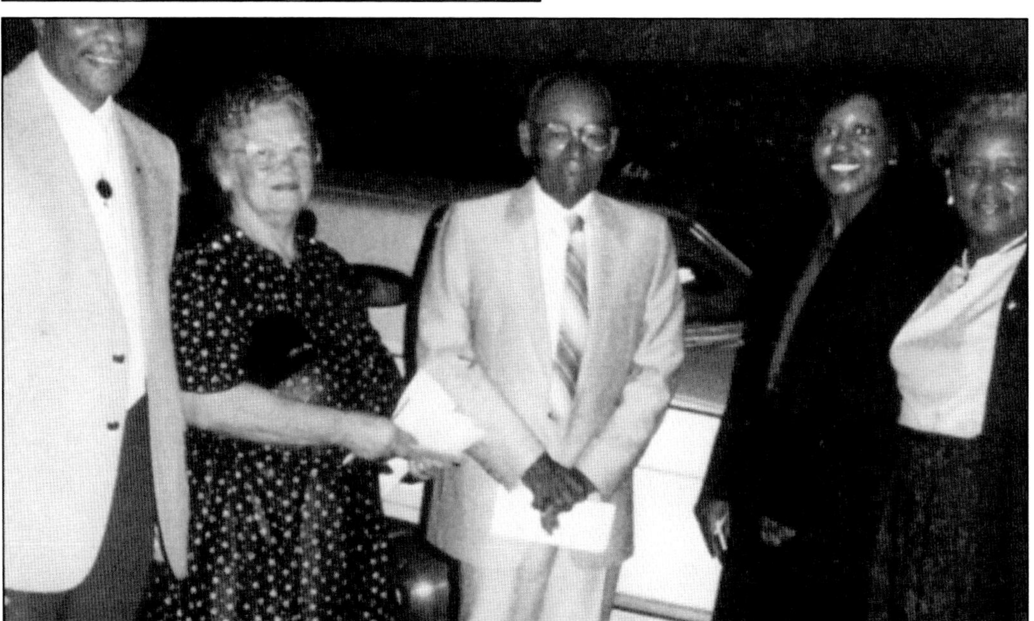

Parishioners of our Lady of Grace Catholic Church were invited to a private audience with Pope John Paul II at the New Orleans Superdome on September 12, 1987. Pictured from left to right are Sterling Simon, Thelma Robinet, Edward Hall, Mary Dorothy Mitchell, and Mona Nicholas. The visit to New Orleans was one of 10 stops on a North American tour by Pope John Paul II. (Courtesy of Mary Dorothy Mitchell.)

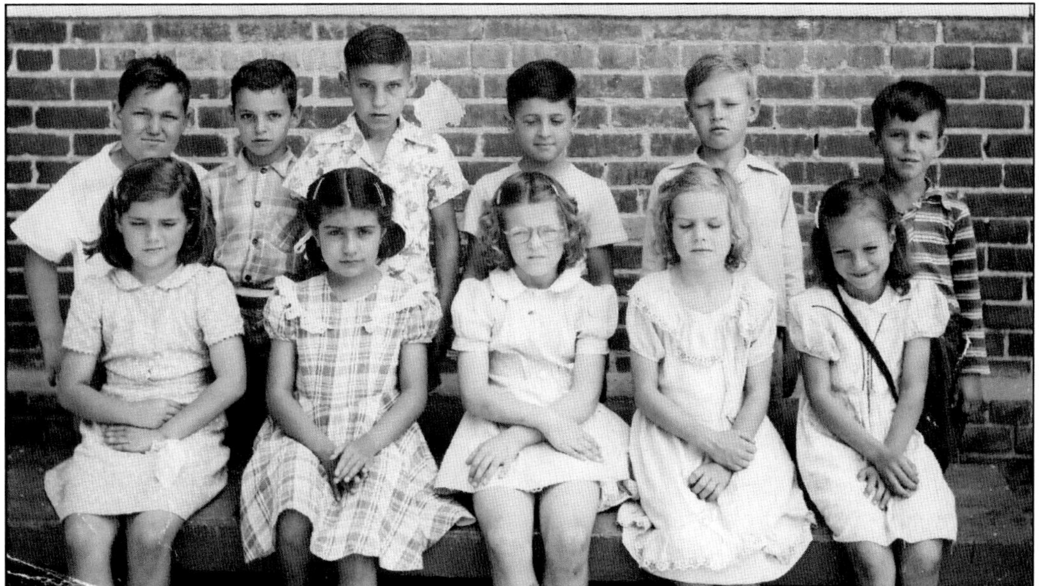

In 1951, the Leon Godchaux Grammar School second grade class included, from left to right, (first row) Mary Ann Landry Brady, Olga Haik Porteous, Natalie Petit, Doris Remondet, and Gloria Oubre; (second row) Pat Breaux, Brent Duhe, Phil Breaux, Michael Jaubert, Elias Duhe, and Jerry Toups. Edna Boutiton served as the school principal at Leon Godchaux Grammar School for 40 years. (Courtesy of Phil Breaux.)

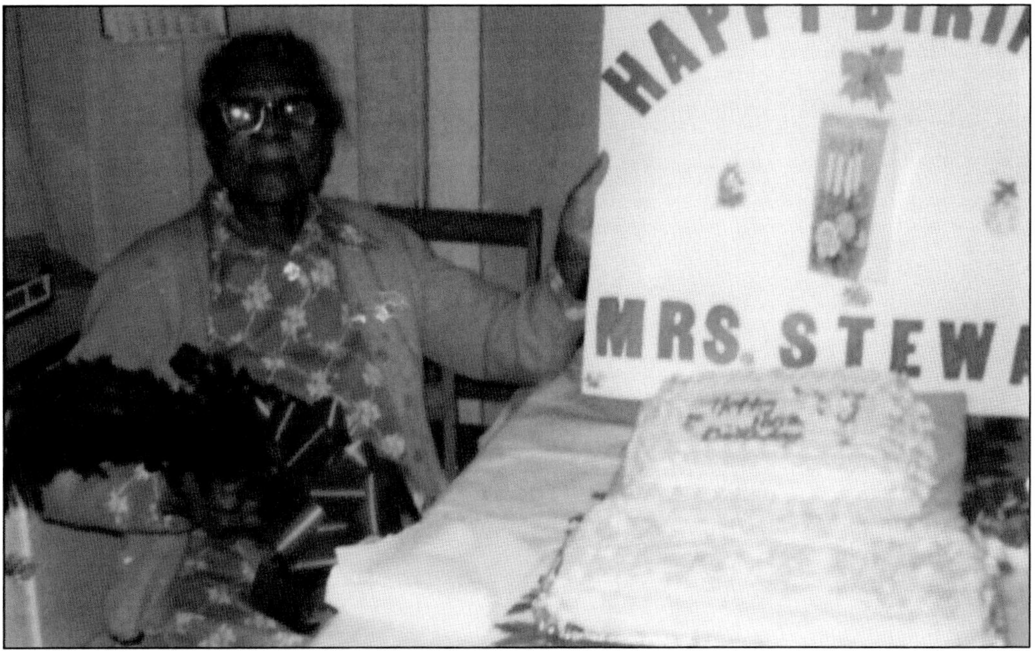

Edwrine Picou Stewart celebrated her 100th birthday with a party on December 13, 1975. She died at the age of 102, and she contributed her longevity to hard work, beginning at an early age cutting sugarcane, picking cotton, doing domestic work, and rearing and babysitting generations of children. In 1893, she married James Stewart, and they reared seven children until his death in 1931. (Courtesy of Ernestine Stewart.)

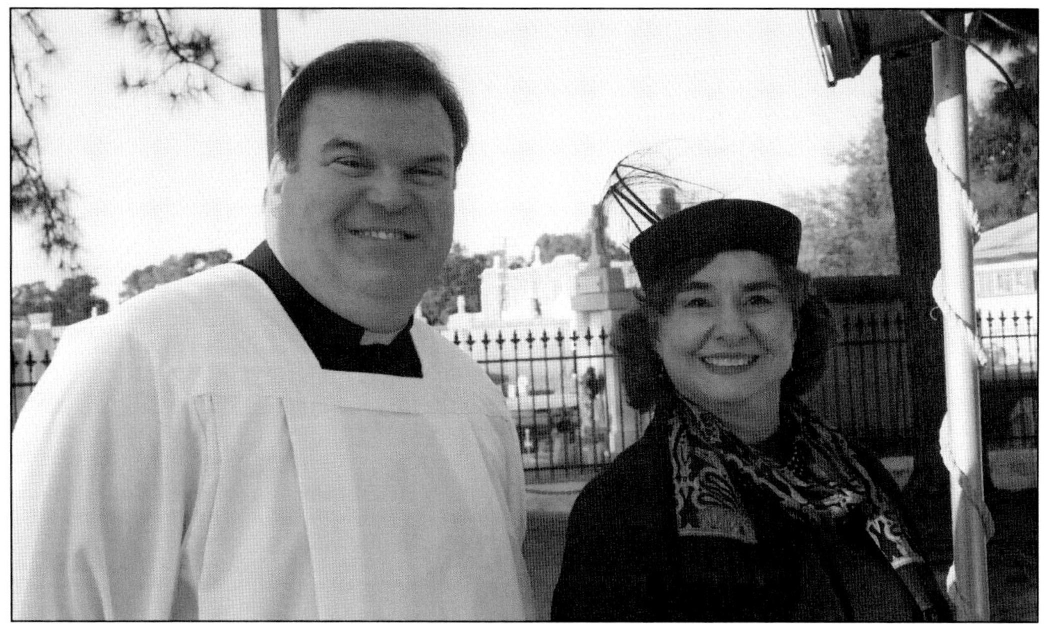

Pictured are Fr. Ray Hymel and Jane Montz Deroche. The son of Ray and Melba Duhe, Father Hymel was a graduate of St. Peter School, East St. John High School, and St. Joseph Seminary. He earned a master of divinity degree from Notre Dame Seminary and was ordained in 1987. Father Hymel is currently on the staff of the Office of Worship and Liturgy of the Archbishop of New Orleans. (Courtesy of Walter Hillary Castay.)

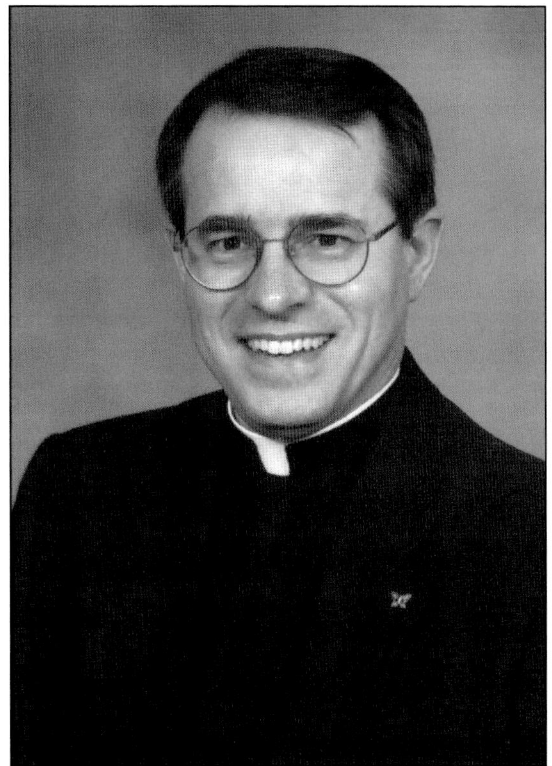

Fr. John Marse was born to James and Doris Vicknair Marse and raised in Reserve. He studied at the University of St. Thomas and St. Mary's Seminary in Houston, Texas, and was ordained on May 16, 1981. He spent several years in parochial ministry and chaplaincy at Memorial Medical Center in New Orleans. Currently, he is the priest-chaplain at East Jefferson General Hospital in Metairie, Louisiana. (Courtesy of Doris Marse.)

Pictured in the 1950s are Anatole Keller (left) and Marshall Lawrence Jr. Keller was well known for his medicinal skills. Called *traiteur* in Cajun French, healers in South Louisiana developed the exchange and adoption of herbal, faith, and magical traditional healing practices. Keller's home apothecary products included herbs, seeds, and different home-remedy ingredients. He treated many ailments, set broken limbs, and gave therapeutic rubs for backaches and sprains. (Courtesy of Mary Dorothy Mitchell.)

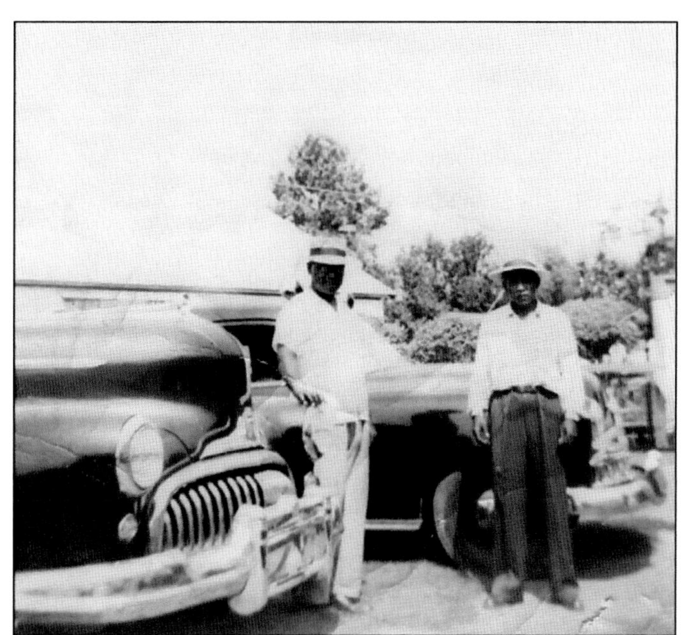

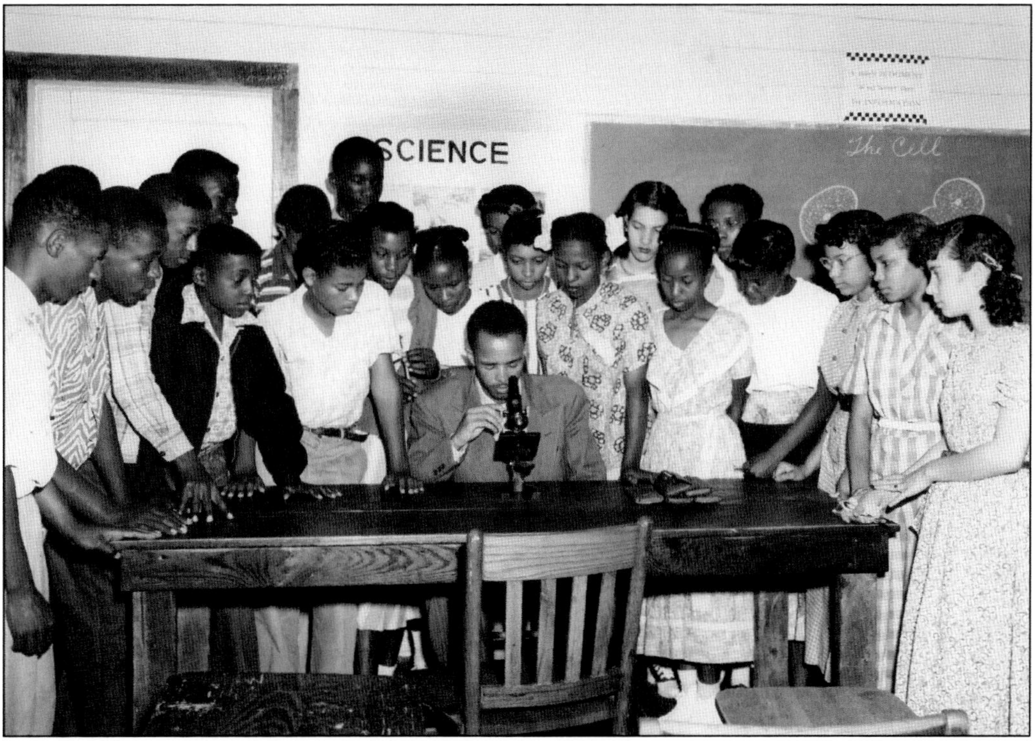

Pictured in the 1950s is Henry Bardell's Fifth Ward High School general science class. Students are, from left to right, (first row) unidentified, Joseph Smith, Raymond Borne, Sidney Sanders, Wilfred Duhe, two unidentified, instructor Henry Bardell, Jacqueline Chandler, unidentified, Geraldine Spears, Alice May Collins, Ernestine Stewart, Esma Hall, Joyce Keller, and Earline Alexander; (second row) unidentified, Willis Johnson, Shirley Walker, Bessie Wilson, and Ernestine Stewart. (Courtesy of Wilhelmina Bernard Armour.)

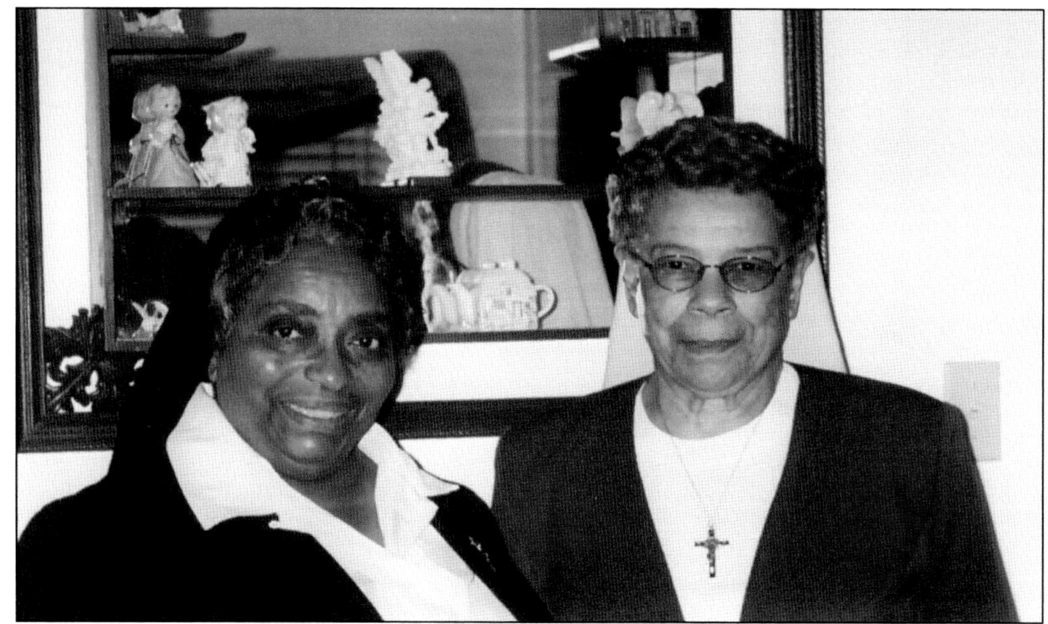

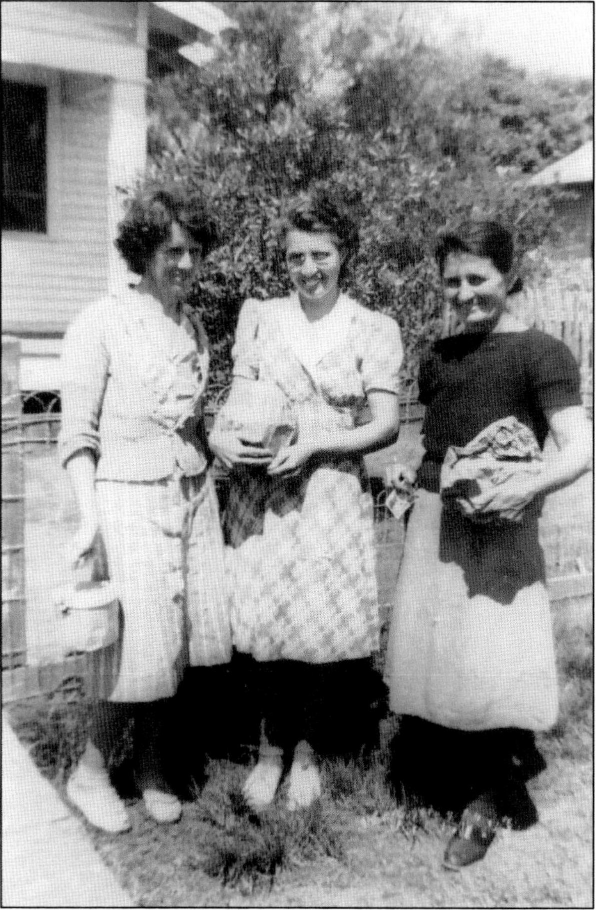

Sr. John Mary Jackson (left) was an Our Lady of Grace Elementary and High School graduate and served as principal at Our Lady of Grace from 1974 to 1977. Sister Jackson joined the Sisters of the Holy Family in 1961. Sr. Mary Cornelia Hall (right) was also a graduate of Our Lady of Grace Elementary School and joined the Sisters of the Holy Family in 1948. (Courtesy of Mary Dorothy Mitchell.)

Pictured from left to right are Odile Jacob, Elma Brady, and Emma Weber. They are waiting in Old Cornland (West First Street) for June Vicknair to pick up hot lunches for their husbands working the day shift at the Godchaux Sugar Refinery. Lunches were picked up at 11:00 a.m., and June was paid 5¢ for every meal delivered. Daily, he delivered 30 meals to the refinery on his bicycle. (Courtesy of Farrel Weber.)

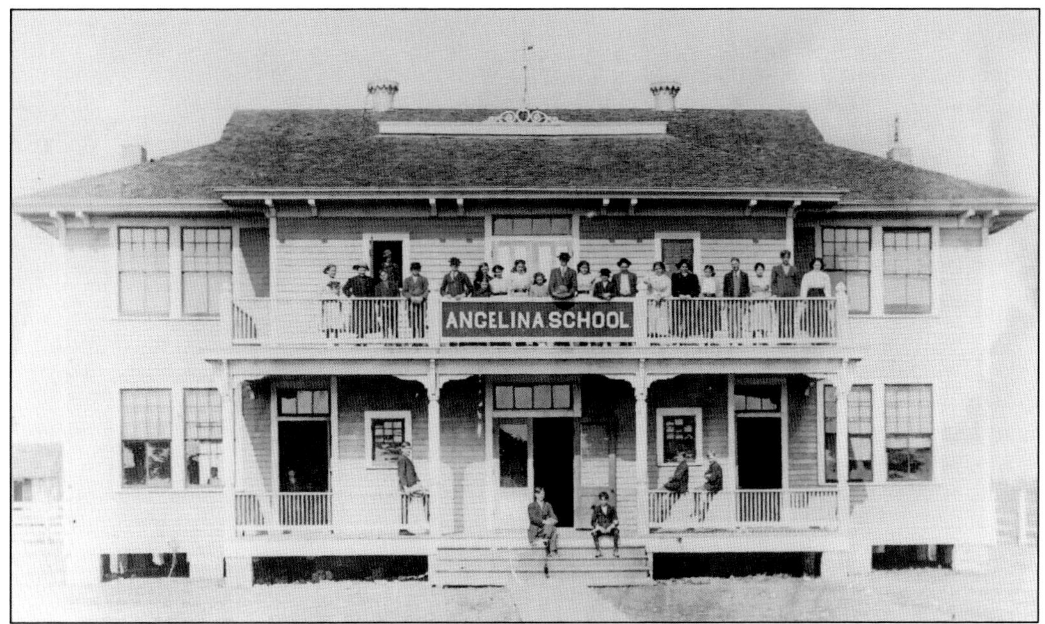

Today, there is little evidence that a German prisoner of war camp existed in Reserve during World War II. Activated on October 25, 1944, the camp was located across the Illinois Central Railroad train station on West Tenth Street. The former Angelina School was moved from Mt. Airy, Louisiana, to house the German prisoners. The camp was officially closed on January 15, 1946. (Courtesy of J.L. and Peggy Robichaux.)

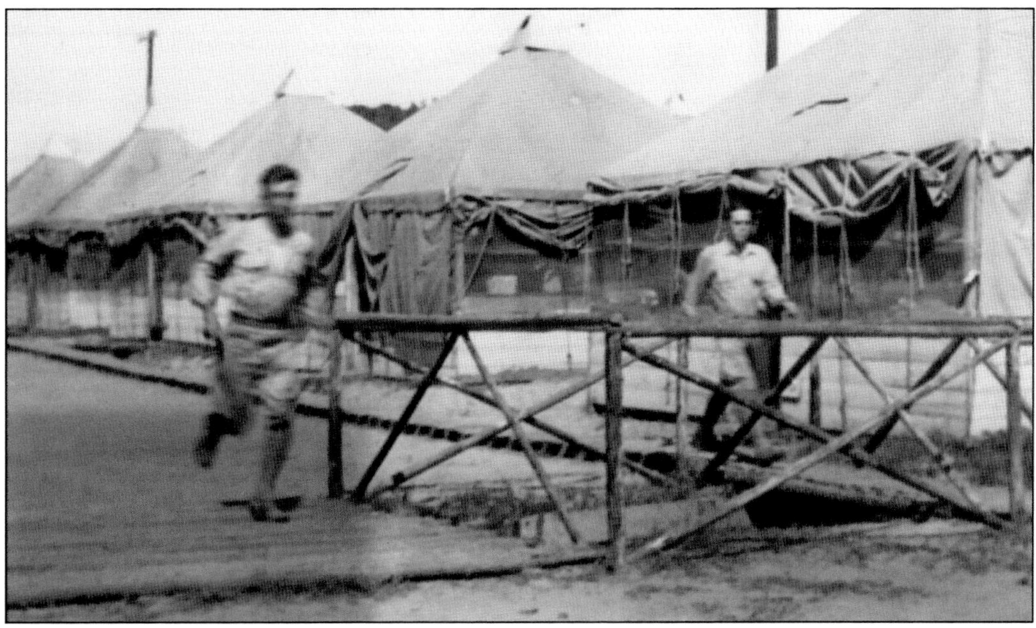

The Reserve prisoner of war camp was under the military command of Capt. Samson Bridgers and later, Lt. Scott Pace. As many as 24–34 soldiers were assigned to Reserve to guard the compound and work details that trucked prisoners to work the sugarcane fields, the Godchaux Sugar Refinery, the ice plant, and farmland in LaPlace, Garyville, and Gramercy, Louisiana. (Courtesy of Dorothy Grady Young.)

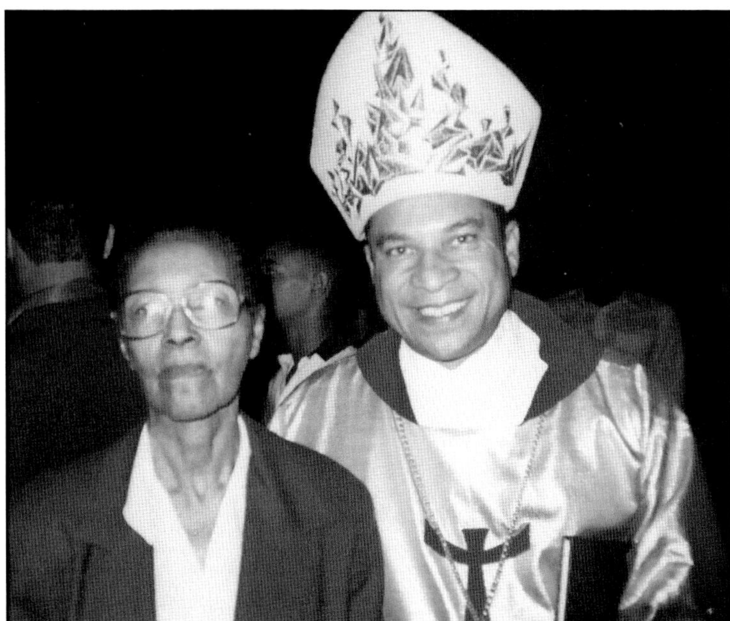

In April 1990, Reservian Mary Dorothy Keller is pictured with family friend Carl A. Fisher, auxiliary bishop of Los Angeles, California. Mary Keller was a member of St. Peter Catholic Church until she became a devoted member of Our Lady of Grace Church in 1937. She worked as a housekeeper in the Godchaux Guest House, Millet's Funeral Home, and Englade's Cleaners. (Courtesy of Mary Dorothy Mitchell.)

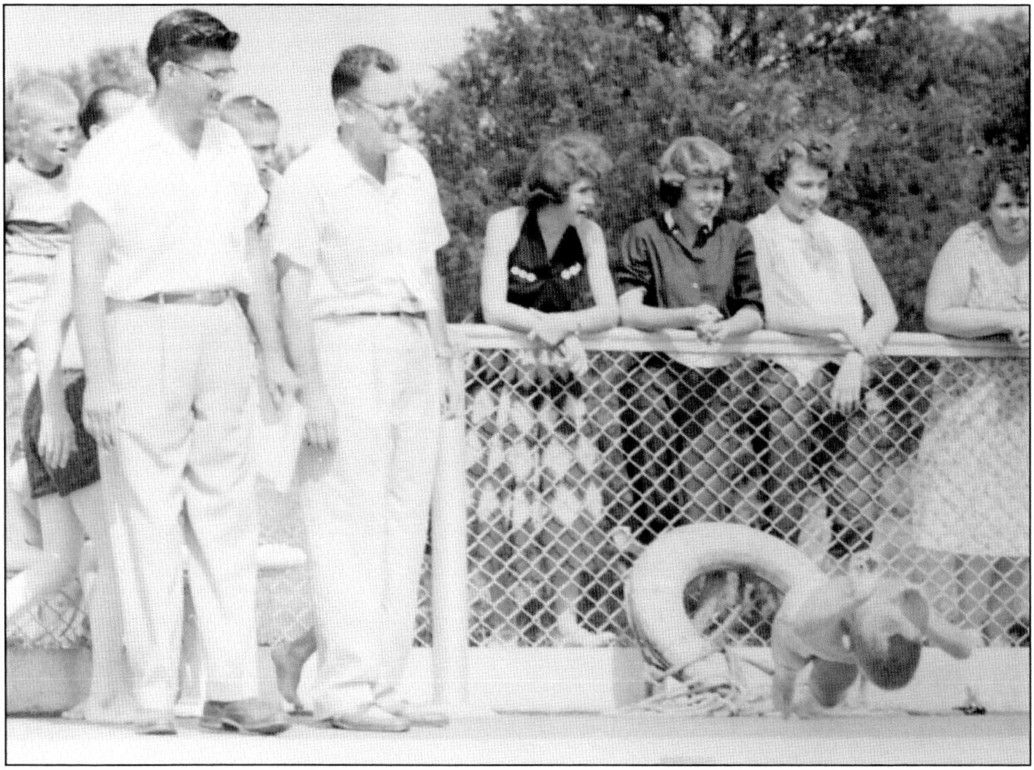

In 1954, swimming pool judges Percy Vicknair, left, and Hamilton J. Boudreaux Jr., right, check out the swimming race at the Godchaux swimming pool during the Fourth of July fair at the Reserve Community Club. Ladies watching the race are, from left to right, Francis Madere Keating, Beverly Jacob Ingraffia, Rita Jacob Cancienne, and unidentified. Events at the swimming pool also included beauty and diving contests. (Courtesy of Hamilton J. Boudreaux Jr. and family.)

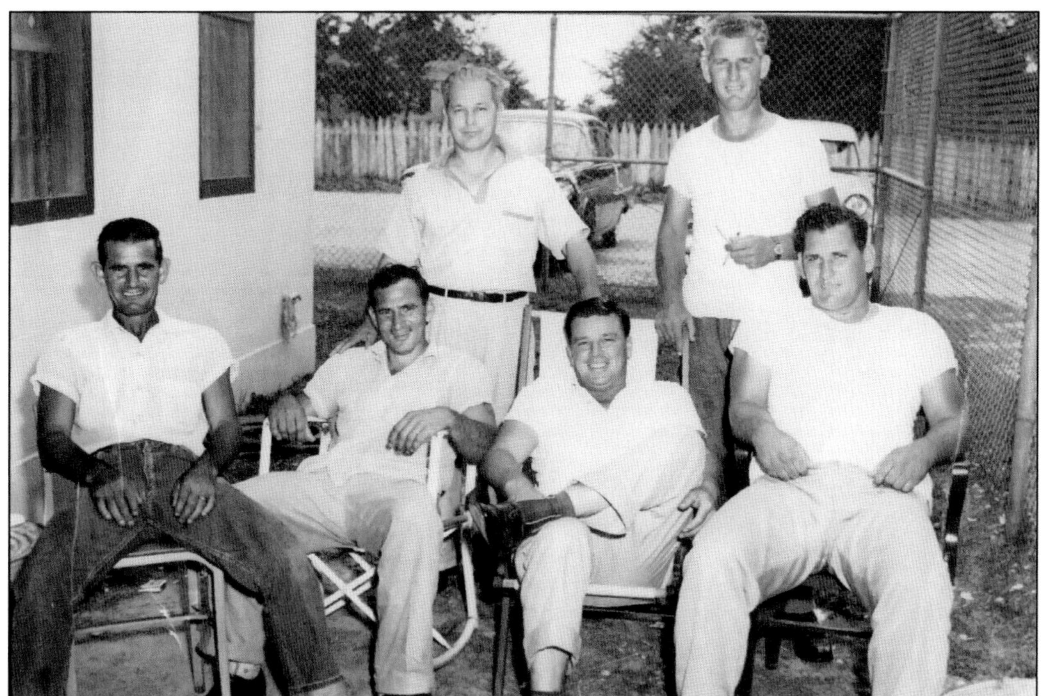

Demanding higher wages, unionized workers at Godchaux Sugar Refinery walked out of the refinery for 10 months in April 1955. The strike turned violent, and some union workers were jailed for skirmishing with a non-striking worker and breaking his leg. The gentlemen seated in the first row were jailed for the incident and include, from left to right, Dewey "Airline" Weber, "Pony" Cambre, Adam Duhe Sr., and Leon Scioneaux. The second row includes Wallace Gauthe (left) and Prentice Tamplain Jr. (Courtesy of Sheryl Tamplain Savoie.)

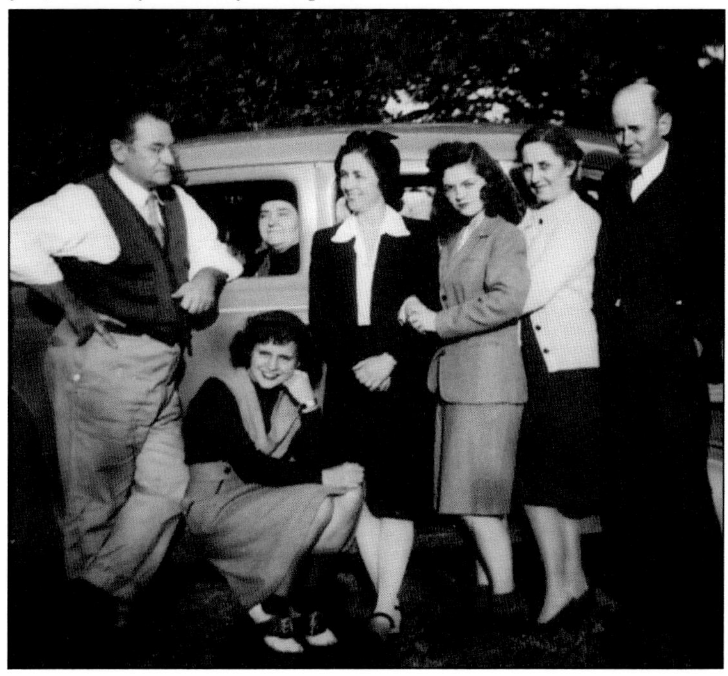

Pictured in the 1940s are, from left to right, Louis J. Maurin Sr., Emma LeBrun Maurin (inside car), Jo-Ann Maurin Montz (sitting on running board), unidentified, Gloria Maurin Oubre, Frances LeBrun Trudeau, and Guy Trudeau. In 1916, Louis Maurin, known as "the Movie Picture Man," brought silent movies to Reserve and operated theaters in Garyville, Lutcher, LaPlace, and Jefferson College. He opened Maurin's Theater in 1931, now the St. John Theatre, a community playhouse. (Courtesy of Gerard Montz.)

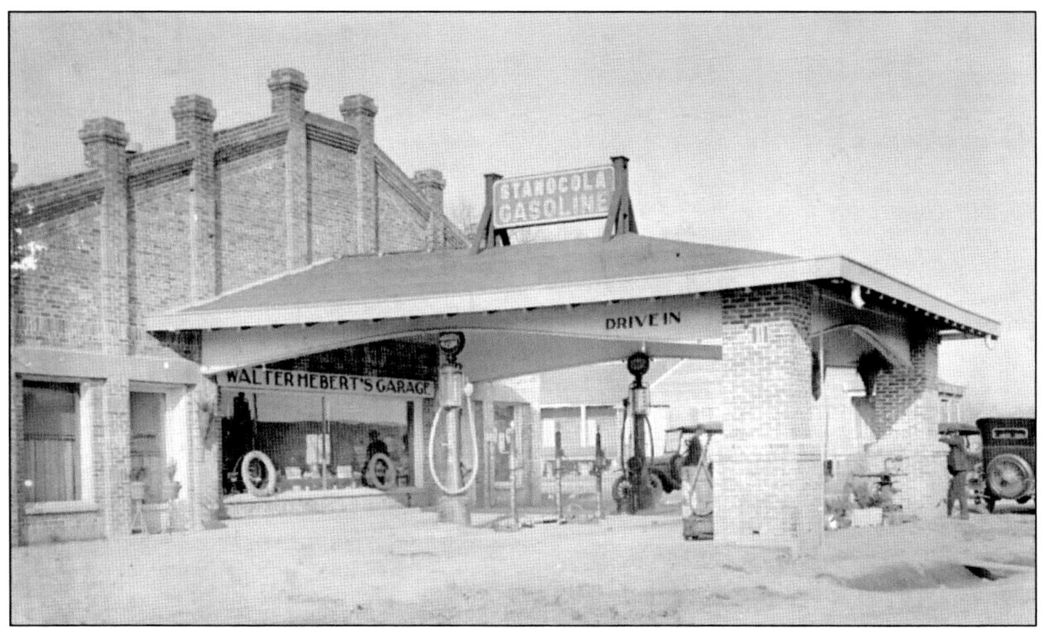

In Lubin Laurent's 1922–1923 *L'Observateur* series of articles entitled "A History of St. John the Baptist Parish," he listed Walter Herbert's Garage as one of three automobile garages in Reserve during the early 1920s. This garage was fully equipped to repair and service automobiles. Interestingly, the service station sold Stanocola gasoline. Stanocola stood for Standard Oil Company of Louisiana, which fell into disarray in 1924.

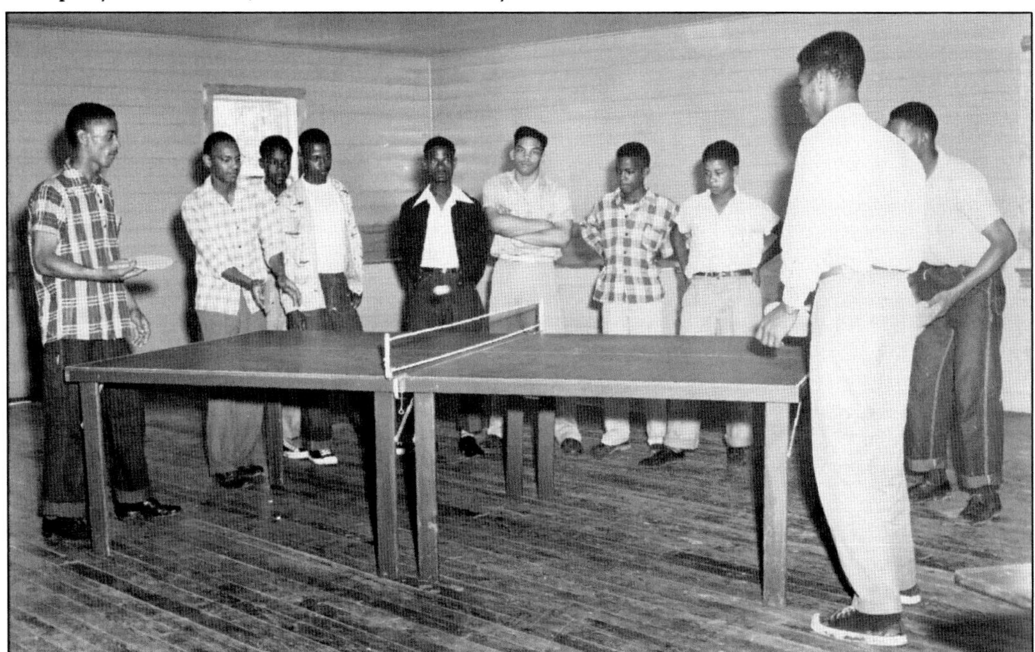

In the 1950s, Fifth Ward High School students are playing a game of table tennis. The opponents are Winthrop Lapeyrolerie (left) and Wilfred Bernard Jr. Spectators waiting their turn include, from left to right, Calvin Keller, Autry Alexis, Leroy Keller, Lucien Madere Jr., McLouis Robinet, Emile Bossier, Wilfred Duhe, and Ferdinand Wallace. (Courtesy of Wilhelmina Bernard Armour.)

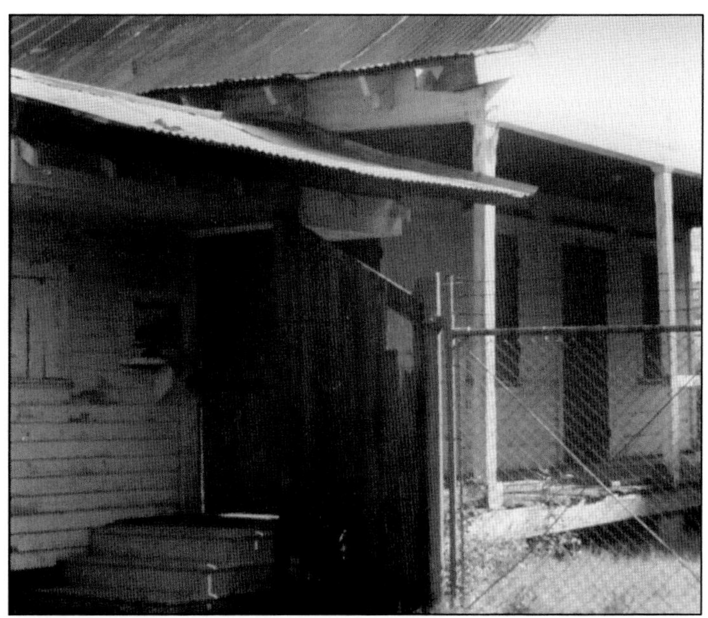

The Bienfaisance Benevolent Association (*bienfaisance* meaning "good will toward others") was organized in January 1873 to assist African American Catholics with medical and spiritual needs. The organization was devoted to the Blessed Mother. The hall was utilized as a public school and served as a meeting and social building for the African American community for 104 years. The organization disbanded in 1977, and the building was demolished in 1979. (Courtesy of Dionne Lapeyrolerie.)

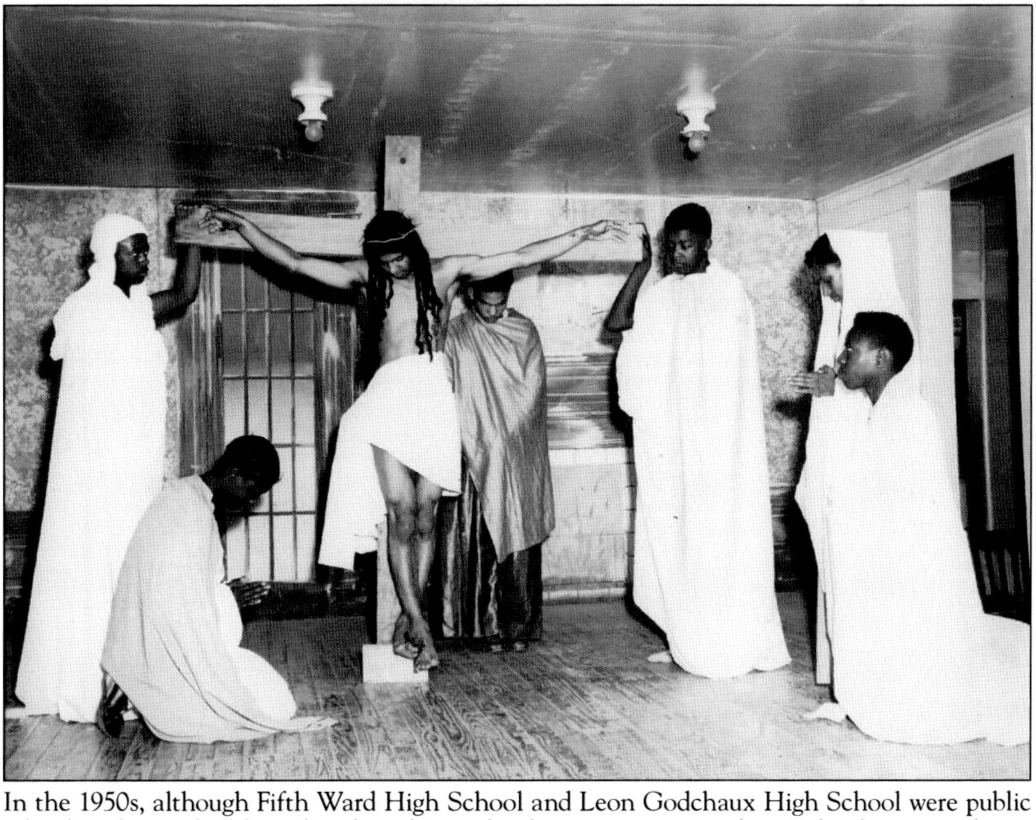

In the 1950s, although Fifth Ward High School and Leon Godchaux High School were public schools, religious holidays played a role in school activities. Pictured is a school passion play at Fifth Ward High. Jesus Christ is portrayed by Calvin Keller. Other students who participated in the play are, from left to right, Leroy Keller, McLouis Robinet, Percy Duhe, Louis Bernard, and Roland Borne. Kneeling is Mildred Beco. (Courtesy of Wilhelmina Bernard Armour.)

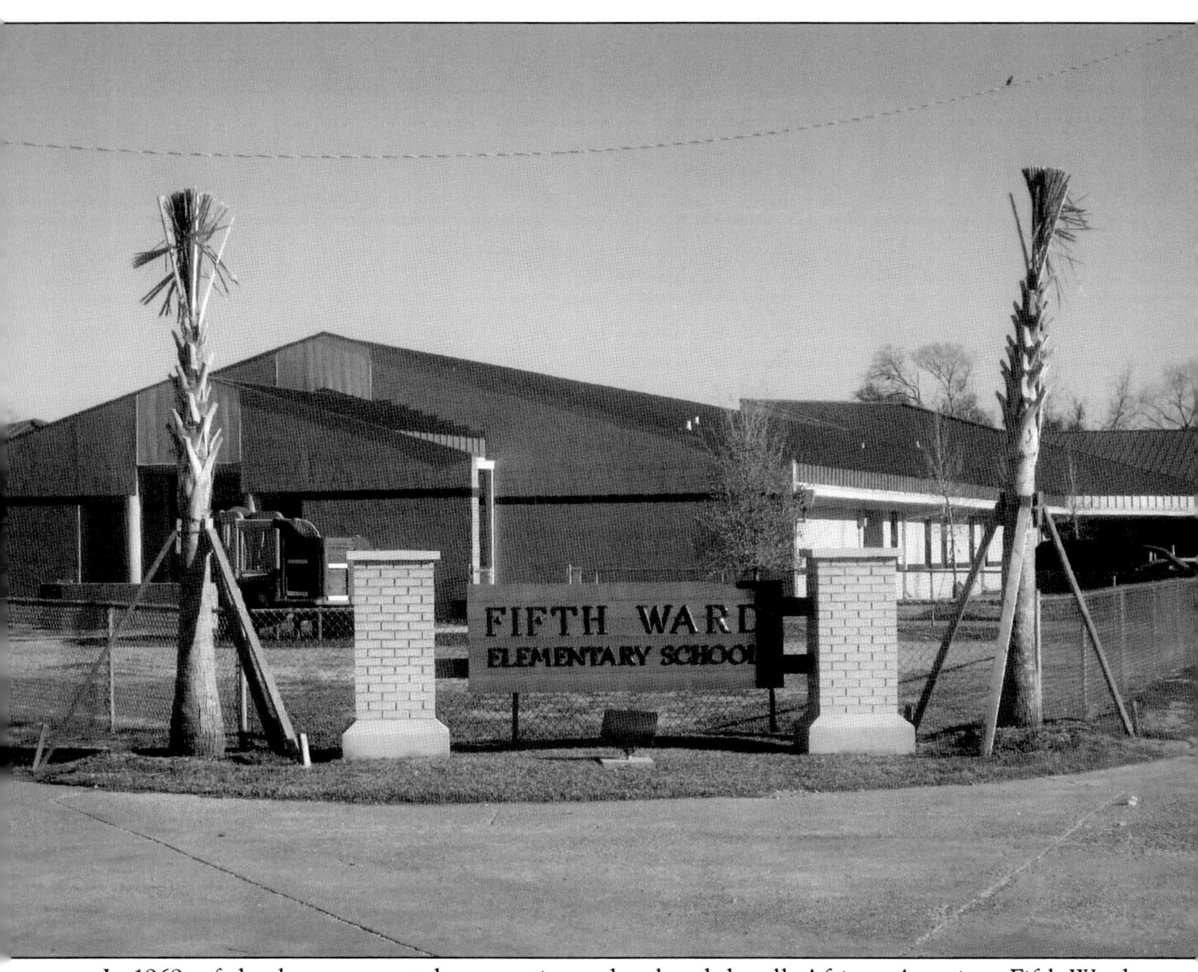

In 1969, a federal government desegregation order closed the all–African American Fifth Ward High School and converted the school to a junior high school, serving grades eight and nine, for all East Bank students. The school was renamed Reserve Junior High School. A parish capital improvement bond election tore down the old brick buildings and gymnasium, and the St. John the Baptist Parish School Board built a new school on the site in 1993. The school was converted to a kindergarten through sixth grade school and renamed Reserve Elementary School. Several years later, the St. John Parish School Board reviewed a petition from Fifth Ward High School graduates and the school community and passed a resolution to rename the school: Fifth Ward Elementary School. Pictured is a current view of Fifth Ward Elementary School with additional capital improvements added to the school. (Courtesy of CSRS.)

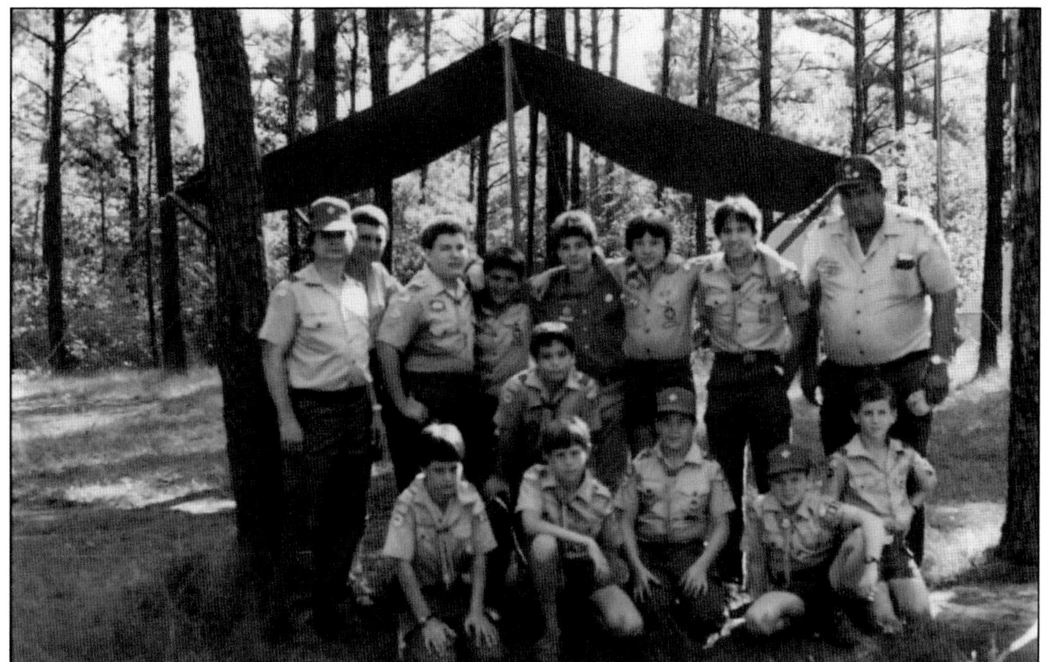

Pictured are the members of Reserve Boy Scout Troop 316 who are attending the annual jamboree at Camp Salmen, near Covington, Louisiana. Scouts attended the jamboree from Sunday until Sunday and engaged in outdoor activities where they earned merit badges. In the second row, assistant Scoutmaster Harris Casseigne Jr. appears at the far left, and Scoutmaster John Waits appears at the far right. Waits served the Scouting community for 32 years. (Courtesy of John Waits.)

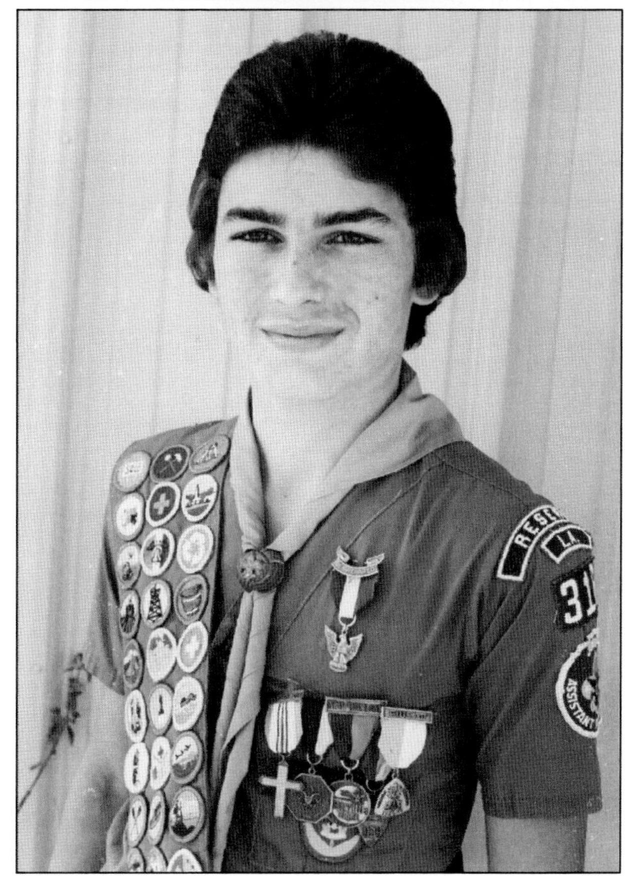

Reserve Eagle Scout Donald Cox received the highest rank attainable in the Boy Scouts of America. Eagle Scouts required at least 21 merit badges, must have been Life Scouts for at least six months, and had to demonstrate Scout spirit. Others in Reserve Troop 316 who earned the Eagle Scout award are Norman Englade Sr., Norman Englade Jr., Pete McGraw, Maxie McGraw, Marvin McGraw, Brent Roussel Jr., and Bertrand Madere. (Courtesy of John Waits.)

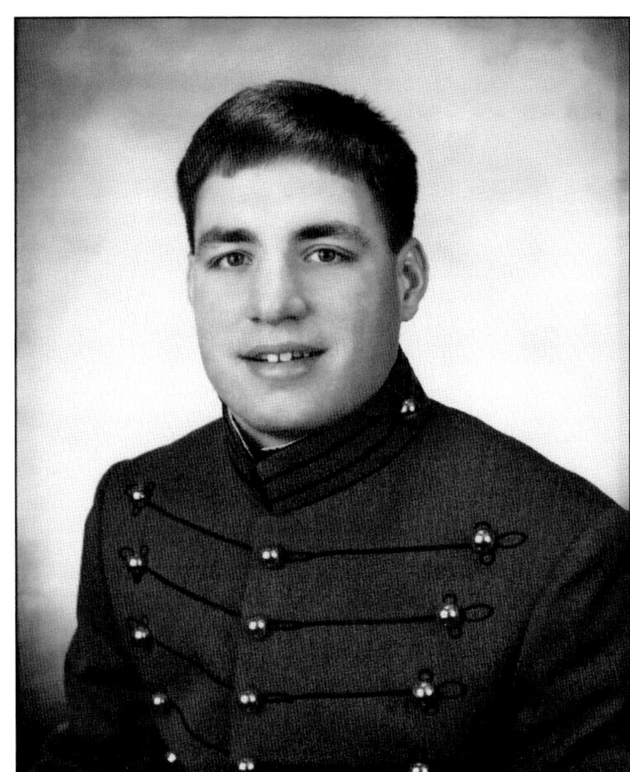

Capt. Patrick Forrest Hymel, a 1987 graduate of Riverside Academy, graduated from the US Military Academy, West Point, in 1992 with a bachelor of science degree in engineering. He received a master's degree from Nicholls State University. He spent seven years as a field artillery officer and taught gunnery skills. He is currently an in-school suspension presider at Prairieville Middle School and a defensive coordinator at Riverside Academy. (Courtesy of Patrick Hymel.)

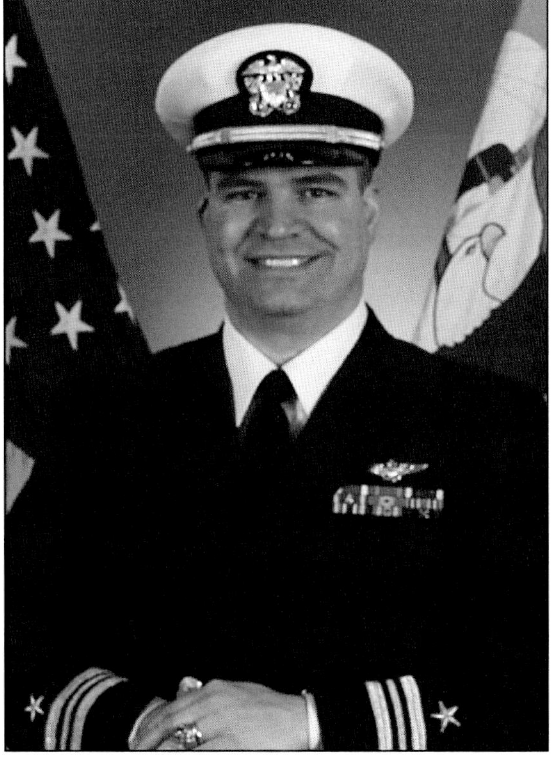

US Navy commander Gregory L. Guidry graduated from the Navy academy in 1995 with an engineering degree. He served on the USS *John C. Stennis* and was the lead planning officer for all intelligence, surveillance, and reconnaissance operations in support of the 2010 Haiti earthquake relief effort. Guidry is married to the former Noel Fromm, of Jacksonville, Florida, and has two sons. (Courtesy of Commander Greg Guidry.)

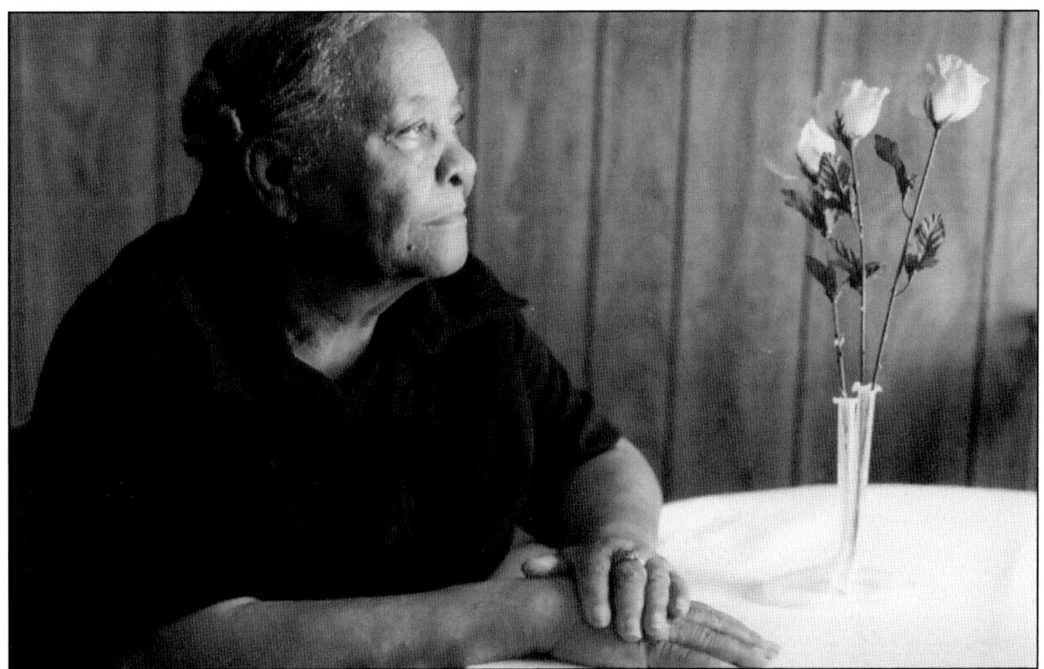

The daughter of Rome and Hortense Davis, Isabella Davis Francois lived to be nearly 100 years old. Isabella grew up on the Belle Pointe Plantation, attended a one-room school, and married Cornelius Francois. She worked in the fields and as a domestic worker to support 10 children. She was a member of Our Lady of Grace Church and created many beautiful afghans for church fundraising events. (Courtesy of Mary Dorothy Mitchell.)

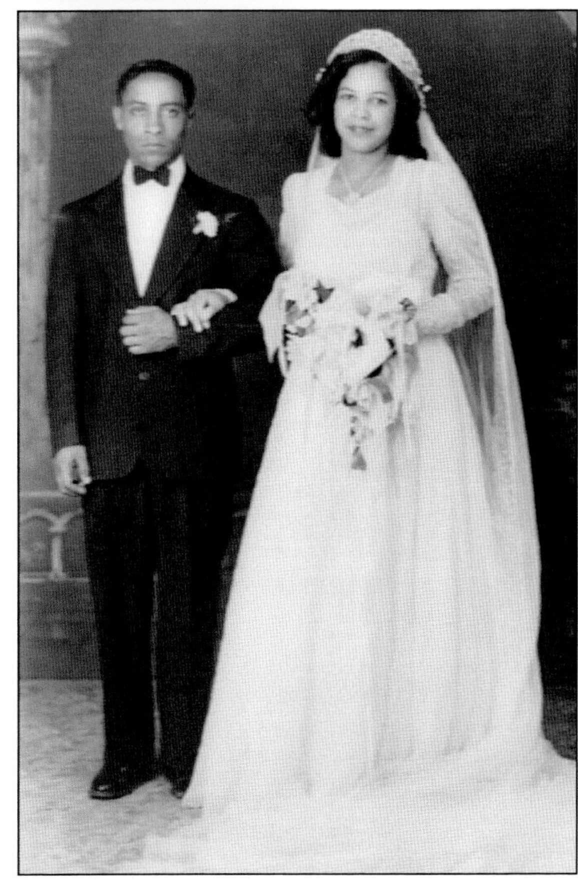

Lennix Madere Sr. married Irene Marmillion, of Gramercy, on July 3, 1946. The couple resided in Reserve and Lennix worked at Godchaux Sugar Refinery for 35 years. Irene was the head baker at St. Peter Parochial School cafeteria from 1958 to 1969. Lennix and Irene raised three children: Linda, Wanda, and Lennix Jr. (Courtesy of Wanda Madere Lee.)

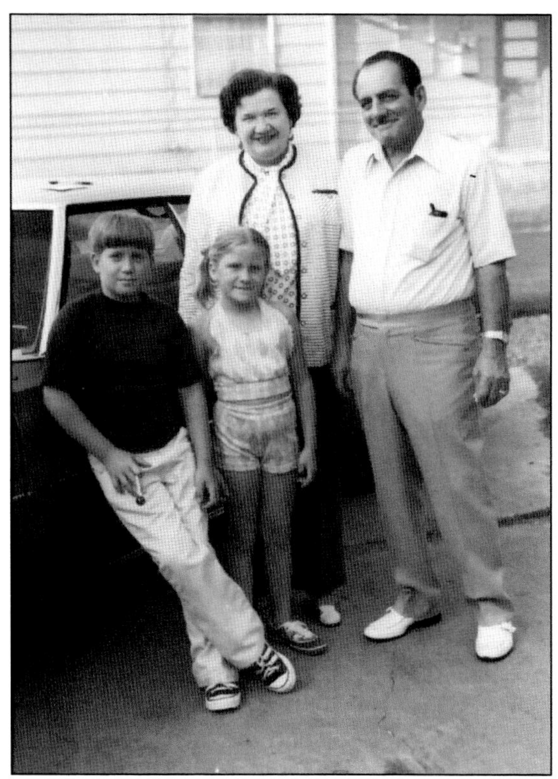

Pictured are Althea Cambre (center), Leonce "Cop" Cambre, and their grandchildren Tommy Jacob (left) and Sydney Jacob. When the Belle Pointe Dairy closed in 1947, Leonce and Althea opened the Reserve Dairy Farm, located on East Twenty-third Street in Reserve. The dairy serviced the community and schools in the area and remained opened into the mid-1960s. (Courtesy of Callan and Diane Cambre Jacob.)

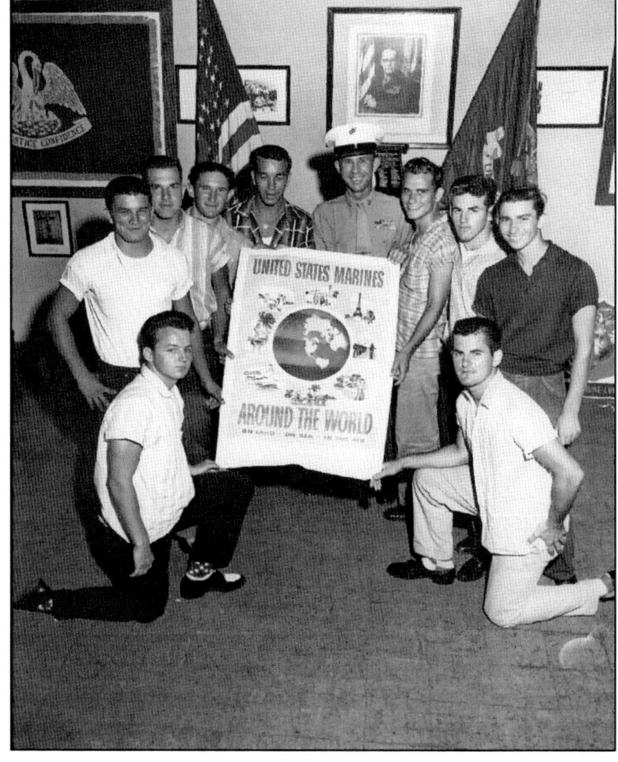

Following their 1957 high school graduation, several Leon Godchaux High School alumni enlisted in the US Marine Corps for two years and were sent to Camp Pendleton, California, for basic training. Shown from left to right are George Terrio (kneeling), Robert "Bob" Vicknair, Farrel "Moonbean" Jacob, Harry Joe Montz, Malcolm Jacob, an unidentified marine recruiter, Darrel Catoire, Armond Brady, Lester Vicknair, and Farrel Weber (kneeling). (Courtesy of Farrel Weber.)

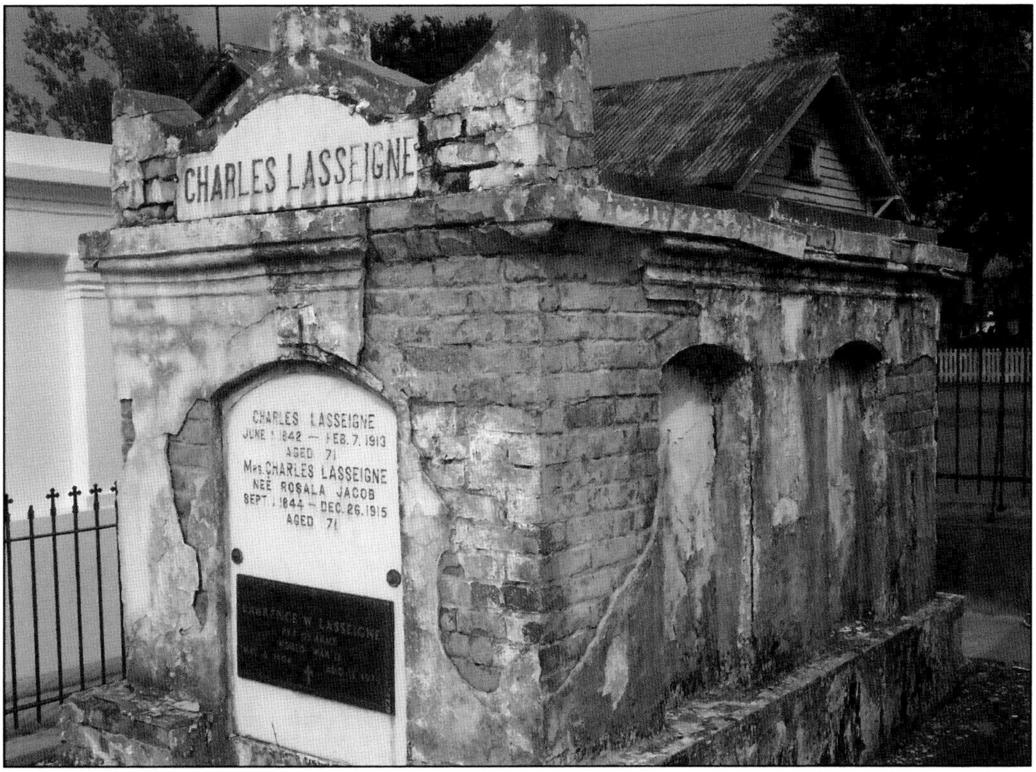

A unique feature of the St. Peter Catholic Church cemetery is aboveground burials. Mississippi River flooding created great problems for belowground burials. Louisiana solved those problems by constructing family vaults. A wooden coffin is placed inside, and within years the occupant is reduced to bone. As space is needed, bones are placed in a sack and pushed to the rear. Old coffin pieces are removed, and another coffin is inserted. (Courtesy of Walter Hillary Castay.)

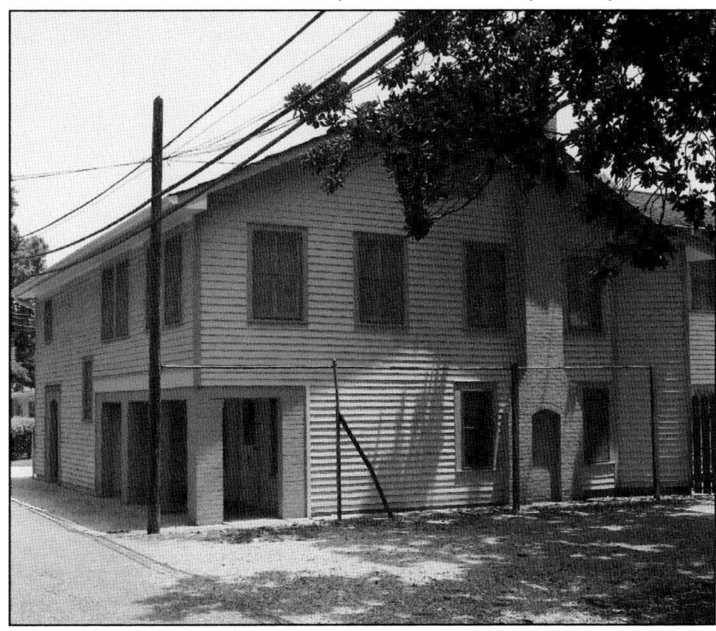

Pictured is the original building of the Reserve Telephone Company on West Fifth Street. Daniel Adam Madere and his wife, Inez Hart Madere, started the independent telephone company in 1935. Madere obtained a franchise for the area of Reserve and Garyville, Louisiana, and the first Reserve telephone book listed 15 customers. Today, the computerized company serves 8,500 customers and is now called Reserve Telecommunication Company. (Courtesy of E. Darroch Watson.)

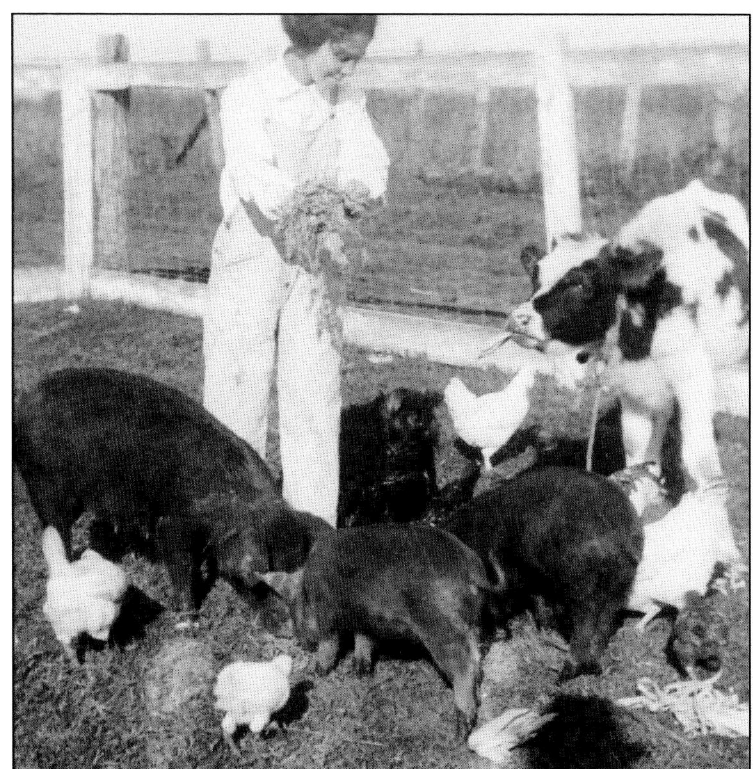

This unknown Reservian from the 1930s represents many in the community who grew their own vegetables and raised their own chickens, hogs, and cows. Cows also supplied the family with milk, butter, and clabber. A tradition maintained by African Americans and French-speaking Cajuns was the butchering of a hog, known as *la boucherie*. Family members and neighbors came to give a *coupe-dimain*, or helping hand. (Courtesy of Dionne Lapeyrolerie.)

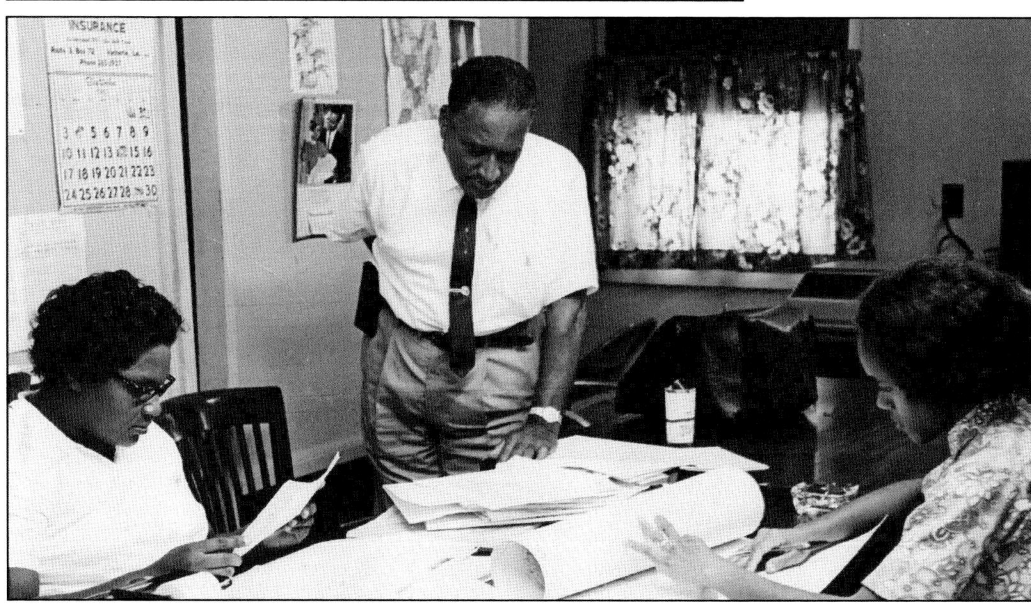

Frank Lapeyrolerie (center) directed the St. John the Baptist Parish Self-Help Federal Housing and Educational Program, which was implemented through the US Department of Health, Education, and Labor in 1965. African American men and women who qualified for the program were taught skills and procedures in surveying, construction, financing, and mortgaging a home. Dorothy Farlough (left) was the head instructor, and Mona Nicholas (right) was the secretary and bookkeeper. (Courtesy of Dionne Lapeyrolerie.)

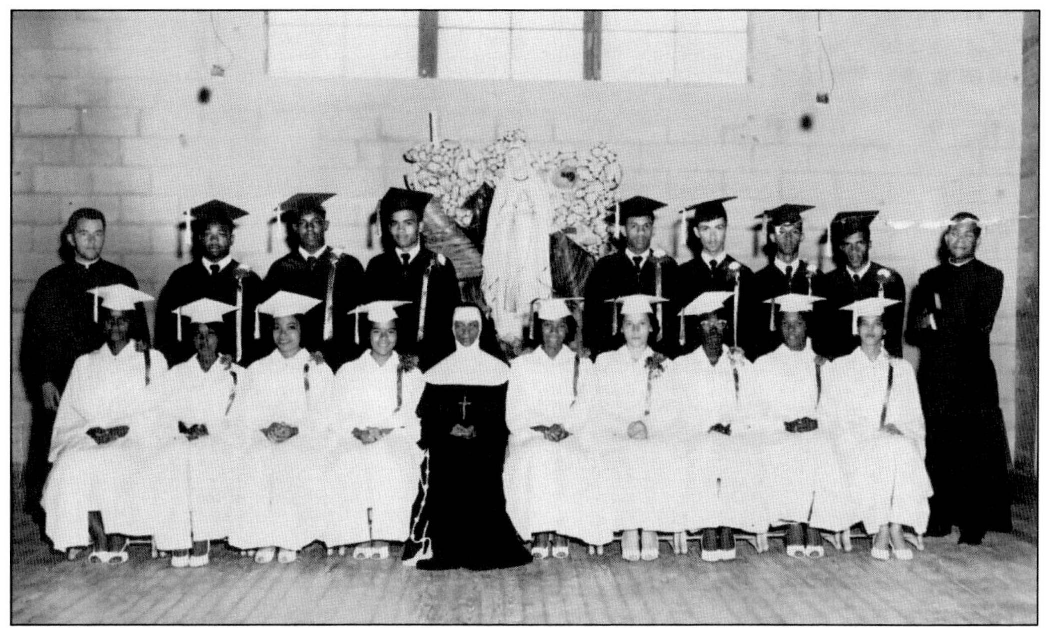

Pictured in 1955 is the first graduating class of Our Lady of Grace. From left to right are (first row) Mary Elizabeth Cambre, Gloria Lewis, Rosalie James, Reah Hall, principal Sr. Mary Louisette, Rose Sanders, Lois Alexander, Betty Gray, Mabel Etienne, and Rosemary Dinvaut; (second row) pastor Rev. Joseph LeFrois, Raymond White, Walter Anderson, Frank Keller, Alvin Lewis, Blaise Duhe Jr., Lucien Gauff Jr., Edward Scioineaux, and unidentified. (Courtesy of Reah Hall Bernard.)

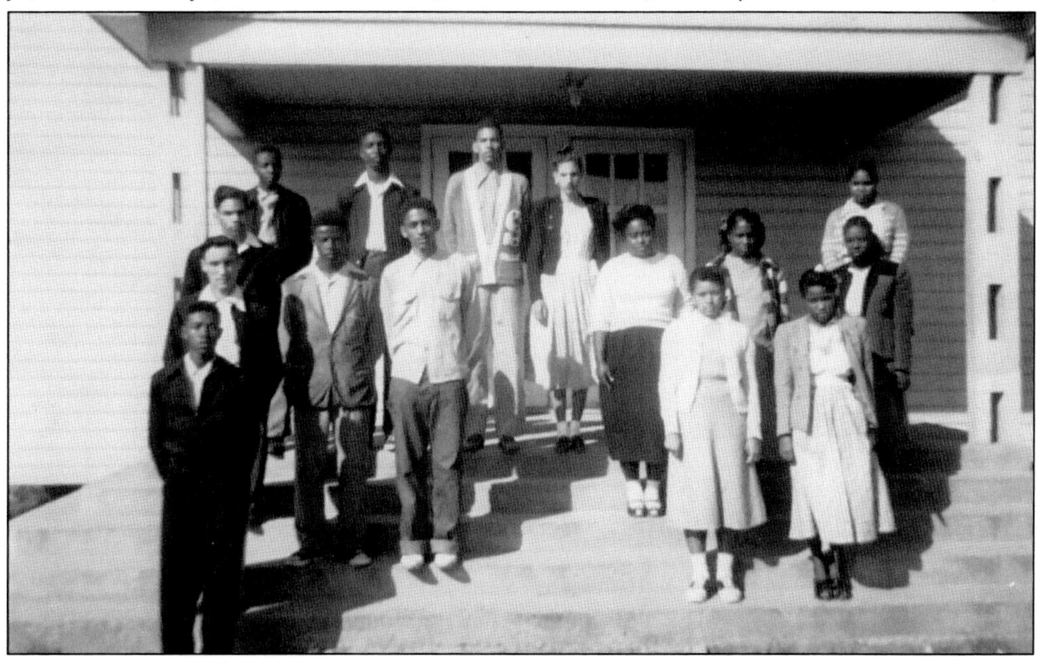

In 1943, parents and community leaders approached the St. John the Baptist Parish School Board for a public high school for African Americans. The Bienfaisance Benevolent Society stepped forward and loaned a church hall so that students could go to high school. Pictured are the first African American students of St. John the Baptist Parish to attend a high school in the parish. (Courtesy of Earline Perrilloux.)

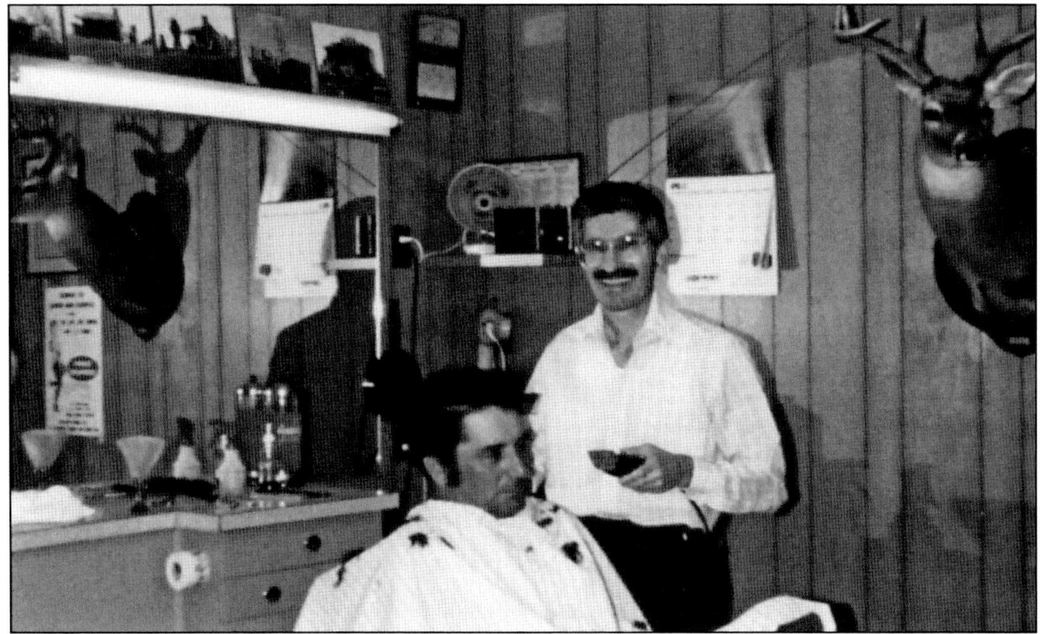

Wesley Breaux rented space from the Pierre Rene' Montz and opened a barbershop near St. Peter Catholic Church in 1932. Wesley remained near the Alltmont Store for the next 65 years and retired at age 87. His son Phil joined his father in 1960 and built a barbershop near West Second Street. Pictured is Phil Breaux cutting Robert Berthelot's hair. (Courtesy of Carla Simon Berthelot.)

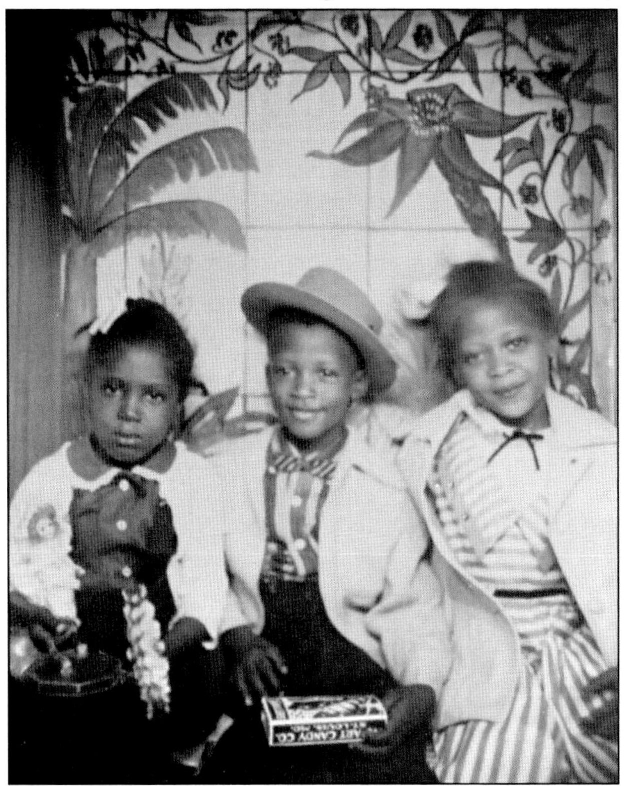

Pictured in the 1950s are, from left to right, Mary Taylor, Robert Taylor, and Sylvia Taylor Steib-Dunn. Judge Sylvia Steib-Dunn received her law degree from Loyola University and became St. John the Baptist Parish's first female African American attorney. She is currently a district judge for the Louisiana Department of Labor for Workers' Compensation claims. (Courtesy of Judge Sylvia Taylor Steib-Dunn.)

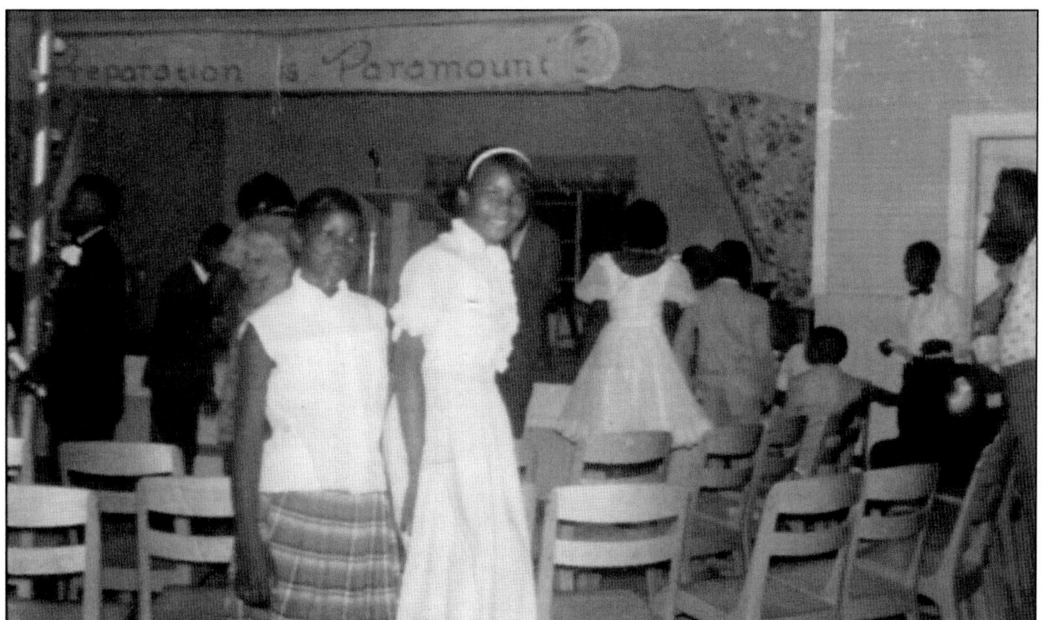

Reserve Rosenwald School was a public elementary school built by the St. John the Baptist Parish School Board for the African American community in the mid-1940s. Located behind the Godchaux Sugar Refinery, brick buildings replaced the school's wooden frame buildings in 1955. Pictured is a graduation exercise held in the 1960s. Reserve Rosenwald closed in the early 1990s, and students were reassigned to Leon Godchaux Grammar School. (Courtesy of Alberta Henderson.)

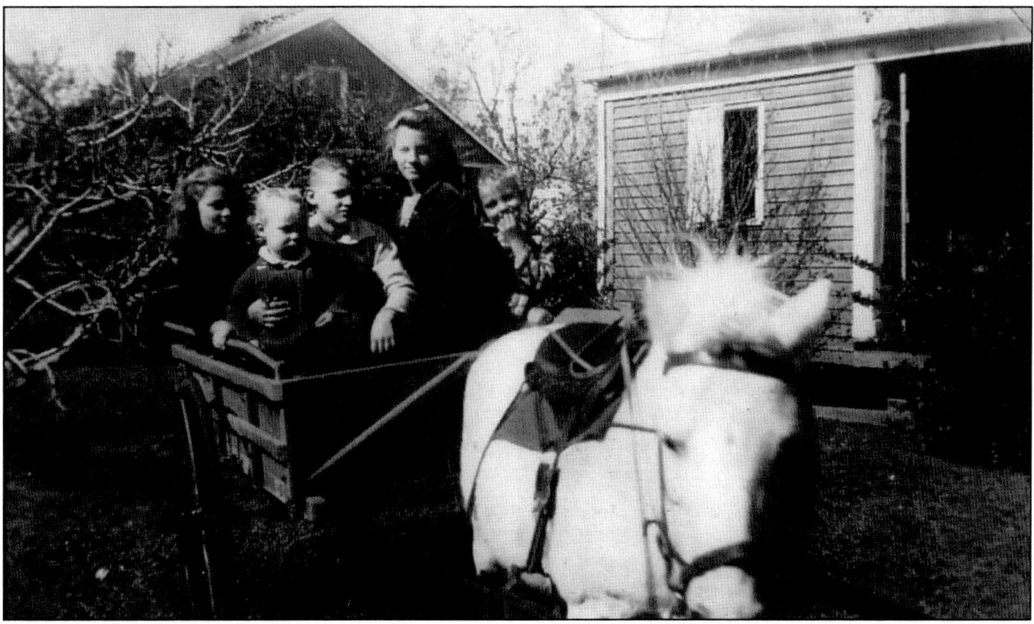

The Haydel family includes, from left to right, Janice, Ralph, Harold "Bubby," Gloria and Bert, and their pony Pal. The family lived on the grounds of the sugar refinery, and Bubby hitched up the wagon and picked up the "slop" at the Reserve prisoner of war camp for their farm animals. He also shaved blocks of ice and sold the German prisoners snowballs. (Courtesy of Harold "Bubby" Haydel.)

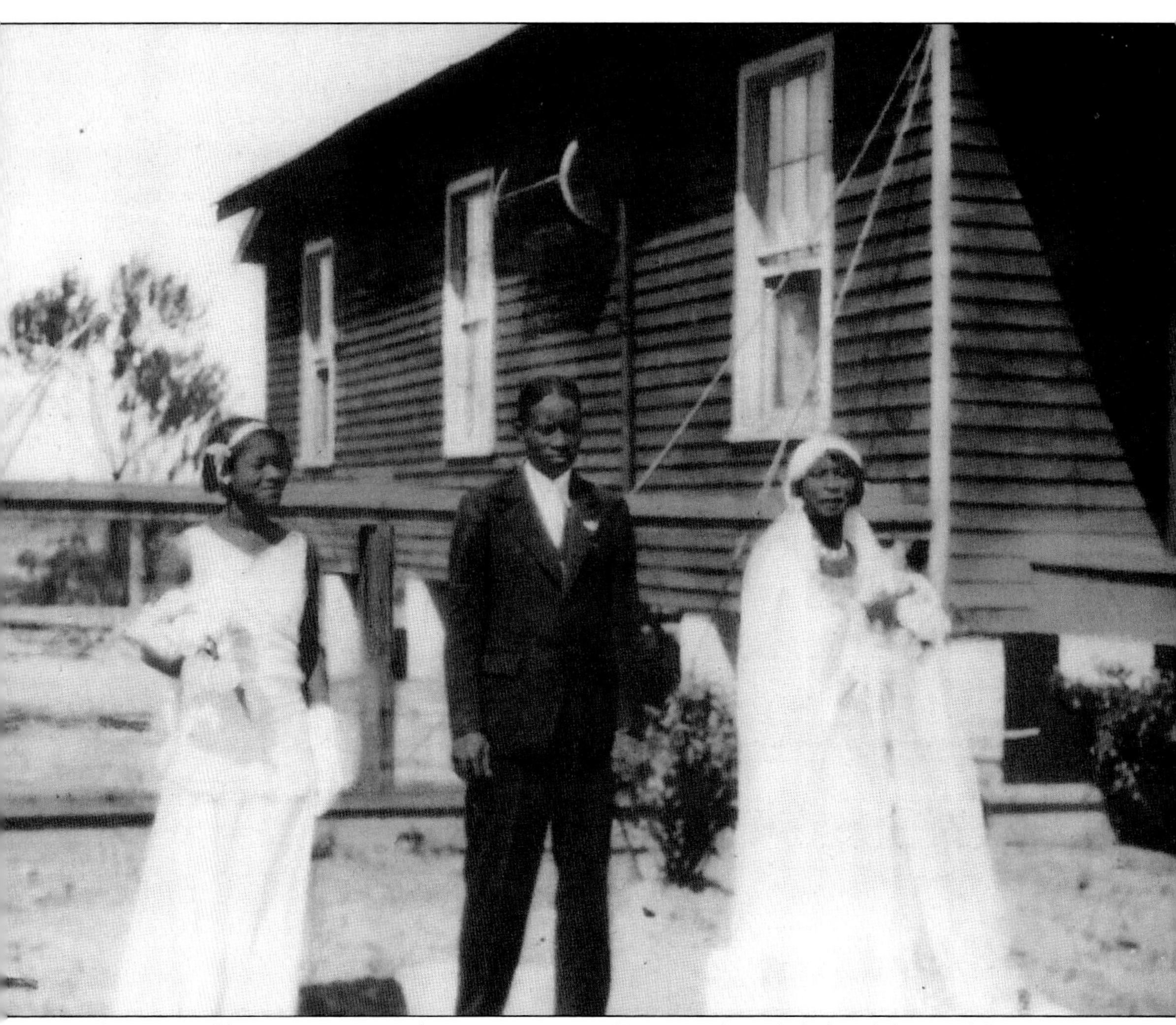

A 1932 wedding picture was taken in a section of Reserve directly behind the Godchaux Sugar Refinery called New Town. The photograph included Grace Frazier (left), groom Henry Harris Sr., and bride Ellian Miles Harris. New Town was a residential section for Godchaux employees, first occupied by African Americans and later by whites. Henry Harris was a Godchaux Sugar Refinery watchman, and he knocked on doors early in the morning to make sure workers were up for their shift. Henry also worked at the Godchaux Guest House and was a chauffeur for Godchaux brothers Edward and Walter. In an era of staunch segregation, African Americans were not allowed entry and could not purchase goods from the Godchaux store on Canal Street. Henry and Ellian were allowed to enter and she picked out her wedding gown and selected other items necessary for the wedding at no cost. One of the Harris children was Albertha "Pinky" Henderson, a long-time public school teacher and political activist. (Courtesy of Albertha "Pinky" Henderson.)

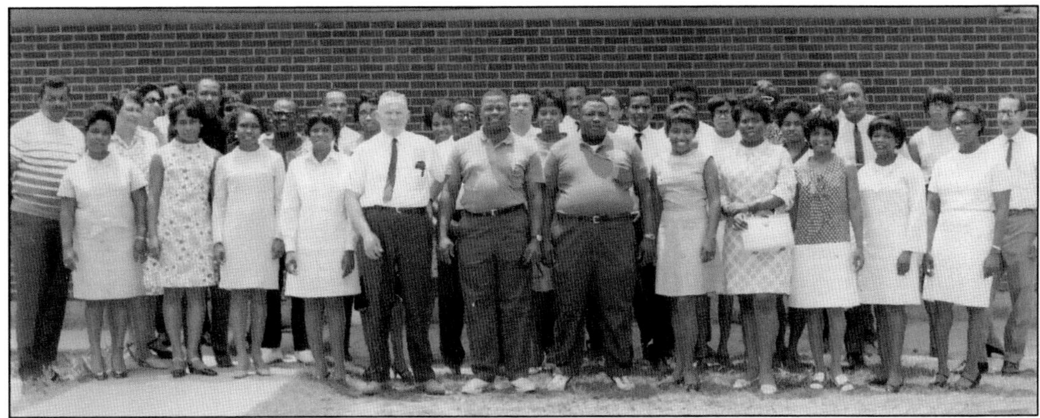

Pictured in 1968–1969 is the last faculty of Fifth Ward High School. In 1943, parents and community leaders approached the St. John the Baptist Parish School Board for a public high school for African Americans. The school board informed residents there were no buildings available. The Bienfaisance Benevolent Society loaned its church hall so that students could go to a high school. (Courtesy of Fifth Ward High School.)

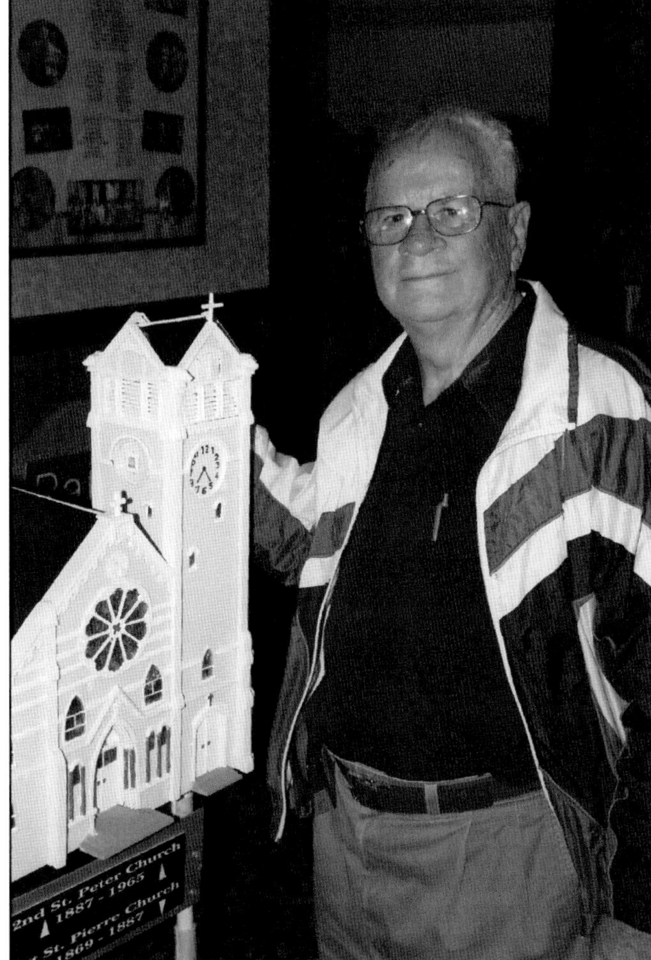

Upon his retirement, Dudley Beadle sought a hobby to occupy his spare time. He began to create scale models of Reserve landmarks. His collection includes the entire Godchaux Sugar Refinery, the Liberty Theatre, Club Café, Ernest Duhe Creole cottage, all three St. Peter churches, Reserve train stations, and several other Reserve landmarks. Pictured is his model of St. Peter Catholic Church. (Photographed by Peter Forest.)

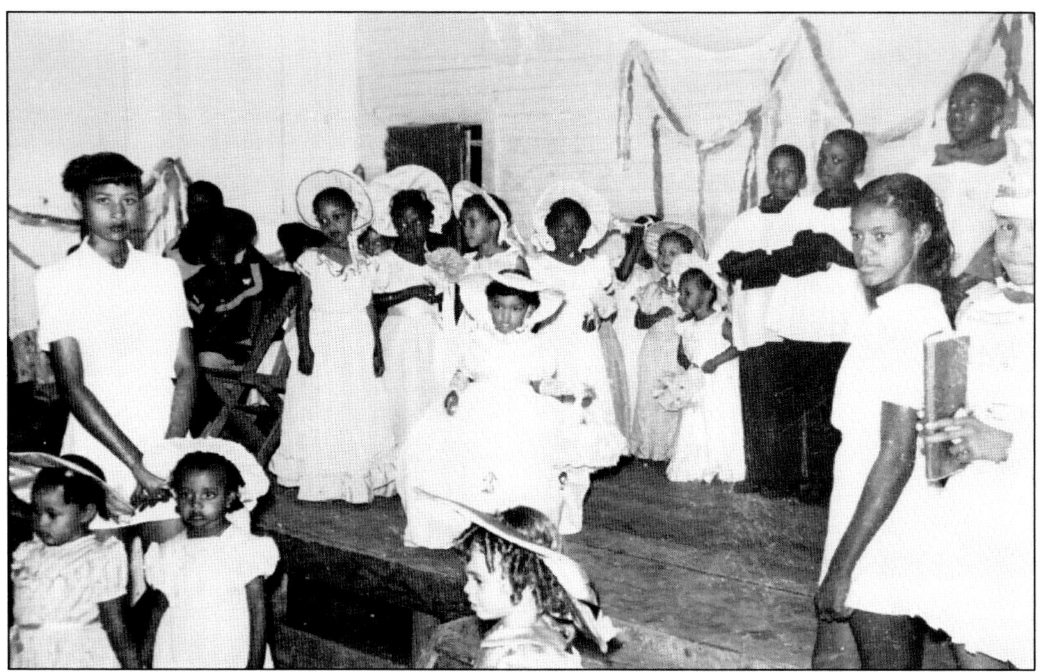

Pictured in 1948 is a Tom Thumb wedding program in which all major wedding roles are played by small children, usually under the age of 10 years old. A church fundraising event and American fad during the 1920s, the program disappeared by the 1970s. The bride is Leah Robottom Rousseve, and the groom is Raymond Frank. (Courtesy of Mary Dorothy Mitchell.)

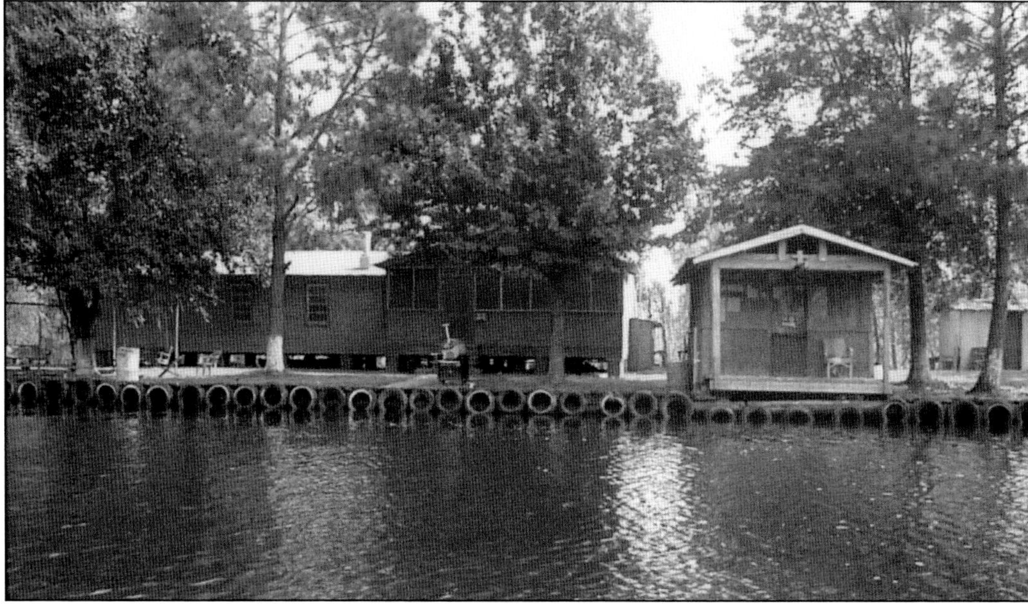

Occupied by the Ambrose "Tatoon" Duhe family for over 50 years, a hunting and fishing camp, located down the Reserve Canal leading to Lake Maurepas, was torched by the Louisiana Department of Wildlife and Fisheries in 2007; the area became a wildlife sanctuary. A five-year litigation case was finally decided when the Louisiana Supreme Court denied an appeal to prevent the state from removing the camp. (Courtesy of Lawrence Duhe.)

Six

Rebirth and Sesquicentennial

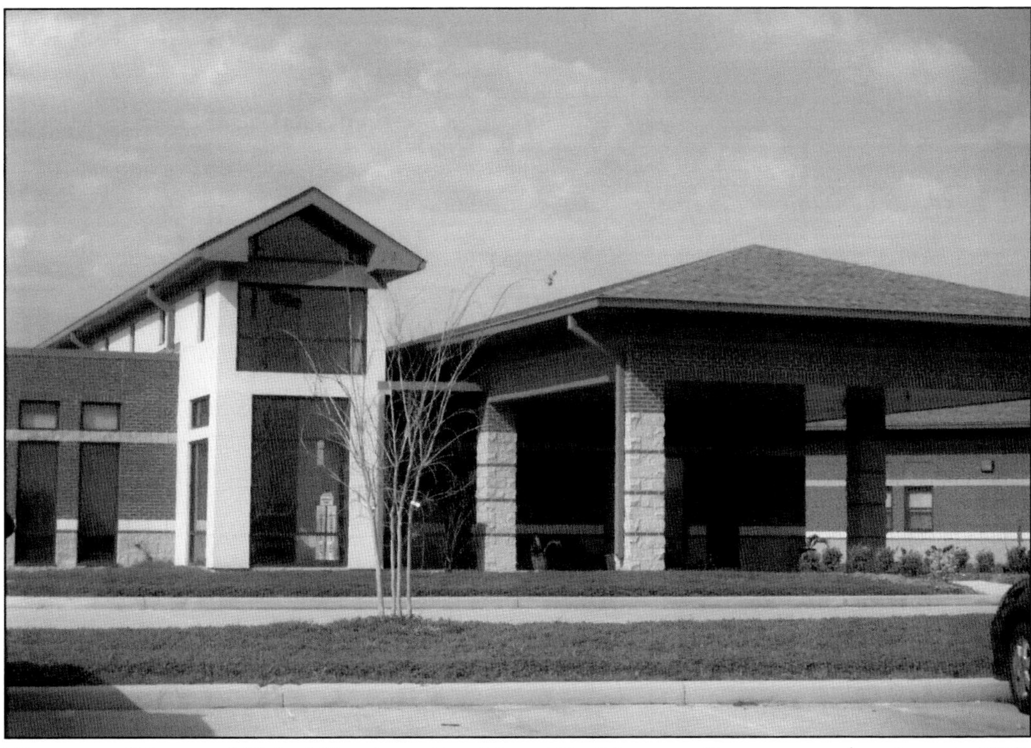

The state-of-the-art, 156-bed Southeast Louisiana War Veterans Home opened on June 4, 2007, and is located on 20 acres of land in Reserve. Only 27 miles from New Orleans, it is conveniently located next to the St. John the Baptist Senior Citizen Center and the Veterans Administration Community Based Outpatient Clinic. The facility offers a wide variety of amenities, including a fishing lake and a large chapel in addition to complete medical care, including skilled nursing, physical therapy, occupational therapy, speech therapy, Alzheimer and dementia care, hospice care, an in-house pharmacy, and transportation services to Veterans Administration specialty-need clinics and the Veterans Hospital in New Orleans. (Courtesy of Darroch Watson.)

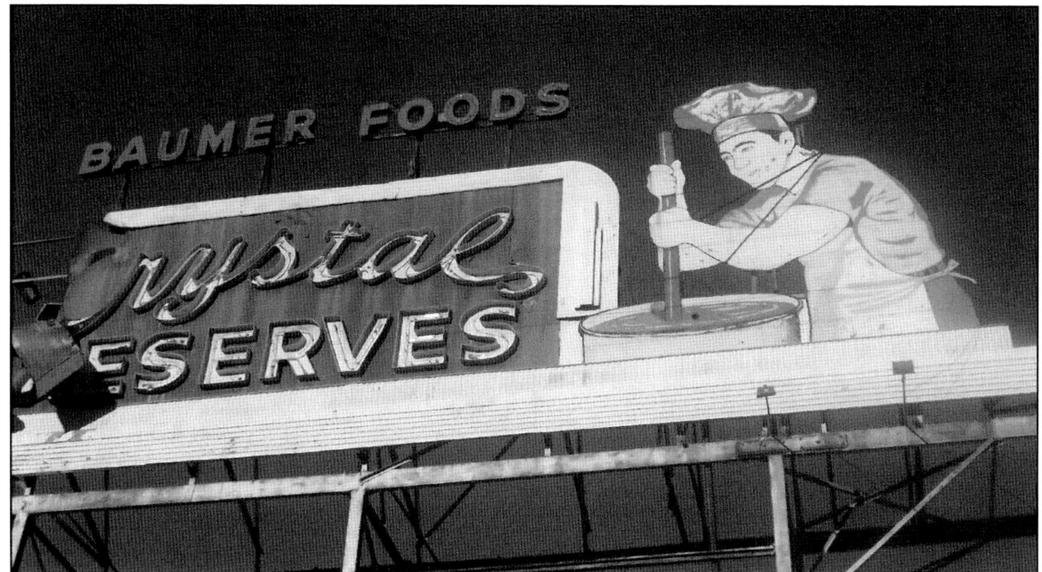

Forced to move as a result of Hurricane Katrina, in 2007, Baumer Foods relocated from New Orleans to the former home of Constar Plastics, Inc., located on West Tenth Street. Baumer Foods is the maker of the six-ounce Crystal Hot Sauce and several other condiments, including Figaro Liquid Smoke, that are shipped worldwide. (Courtesy of Baumer Foods.)

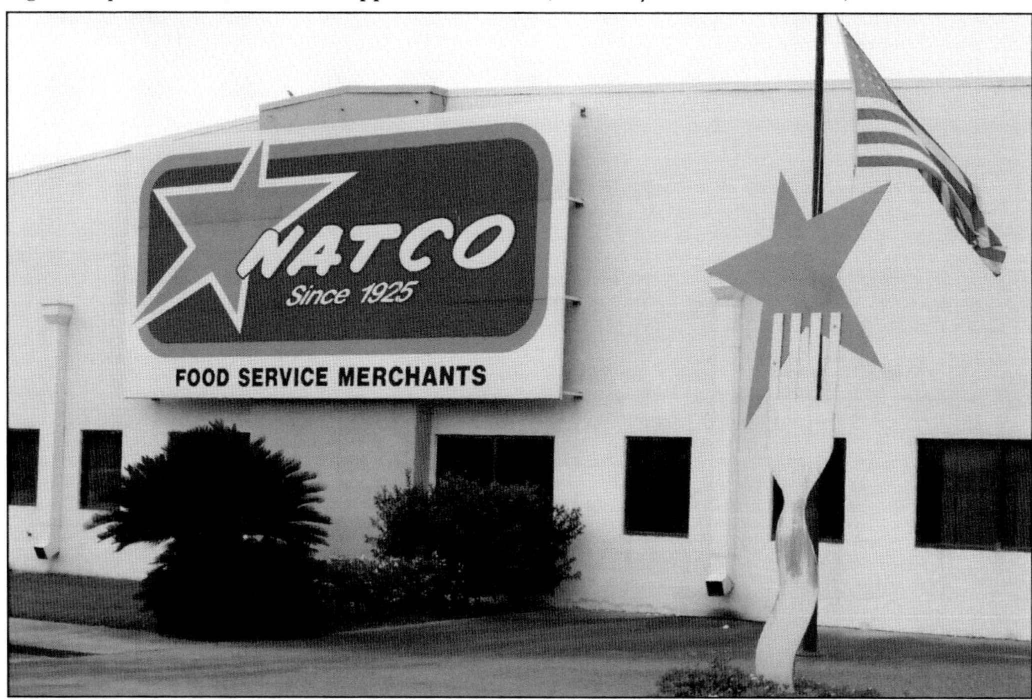

With the help of the State of Louisiana, St. John the Baptist Parish, and the Port of South Louisiana, NATCO Food Service Merchants now calls Reserve home. A family-operated business since 1925, the company is a meat processor and distributor that caters to high-end restaurants. Employing approximately 75 workers, the distributorship can customize any beef, pork, lamb, or veal products. (Courtesy of Gerald Keller.)

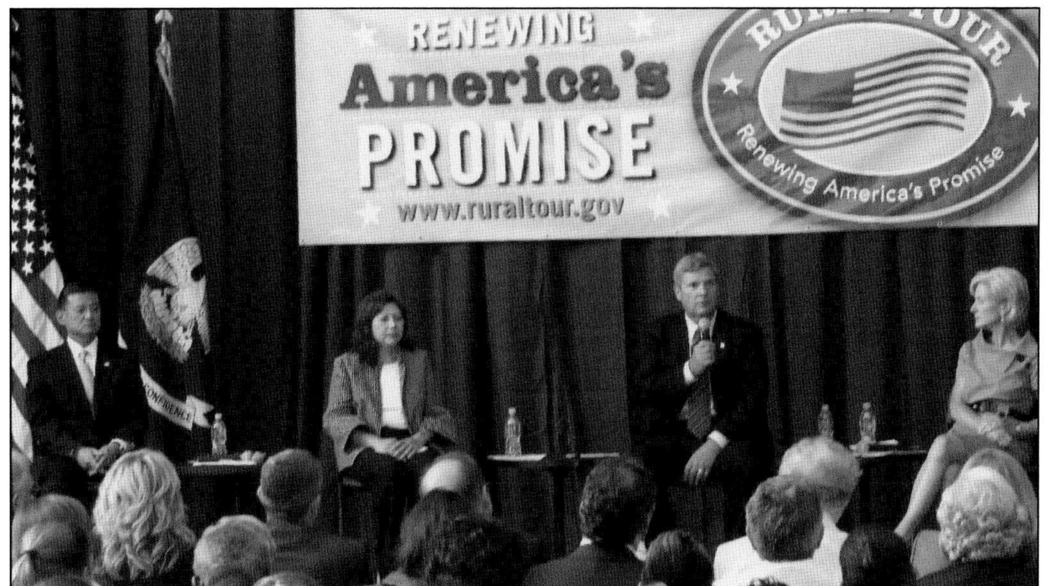

Cabinet secretaries from Pres. Barack Obama's administration visited Reserve on July 20, 2010, as part of the Rural America Tour. The spirited event featured a panel discussion and town hall–style question and answer session. From left to right are Secretary of the Department of Veterans Affairs Eric Shinseki; Secretary of the Department of Labor Hilda Solis; Secretary of the Department of Agriculture Tom Vilsack; and Secretary of the Department of Health and Human Services Kathleen Sebelius. (Courtesy of *L'Observateur*.)

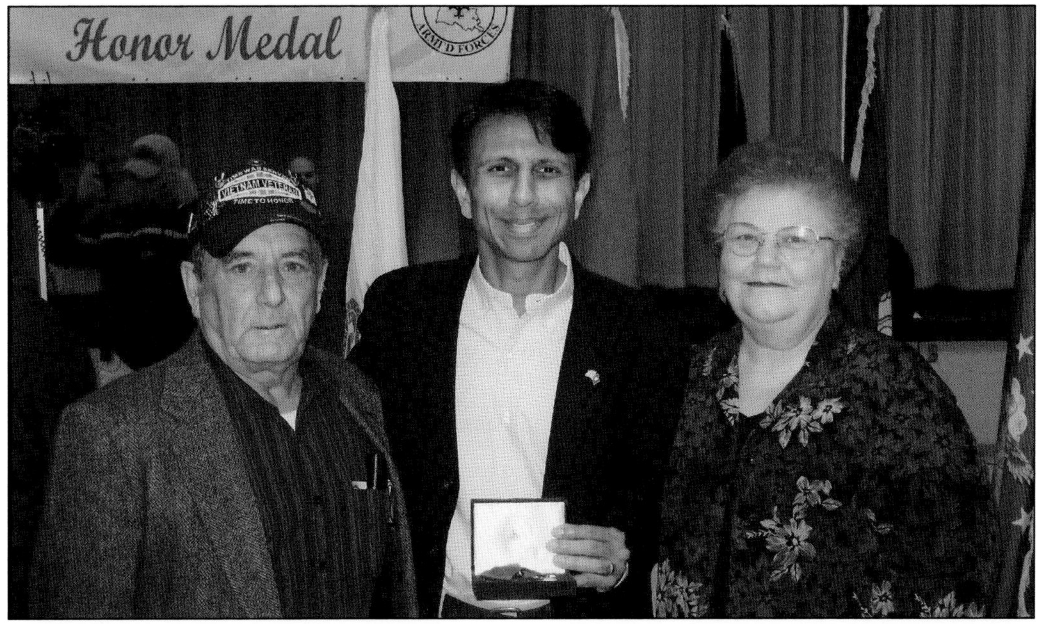

On January 11, 2011, Louisiana governor Bobby Jindal (center) presented Sgt. Robert Berthelot (left) with the Louisiana Veterans Honor Medal, from the Louisiana Department of Veterans Affairs. The medal was given to brave men and women who served their country with honor. Berthelot served in the Mekong Delta of Vietnam from 1967 to 1968 and received two Purple Hearts. Also pictured is his wife, Carla. (Courtesy of Gail and Norman Hill.)

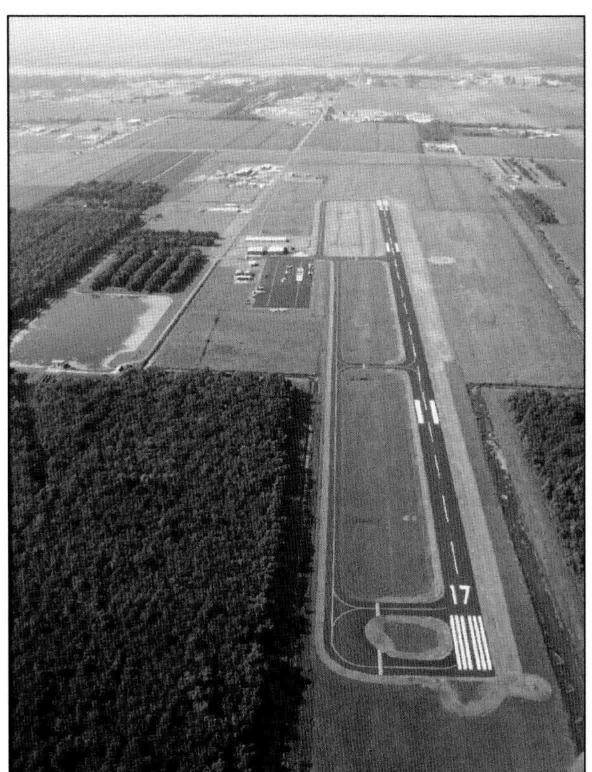

The St. John the Baptist Parish (Reserve) Airport was recognized as an outstanding Louisiana airport in 2004 by the Federal Aviation Administration. Managed by Rick Moran, its strength lies in its close proximity to New Orleans. The parish is lengthening the runway to allow easier access by small jets, and the construction of an Interstate 10 exchange through Reserve should increase the scope and growth of the airport. (Courtesy of Gene Beaver Borne.)

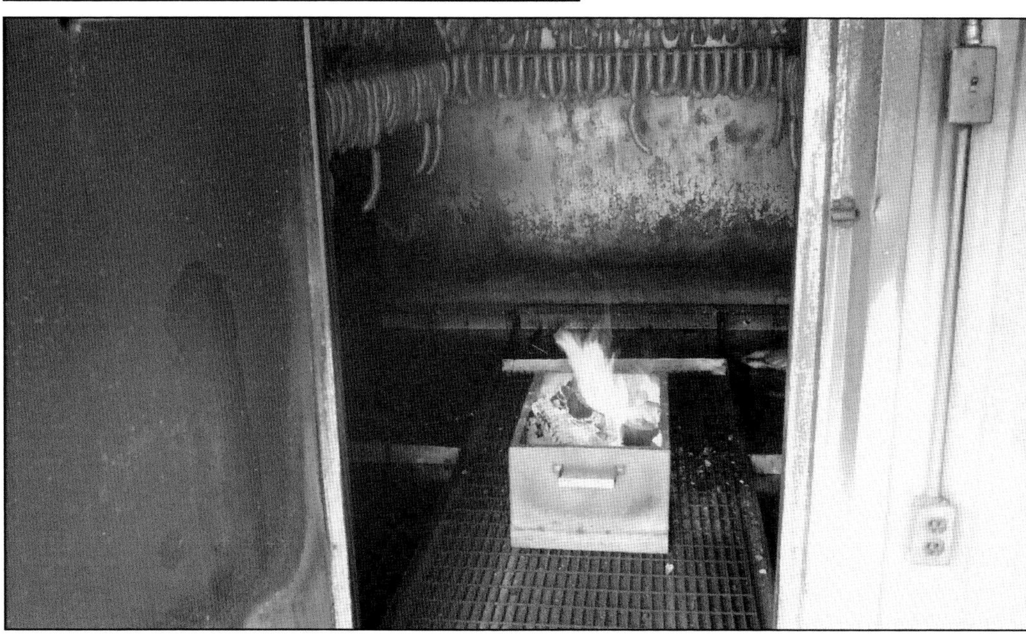

In a tradition dating back to the Germans who came to the Bonnet Carré (Reserve) region in the early 1700s, these settlers contributed the well-seasoned, heavily smoked pork andouille (pronounced *ahn-doo-ee*) sausage used in Creole gumbo, red beans, and jambalayas. Major manufactures of andouille in Reserve are Don's Country Store and Cox's Meat Market. Pictured is Don's smokehouse, which has served the Reserve community for 60 years. (Courtesy of Gerald Keller.)

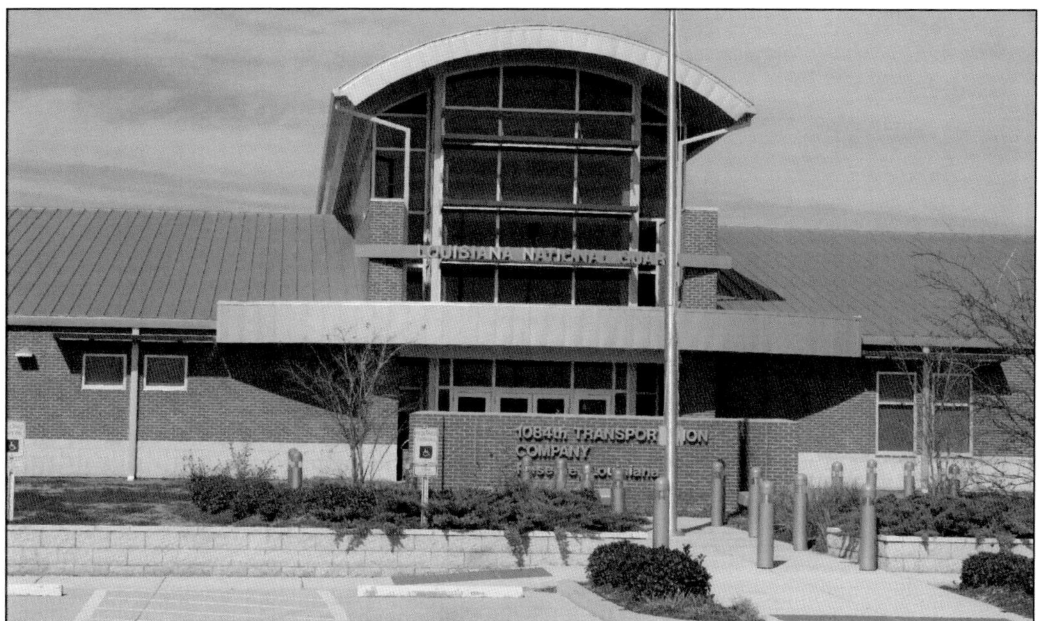

A $15.9-million National Guard Readiness Center, constructed in 2009, can be used to position supplies and equipment needed for a national emergency. The facility houses 113 Guardsmen from the 1084th Transportation Company that reports during annual training and drill weekends. The facility is nested with a veterans retirement home and outpatient clinic, and it sits next to the Reserve Airport. (Courtesy of Gene Beaver Borne.)

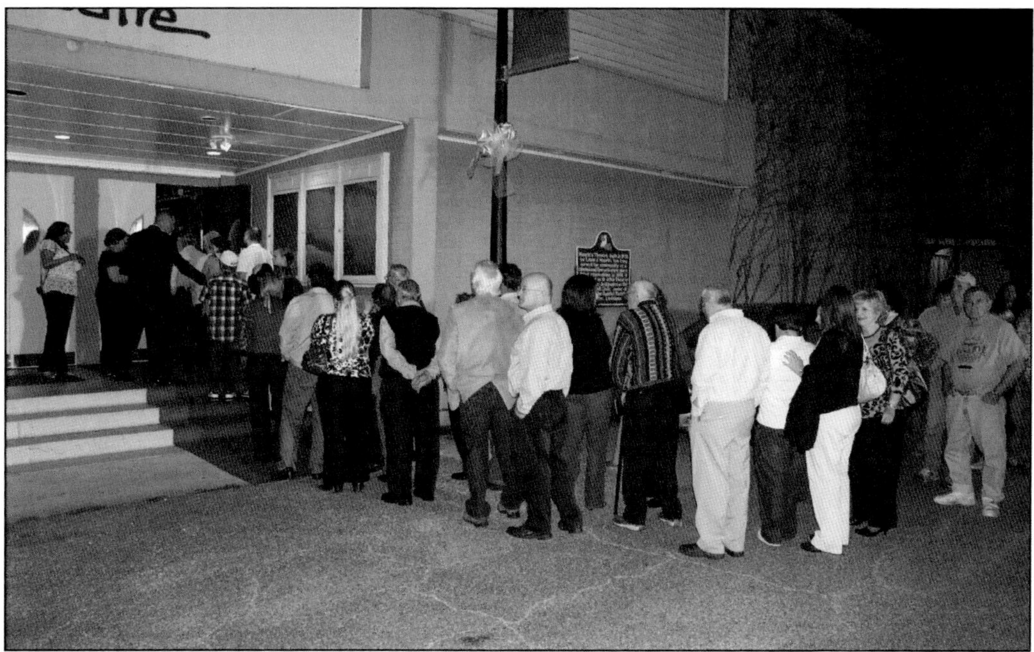
A crowd is entering St. John Theatre for the Reserve150 movie premiere. A full-capacity crowd viewed the movie production that was filmed by Lennen Madere and produced by Jeff Duhe. The pair gathered old photographs and conducted personal interviews of many lifetime residents of the Reserve community. (Photograph by Peter Forest.)

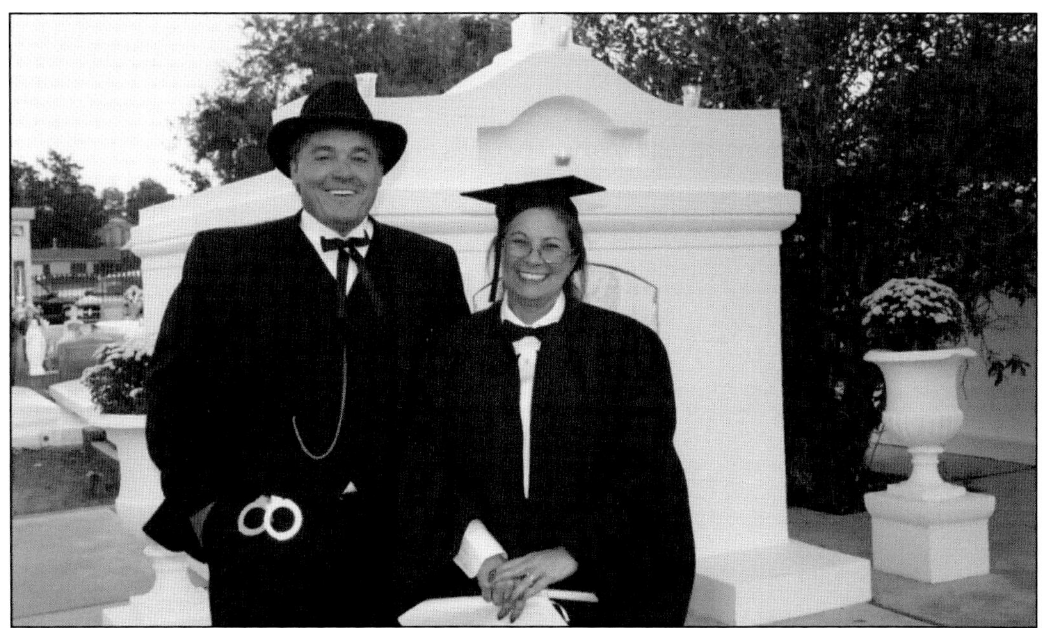

The St. Peter Catholic Church Cemetery Walk was a sesquicentennial event created by Gail Boudreaux Castay and Jane Montz Deroche. Residents, dressed in period costume, gave brief histories of their families, and the event concluded with a candlelight service. Pictured are John Boudreaux (left), who portrayed sheriff Billy Hart, and Marcelle Millet Bailey, who portrayed Noelie Hart. The two gave a brief history of their Hart family. (Courtesy of Walter Hillary Castay.)

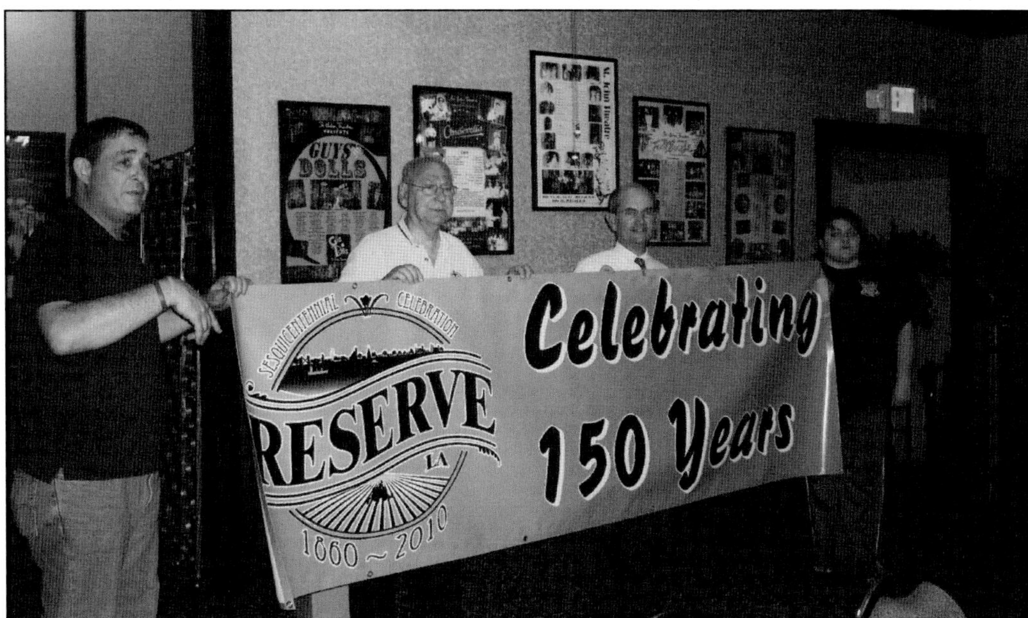

Pictured are members of the Reserve150 Sesquicentennial Committee holding up a banner advertising the Reserve150 sesquicentennial celebration. Pictured from left to right are Jamey Boudreaux, Dr. Gerald Keller, chairman Judge Sterling Snowdy, and Dawn Remondet. Members of the committee conducted a series of meetings over a period of six months to plan activities to celebrate Reserve's sesquicentennial. (Courtesy of Gerald Keller.)

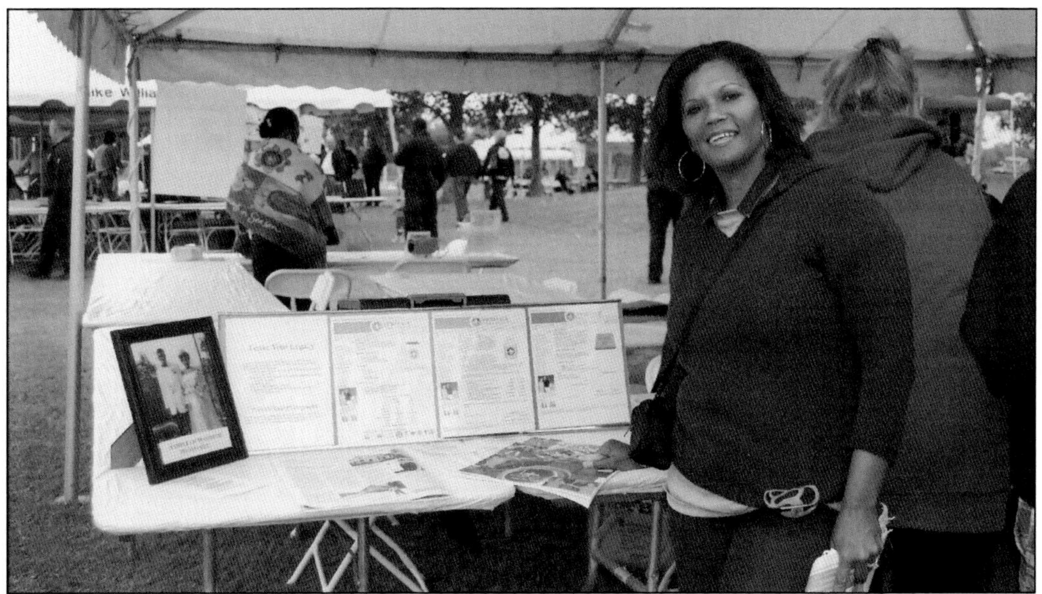

Fun Day was a Reserve sesquicentennial event that invited the community to Regala Park in Reserve for wholesome fun. Pictured is Rita Perrilloux, a member of the Reserve150 Sesquicentennial Committee and wife of Rev. Steven Perrilloux, pastor at Reserve Christian Center. Rita Perrilloux chaired the Reserve150 time capsule event, where residents buried personal items such as letters, newspapers, CDs, DVDs, and family pictures in a time capsule that will be opened in the year 2060. (Courtesy of Rita Perrilloux.).

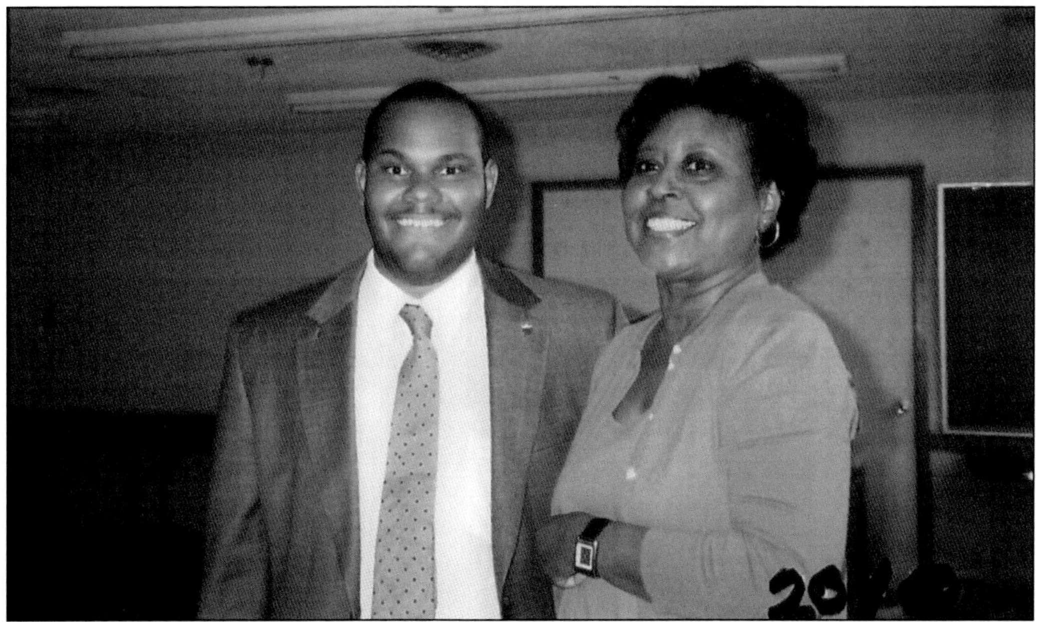

Pictured are Jari Honora (left) and Mary Mitchell. Honora was one of several 2010 guest lecturers for the Reserve150 lecture series. He provided an overview of Louisiana African American Catholics, the impact of the Josephite Fathers, and the history of Our Lady of Grace Church. Mitchell is a member of the Reserve150 Historical Committee and a Sesquicentennial Committee member. (Courtesy of Mary Dorothy Mitchell.)